PREFACE

1. Scope

This publication provides fundamental principles and guidance for combating weapons of mass destruction (CWMD) and their means of delivery.

2. Purpose

This publication has been prepared under the direction of the Chairman of the Joint Chiefs of Staff. It sets forth CWMD doctrine to govern the activities and performance of the Armed Forces of the United States in joint operations and provides the doctrinal basis for interagency coordination and for US military involvement in multinational operations. It provides military guidance for the exercise of authority by combatant commanders and other joint force commanders (JFCs) and prescribes joint doctrine for operations. It provides military guidance for use by the Armed Forces in preparing their appropriate plans. It is not the intent of this publication to restrict the authority of the JFC from task organizing the force and executing the mission in a manner the JFC deems most appropriate to ensure unity of effort in the accomplishment of the overall objective.

3. Application

a. Joint doctrine established in this publication applies to the Joint Staff, commanders of combatant commands, subunified commands, joint task forces, subordinate components of these commands, and the Services.

b. The guidance in this publication is authoritative; as such, this doctrine will be followed except when, in the judgment of the commander, exceptional circumstances dictate otherwise. If conflicts arise between the contents of this publication and the contents of Service publications, this publication will take precedence unless the Chairman of the Joint Chiefs of Staff, normally in coordination with the other members of the Joint Chiefs of Staff, has provided more current and specific guidance. Commanders of forces operating as part of a multinational (alliance or coalition) military command should follow multinational doctrine and procedures ratified by the United States. For doctrine and procedures not ratified by the United States, commanders should evaluate and follow the multinational command's doctrine and procedures, where applicable and consistent with US law, regulations, and doctrine.

For the Chairman of the Joint Chiefs of Staff:

STANLEY A. MCCHRYSTAL
Lieutenant General, USA
Director, Joint Staff

Intentionally Blank

- Highlights the *National Strategy to Combat Weapons of Mass Destruction* and the *National Military Strategy to Combat Weapons of Mass Destruction* as critical pieces of combating weapons of mass destruction strategic guidance

- Introduces the combating weapons of mass destruction (WMD) construct, consolidating the discussion of the three pillars of combating weapons of mass destruction: nonproliferation, counterproliferation, and WMD consequence management

- Discontinues the discussion of tasks as part of the three pillars

- Introduces "military strategic objectives," "strategic enablers," and "military mission areas" as part of the combating weapons of mass destruction strategic framework

- Replaces combating weapons of mass destruction enablers of "command, control, intelligence, surveillance, and reconnaissance;" "information operations;" "interoperability;" "readiness;" "mobility;" and "sustainment" with strategic enablers of "intelligence," "partnership capacity," and "strategic communications support"

- Describes the relationship between combating weapons of mass destruction, the war on terrorism, and homeland defense

- Expands discussion of weapons of mass destruction consequence management, to include domestic WMD consequence management, foreign WMD consequence management, and Department of Defense (DOD) led consequence management operations

- Introduces "traditional" and "nontraditional threats"

- Introduces proliferation networks as part of the combating weapons of mass destruction threat

- Highlights the role of deterrence against state and non-state actors

- Introduces DOD combating weapons of mass destruction organizational and command relationships

- Describes the critical role of interagency and intergovernmental cooperation in combating weapons of mass destruction success

- Establishes enhanced definitions and critical distinctions for the eight military mission areas of combating WMD

- Introduces importance of integrating combating weapons of mass destruction planning into all types of military operations

- Discusses the unique combating weapons of mass destruction aspects of offensive and defensive operations

- Consolidates the planning considerations for nonproliferation, counterproliferation and consequence management into a single chapter on combating weapons of mass destruction planning considerations

- Eliminates chapter on combating weapons of mass destruction training and exercises

- Incorporates the *Joint Weapons of Mass Destruction Elimination Handbook* into the publication as an appendix.

- Introduces an appendix for weapons of mass destruction interdiction operations

- Establishes new definitions for the terms "chemical, biological, radiological, and nuclear passive defense," "nuclear reactor," "proliferation," "threat reduction cooperation," "weapons of mass destruction active defense," "weapons of mass destruction consequence management," "weapons of mass destruction elimination," "weapons of mass destruction interdiction," weapons of mass destruction offensive operations," and "weapons of mass destruction security cooperation and partner activities"

- Modifies the definitions for the terms "counterproliferation," "nonproliferation," "weapons of mass destruction,"

- Removes the terms "balance," "tacit arms control agreement," and "unilateral arms control measure" from Joint Publication 1-02, *Department of Defense Dictionary of Military and Associated Terms*

TABLE OF CONTENTS

CHAPTER V
COMBATING WEAPONS OF MASS DESTRUCTION PLANNING
CONSIDERATIONS

APPENDIX

GLOSSARY

FIGURE

Intentionally Blank

EXECUTIVE SUMMARY
COMMANDER'S OVERVIEW

- **Provides an Overview of Combating Weapons of Mass Destruction (CWMD)**

- **Discusses the Challenge of Weapons of Mass Destruction Threats**

- **Discusses CWMD Organizational and Command Relationships**

- **Discusses CWMD Planning and Execution**

- **Discusses CWMD Planning Considerations**

- **Provides Further Guidance on CWMD Elimination Operations**

- **Provides a CWMD Interdiction Operations Reference for Staff Officers**

Overview

Combating weapons of mass destruction (CWMD) is a continuous campaign conducted and supported by the entire United States Government.

Combating weapons of mass destruction (CWMD) and their means of delivery is one of the greatest challenges the United States (US) faces. Weapons of mass destruction (WMD) have the potential to severely disrupt and damage the United States, its forces, allies, multinational partners, and other friendly nations. It is important for commanders and their staffs to keep the perspective that WMD is not an adversary, but a capability an adversary can use. Adversaries may use WMD as a tool to inflict casualties on civilian populations, degrade the instruments of our national power, or to counter US military superiority.

CWMD is a global mission that requires the coordinated action of interagency and multinational partners; and integrated, synchronized effort to be effective.

CWMD is a global mission crossing geographic areas of responsibility (AORs) boundaries, requires an integrated and synchronized effort, and requires numerous interagency and multinational partners for effective mission accomplishment. Rather than a discrete, specialized mission, CWMD requires a continuous campaign conducted and supported by the entire United States Government (USG). CWMD actions are conducted across the range of military operations and DOD will often be acting in support of another lead agency, or even supporting a multinational effort.

The National Security Strategy (NSS) of the United States of America identifies as an essential task to "prevent our enemies from threatening us, our allies, and our friends with weapons of mass destruction" for ensuring national security. The United States advances this strategy through strengthened alliances, the establishment of new partnerships, proactive counterproliferation (CP) efforts, modern technologies, and increased emphasis on intelligence collection and analysis. *The National Strategy to Combat Weapons of Mass Destruction* (NS-CWMD) provides additional guidance concerning CWMD: nonproliferation (NP), CP, and WMD consequence management (CM), as highlighted in the NSS, and introduces the construct of the three pillars which provides a common framework for the interagency conduct of CWMD activities. *The National Military Strategy to Combat Weapons of Mass Destruction* (NMS-CWMD) provides Department of Defense (DOD) components with guidance and a strategic framework for CWMD. The NMS-CWMD uses an ends, ways, and means approach to planning, executing, resourcing, and emphasizes those CWMD missions in which the military plays a prominent role. It defines strategic end states, strategic enablers, military strategic objectives, and eight military mission areas (MMAs) the Armed Forces of the United States may be called upon to perform.

Shaping, nonproliferation, counterproliferation, and consequence management provide the United States (US), its forces, allies, partners, and interests with ways to avoid coercion or attack from those armed with weapons of mass destruction

Shaping activities are performed to dissuade or deter potential adversaries and to assure or solidify relationships with friends and allies. NP activities are those actions taken to prevent the proliferation of WMD by dissuading or impeding access to, or distribution of, sensitive technologies, material, and expertise. CP activities are those actions taken to defeat the threat and/or use of WMD against the United States, our forces, allies, and partners. WMD CM activities are those actions authorized by the President or Secretary of Defense (SecDef) to mitigate the effects of a weapon of mass destruction attack or event and provide temporary essential operations and services at home and abroad. DOD can act as both a supported and a supporting entity during CWMD operations outside of the United States. Moreover, CWMD must be synchronized with the homeland defense (HD) mission to prevent a terrorist group from striking the US homeland with WMD. This normally omits high-yield explosive (HYE) weapons as a WMD-CM consideration; however, certain domestic response plans include HYE and other weapons. When CWMD operations involve significant or complex interactions with foreign civil authorities or intergovernmental organizations (IGOs), the commander should consider forming a civil-military operations center (CMOC) or supplementing an existing CMOC with CWMD expertise.

The Challenge

While the challenges of combating weapons of mass destruction may be daunting, they are defined and can be countered through strong partnership action between the US, its allies, and other friendly nations.

The primary challenges facing the joint force commander (JFC) are: the diversity of threat actors, including the emergence of nontraditional WMD threats; the varied nature of WMD demands a varied approach to deterrence; a complex WMD proliferation continuum; the dual-use nature of much of the related technology and expertise; and the increasing complexity and number of WMD proliferation networks.

State actors and their associated WMD programs vary in their level of activity and sophistication and remain a credible threat to the United States. Since the fall of the Soviet Union in 1991, and with the possible decline of authority in other states with WMD programs, the US faces an increasingly challenging dilemma involving states that may not be able to control their chemical, biological, radiological, and nuclear (CBRN) weapons, material, technology, or expertise. In such cases, these items can fall into the hands of other states or non-state actors. Proactive actions can be taken at every stage of the proliferation continuum to successfully combat the WMD proliferation. However, the JFC should look to combat these threats early in the continuum to minimize risk of further proliferation or use. The generic activities include: a decision to pursue WMD capability; infrastructure and expertise development; production; weaponization; deployment; and employment.

Proliferation networks are multifunctional and multidimensional; consist of state and, increasingly, independent non-state actors; are dynamic, adaptive, and can be transnational; have differing motivations and desired end states; and operate in secrecy to avoid detection and counteraction.

Effective strategic communications, robust active weapons of mass destruction (WMD) defense; complementary

The JFC must consider the changing role of deterrence against state actors and, more importantly, the role of deterrence against non-state actors. The general principles of deterrence against a state actor have not significantly changed.

passive chemical, biological, radiological, and nuclear defense; and effective consequence management are important in deterring WMD use or effort to obtain WMD capability.

Deterring non-state actors is a difficult challenge because it may not be possible to deter the most devoted violent extremists. However, a measure of WMD deterrence may be achieved by demonstrating capabilities such as robust WMD active defense and CBRN passive defense, as well as exercising WMD.

Organizational and Command Relationships

The Secretary of Defense, the Chairman of the Joint Chiefs of Staff, the Services, combatant commanders, and combat support agencies play important and continuing roles in CWMD.

The Office of the Secretary of Defense (OSD) develops, coordinates, and oversees implementation and integration of DOD CWMD policy. The Chairman of the Joint Chiefs of Staff (CJCS) serves as the principal military advisor to the President, National Security Council, and SecDef regarding CWMD activities and apportions CWMD resources for planning and execution of the mission.

CWMD operations are planned and executed by geographic combatant commanders

Geographic combatant commanders (GCCs) plan and execute CWMD operations within their AORs. GCCs also provide for movement of specialized CWMD personnel and equipment and coordinate transition of WMD-related material for short- to long-term storage, protection, dismantlement, destruction, or disposal. Combatant commanders (CCDRs) coordinate with OSD and the Joint Staff to plan for transition or transfer of responsibility of CWMD operations. When applicable, they develop threat reduction and cooperation plans to allow for transfer and termination of CWMD missions.

Expertise in synchronizing CWMD planning; advocating capability; transportation; locating, tagging, and tracking WMD; direct-action operations; and other specialized capabilities are provided by the functional combatant commands.

The functional combatant commanders have specific roles in CWMD: United States Strategic Command (USSTRATCOM) is responsible for synchronizing DOD CWMD planning and advocating for CWMD capabilities.

Commander, United States Joint Forces Command in coordination with USSTRATCOM, develops and makes recommendations to the CJCS regarding joint force integration for CWMD. As the joint force provider, United States Joint Forces Command provides forces, resources, and capabilities, as directed, to the supported CCDR's CWMD operations. United States Transportation Command (USTRANSCOM) plans and executes the common user transportation aspects of global CWMD operations. As the mobility force provider, USTRANSCOM supports intertheater and intratheater transportation of CWMD forces, equipment, and material, including specialized WMD shipments or certified containers provided by the appropriate agency. USTRANSCOM is prepared to expeditiously conduct retrograde movements of samples and specialized WMD tools for identification and attribution, providing in-transit visibility for positive control of CWMD shipments.

United States Special Operations Command (USSOCOM) is the lead combatant command for planning, synchronizing, and, as directed, executing global operations against terrorist networks. USSOCOM provides the following CWMD capabilities: expertise, material, and teams to supported GCC teams to locate, tag, and track WMD, as required; capabilities to conduct direct action operations in limited access areas, as required; and other specialized CWMD capabilities.

The Services organize, train, equip, and otherwise prepare their respective forces to combat WMD, means of delivery, and related materials. Specifically, the Services provide forces with the capability to conduct WMD interdiction, WMD elimination, WMD offensive operations, WMD active defense, CBRN passive defense, and WMD CM operations.

There are two principal combat support agencies with significant responsibilities related to CWMD: the Defense Threat Reduction Agency (DTRA) and the Defense Intelligence Agency (DIA). DTRA's mission is to provide capabilities to reduce, eliminate, and counter the WMD threat, and mitigate its effects. DIA advises SecDef, CJCS, and CCDRs on WMD intelligence and provides military intelligence support for CWMD planning. They support CCDR preparation of strategic estimates, priorities, and joint operation plans for CWMD operations.

Coordination is critical to the success of CWMD operations.

Coordination between DOD and other government agencies (OGAs), nongovernmental organizations, and IGOs is critical to the success of CWMD operations. In particular, security cooperation and partner activities; threat reduction cooperation; and the WMD elimination, interdiction, and consequence management missions require significant interagency and intergovernmental coordination.

Command relationships are established as appropriate to the situation. US forces supporting other agencies will normally remain under Department of Defense (DOD) command structures.

Specific command relationships for CWMD operations are established by tasking orders, CCDR plans, and operation orders, as appropriate. Because of the interagency aspects of CWMD operations, agencies other than DOD may lead efforts with DOD providing support; however, US military forces; other than National Guard forces due to their unique status when operating under Title 32, United States Code authority, will remain under the DOD command structure while supporting other agencies. SecDef, a CCDR, a subordinate unified command commander, or an existing commander, joint task force can establish a joint task force to execute a specific CWMD mission or when CWMD operations require joint resources on a significant scale.

Protection of the homeland is provided by DOD through actions in homeland defense and through civil support.

DOD protects the homeland through two distinct but interrelated missions: HD and civil support. The purpose of HD is to protect against, and mitigate the impact of, incursions or attacks on sovereign territory, the domestic population, and critical defense infrastructure. DOD is the federal agency with lead responsibility, supported by other agencies, in defending against external threats or aggression. DOD provides support to civil authorities for domestic emergencies and for designated law enforcement and other activities.

Planning and Execution

Eight military mission areas provide logical grouping for planning for CWMD, help joint force commanders relate CWMD capability with the strategic pillars, determine operational tasks, integrate activities, and inform their decisions.

This chapter translates strategic CWMD guidance into an operational approach leveraging capabilities from the six joint functions across campaign phases and across the range of military operations. The **eight CWMD MMAs** provide JFCs with a logical grouping of CWMD activities. These enhanced descriptions offer the JFC a more precise and operational perspective to combat WMD: **WMD security cooperation and partner activities** (activities to improve or promote defense relationships and capacity of allied and partner nations to execute or support the other MMAs to combat WMD through military-to-military contact, burden sharing arrangements, combined military activities, and support to international activities); **threat reduction cooperation** (activities undertaken with the consent and cooperation of host nation (HN) authorities in a permissive environment to enhance physical security, and to reduce, dismantle, redirect, and/or improve protection of a state's existing weapons of mass destruction program, stockpiles, and capabilities); **WMD interdiction** (operations to track, intercept, search, divert, seize, or otherwise stop the transit of WMD, its delivery systems, or related materials, technologies, and expertise. In peacetime, WMD interdiction operations are planned and executed in order to intercept dual-use materials and expertise in transit aboard nonmilitary transports); **WMD offensive operations** (actions to disrupt, neutralize, or destroy a WMD threat before it can be used, or to deter subsequent use of such weapons improves or promotes relationships and capacity); **WMD elimination** (actions undertaken in a hostile or uncertain environment to systematically locate, characterize, secure, and disable, or destroy WMD programs and related capabilities); **WMD active defense** (active measures to defeat an attack with chemical, biological, radiological, or nuclear weapons by employing actions to divert, neutralize, or destroy those weapons or their means of delivery while en route to their target); **CBRN passive defense** (passive measures taken to minimize or negate the vulnerability to, and effects of, chemical, biological, radiological, or nuclear attacks causing a high order of destruction or mass casualties. This mission area focuses on maintaining the joint force's ability to continue military operations in CBRN environments); and **WMD consequence management.** (actions authorized by the SecDef to mitigate the effects of a WMD attack or event and restore essential operations and services.)

The CWMD MMAs are useful to the JFC as logical groupings of capabilities and in order to relate them to the strategic pillars. However, the distinctions and subtleties between several of CWMD MMAs are also important in determining the operational tasks and related activities to a successful CWMD program. It also informs JFC decisions for future actions, some of which may have diplomatic implications. And finally, it provides architecture within which to frame, organize, mass, and optimize friendly capabilities necessary for the CWMD program. CWMD actions and activities must not be planned or executed in isolation but must be integrated throughout the range of military operations. CWMD must be integrated into all types of military operations.

CWMD planning is not a separate process; it is the integration of WMD-specific knowledge, experience, and capabilities into the existing joint operation planning process. Commanders at every level must be aware that in a world of constant, immediate communications, any single action may have consequences at all levels.

Joint intelligence preparation of the operational environment is also critical to CWMD operations success.

Joint intelligence preparation of the operational environment (JIPOE) underpins planning for CWMD operations. JIPOE is the analytical process used by joint intelligence organizations to produce intelligence assessments, estimates, and other intelligence products in support of the JFC's decision-making process.

Planning for CWMD promotes unified action by clarifying the relationship between strategic objectives and CWMD tasks.

JFCs approve strategic military objectives which comprise the military end state. The military end state (whether focused specifically on WMD or not) is the point in time, or circumstances, beyond which the President does not require the military instrument of national power to achieve the remaining objectives of the national strategic end state. The identification of desired and undesired effects clarifies the relationship between objectives and tasks and helps commanders and their staffs gain a common picture and shared understanding of the operational environment that promotes unified action.

WMD-related targets represent highly sensitive and critical capabilities of many states and non-states and carry unique targeting considerations. Holding these targets at risk is a priority for the JFC and requires a wide array of capabilities, both lethal and nonlethal. A detailed analysis to determine the potential release of hazards when targeting adversary WMD storage sites, weapon systems, or production facilities is required; the utility of employing agent defeat weapons to minimize the dispersal and collateral effects of CBRN hazards should be considered. JFCs should seek to minimize collateral damage consistent with higher-level guidance as well as plan for follow-on WMD CM operations, as appropriate.

Logical lines of operation (LOOs) are often the most appropriate for CWMD operations or campaigns. A LOO depiction at this level can help the commander and staff discuss the relationship and status of decisive points or key tasks, as required. CWMD operations can occur throughout all phases of a campaign or operation. Phasing is most directly related to arranging of operations and LOOs during operational design. Many plans require adjustment beyond the initial stages of the operation. Consequently, JFCs build flexibility into their plans by developing branches and sequels to preserve freedom of action in rapidly changing conditions. Branches and sequels directly relate to phasing. Flexible deterrent options are preplanned, deterrence-oriented actions carefully tailored to bring an issue to early resolution without armed conflict.

Strategic communication planning is critical to CWMD and must create a responsive and agile whole-of-government effort to synchronize crucial themes, messages, images, and actions. JFC planning must consider public diplomacy, public affairs (PA), and information operations requirements when confronting the WMD threat or use. Public interest in WMD-related developments may be intense and may affect US and multinational partner decision-making. Therefore, the JFC must be a source of timely, accurate information, with particular emphasis on the explanation of actions taken in response to WMD threats or use.

Force planning for CWMD encompasses all those activities performed by the supported CCDR, subordinate component commanders, and OGAs to select (source and tailor), prepare, integrate, and deploy forces and capabilities required to accomplish CWMD-related missions. It should provide an active, layered defense against WMD and prepare for the possibility of rapid escalation to counter or respond to WMD use by an adversary. A challenge for the JFC is in managing expectations for employing CBRN-specific forces. An additional, yet related, challenge is balancing the use of low-density, CBRN-specific units with assigned forces that can accomplish many of the CWMD related tasks. An additional, yet related, challenge is balancing the use of low-density, CBRN-specific units with assigned forces that can accomplish many of the CWMD related tasks.

CWMD integration and synchronization must be carefully considered and executed in support of the military objectives of each and all types of military operations.

Successful shaping activities can be a very cost effective approach to combating WMD by investing relatively few resources in engagement versus costly responses to adversary use of WMD. CWMD MMAs that support shaping the environment can include security cooperation, threat reduction cooperation, and WMD interdiction. Success in CWMD relies heavily on military engagement opportunities. Military engagement is the routine contact and interaction between individuals or elements of the

Armed Forces of the United States and those of another nation's armed forces, or foreign and domestic civilian authorities or agencies to build trust and confidence, share information, coordinate mutual activities, and maintain influence. Security cooperation is a key element of global and theater shaping operations and the WMD security cooperation MMA. Security cooperation involves all DOD interactions with foreign defense establishments to build defense relationships that promote specific US security interests, develop allied and friendly military capabilities for self-defense and multinational operations, and provide US forces with peacetime and contingency access to a HN. Deterrence prevents an action by an adversary through the perception of cost imposition, benefit denial, or the consequences of restraint. Having a credible threat of response in the form of WMD interdiction, WMD elimination, WMD offensive operations, WMD active and CBRN passive defense, and WMD CM capabilities supports the overall USG deterrence goal

CWMD MMAs that support crisis response and limited contingency operations include WMD interdiction, WMD offensive operations, WMD active defense, CBRN passive defense, and WMD CM. CWMD in crisis response and limited contingency operations includes: peace operations, consequence management operations, defense support of civil authorities, homeland defense, strikes, and raids

When required to achieve national strategic objectives or protect national interests, US national leadership may decide to conduct a major operation or campaign. In such cases, the goal is to prevail against the adversary as quickly as possible, conclude hostilities, and establish conditions favorable to the HN, United States, and multinational partners. Establishing these conditions often requires CWMD considerations for termination objectives and end states. All eight CWMD MMAs could be part of a major operation or campaign. While offensive CWMD operations support the decisive operation, defensive CWMD operations protect friendly force critical assets and centers of gravity. Conducting offensive and defensive operations independently detracts from the efficient employment of CWMD assets. At best, independent operations expend more resources than would be required if done in concert. At worst, uncoordinated efforts increase conflicts and mutual interference. In the extreme, they may compromise friendly intentions or result in loss of operational momentum. Fully integrating CWMD offensive and defensive operations requires JFCs and their staffs to treat CWMD as a single, integrated function.

CWMD Planning Considerations

Planning for CWMD military operations are complicated by being only part of a comprehensive US government effort and by the very broad range of considerations particularly important to joint task forces.

CWMD operations are a component of a comprehensive USG effort requiring a coordinated interagency approach and the cooperation of the international community. These activities require early coordination with these OGAs and often require the participation of multinational partners during planning. The staff judge advocate should be involved throughout the planning process, including mission analysis and course of action development, to ensure the JFC is aware of potential CWMD related legal issues. International law, policies, treaties, and agreements to which the United States is a signatory identify certain rights and obligations that may impact joint operations. These legal requirements may pose constraints and restraints. Arms control and NP treaties and regimes establish global norms against the proliferation of WMD precursors, weapons, their means of delivery, and weapons manufacturing equipment. Treaties provide international standards to gauge and address the activities of potential proliferators. Through security assistance activities, the Armed Forces of the United States can help multinational partners develop the ability to cope with a WMD attack as well as reduce their vulnerability to armed aggression. An important aspect of NP is preventing the spread of WMD technology through physical security and export controls. NP and CP initiatives: various international cooperation programs have been initiated to defeat the proliferation of WMD and the materiel, technology, and expertise necessary to create and sustain a WMD program

Operational planning considerations of particular importance to the JFC are: task organization; intelligence, surveillance & reconnaissance; military operations; logistics operations; PA; civil-military operations; meteorological and oceanographic operations; environmental considerations; health service support; consequence management; and interagency coordination.

CONCLUSION

This publication establishes joint doctrine for the conduct of CWMD operations across the range of military operations.

CHAPTER I
INTRODUCTION TO COMBATING WEAPONS OF MASS DESTRUCTION

> *"There are few greater challenges than those posed by chemical, biological, and particularly nuclear weapons. Preventing the spread of these weapons, and their use, requires vigilance and obligates us to anticipate and counter threats. Whenever possible, we prefer nonmilitary options to achieve this purpose."*
>
> **National Defense Strategy, 2008**

1. General

a. Combating weapons of mass destruction (CWMD) and their means of delivery is one of the greatest challenges the United States (US) faces. Weapons of mass destruction (WMD) have the potential to severely disrupt and damage the US, its forces, allies, multinational partners, and other friendly nations. Adversaries may use WMD to inflict casualties on civilian populations, degrade the instruments of our national power, or counter US military superiority.

b. This publication forms the foundation for all other joint and Service doctrine for CWMD and provides overarching guidelines and principles to assist in planning and conducting operations to combat WMD. **WMD are defined as chemical, biological, radiological, or nuclear (CBRN) weapons or devices capable of a high order of destruction WMD and/or causing mass casualties and exclude the means of transporting or propelling the weapon where such means is a separable and divisible part from the weapon. CWMD does not include countering the employment of high-yield explosives (HYE).** Efforts to combat WMD must take into account an actor's motivations for and decision to undertake efforts to engage in WMD-related activities, as well as the weapons themselves. The existence of CBRN materials and the potential for adversaries willing to employ them as a weapon precipitates the need to plan, prepare for, and combat their use. CWMD entails those activities conducted across the US Government (USG) to ensure the US, its Armed Forces, allies, partners, and interests are neither coerced nor attacked with WMD. Thus, CWMD operations should be considered a set of activities integrated into all joint operations. This chapter provides a brief synopsis of relevant national-level and Department of Defense (DOD) guidance for CWMD, highlights some overarching CWMD constructs, and discusses the relationship of CWMD with the war on terrorism (WOT) and homeland defense (HD).

c. It is important for commanders and their staffs to keep the perspective that WMD is not an adversary, but a capability an adversary may use. CWMD is a global mission crossing geographic areas of responsibility (AORs) boundaries, requires an integrated and synchronized effort, and requires numerous interagency and multinational partners for effective mission accomplishment. Rather than a discrete, specialized mission, CWMD requires a continuous campaign conducted and supported by the entire USG. CWMD actions are conducted across the range of military operations and DOD will often be acting in support of another lead agency, or even supporting a multinational effort.

d. WMD proliferation is the *transfer* of WMD, related materials, technology, and expertise from one actor to another. The actors may be state or non-state. WMD proliferation represents an adversarial intent to either possess WMD, develop WMD programs, or to endorse WMD possession and/or programs to other actors.

2. National Strategy and Guidance

a. ***The National Security Strategy (NSS) of the United States of America*** identifies as an essential task to "prevent our enemies from threatening us, our allies, and our friends with weapons of mass destruction" for ensuring national security. To achieve this goal, the NSS of the United States of America sets forth an active strategy to counter transnational terror networks, rogue nations, and aggressive states that possess, or are working to acquire, WMD. The United States advances this strategy through strengthened alliances, the establishment of new partnerships, proactive counterproliferation (CP) efforts, modern technologies, and increased emphasis on intelligence collection and analysis. The NSS highlights nonproliferation (NP) concerns in its examination of the Treaty on the Nonproliferation of Nuclear Weapons (NPT) and its special emphasis on stemming the spread of nuclear weapons and fissile materials, and the diversion of nuclear energy materials to nuclear weapons programs. Both *proactive* CP and *improved protection* are reemphasized in order to "defend against and defeat WMD and missile threats before they are unleashed," and "to mitigate the consequences of WMD use," respectively.

b. The ***National Strategy to Combat Weapons of Mass Destruction*** (**NS-CWMD**) provides additional guidance concerning CWMD: NP, CP, and WMD consequence management (CM), as highlighted in the NSS, and introduces the construct of the three pillars which provides a common framework for the interagency conduct of CWMD activities. It describes how critical enabling functions (improved intelligence collection and analysis; research and development (R&D); strengthened international cooperation; and targeted strategies against proliferants) help to integrate the three pillars into one seamless, comprehensive approach to CWMD. In order for this strategy to be successful, DOD will dissuade the development and production of WMD; deter its use or mitigate its effects; prevent or reverse its proliferation; ensure stockpiles are secure and progressively reduced or destroyed. If WMD is used against the United States, DOD will defend against it, mitigate its consequences, and respond appropriately. These three pillars are discussed in detail later in this chapter.

c. The ***National Strategy for Combating Terrorism*** articulates four priorities of action that the USG intends to take in reference to combating terrorism. One of them is to deny WMD to rogue states and terrorist allies who seek to use them. This priority identifies the need to develop a comprehensive approach for addressing WMD terrorism, specifically through six objectives that are intended to drive focus and action from the international community:

(1) Determine terrorists' intentions, capabilities, and plans to develop or acquire WMD.

(2) Deny terrorists access to the materials, expertise, and other enabling capabilities required to develop WMD.

(3) Deter terrorists from employing WMD.

(4) Detect and disrupt terrorists' attempted movement of WMD-related materials, weapons, and personnel.

(5) Prevent and respond to a WMD-related terrorist attack.

(6) Define the nature and source of a terrorist-employed WMD device.

3. Military Strategic Guidance

a. **The *National Military Strategy to Combat Weapons of Mass Destruction* (NMS-CWMD)** provides DOD components with guidance and a strategic framework for CWMD, as outlined in Figure I-1. The NMS-CWMD uses an "ends, ways, and means" approach to planning, executing, resourcing, and emphasizes those CWMD missions in which the military plays a prominent role. It defines strategic end states, strategic enablers, military strategic objectives (MSOs), and eight military mission areas (MMAs) the Armed Forces of the United States may be called upon to perform.

(1) The **MSOs** identified in the NMS-CWMD serve as the "ways" in the "ends, ways, means" approach to achieving the US strategic CWMD goal. These are conducted across all three pillars and the eight MMAs and may cut across all phases of joint operations (shape, deter, seize the initiative, dominate, stabilize, and enable civil authority).

(a) **Prevent, Dissuade, or Deny WMD Proliferation or Possession.** The purpose of this MSO is to keep WMD out of the hands of adversaries and potential adversaries, while simultaneously increasing multinational partner capability and support for CWMD activities. This includes conveying to current and potential adversaries the futility of using WMD possession or proliferation is not an avenue to impose their will on the United States. Moreover, the US will assure multinational partners that they do not need to possess WMD to ensure their security or stability. The WMD offensive operations, WMD interdiction, and WMD security cooperation MMAs link directly to this MSO. The activities associated with this MSO principally occur in phase 0 (Shape) and phase 1 (Deter) operations. Successfully attaining this MSO requires significant interagency coordination, especially between DOD and the Department of State (DOS).

For further guidance to indicate what different phases are and where they are defined, refer to Joint Publication (JP) 3-0, Joint Operations, *Chapter IV*, Planning, Operational Art and Design, and Assessment.

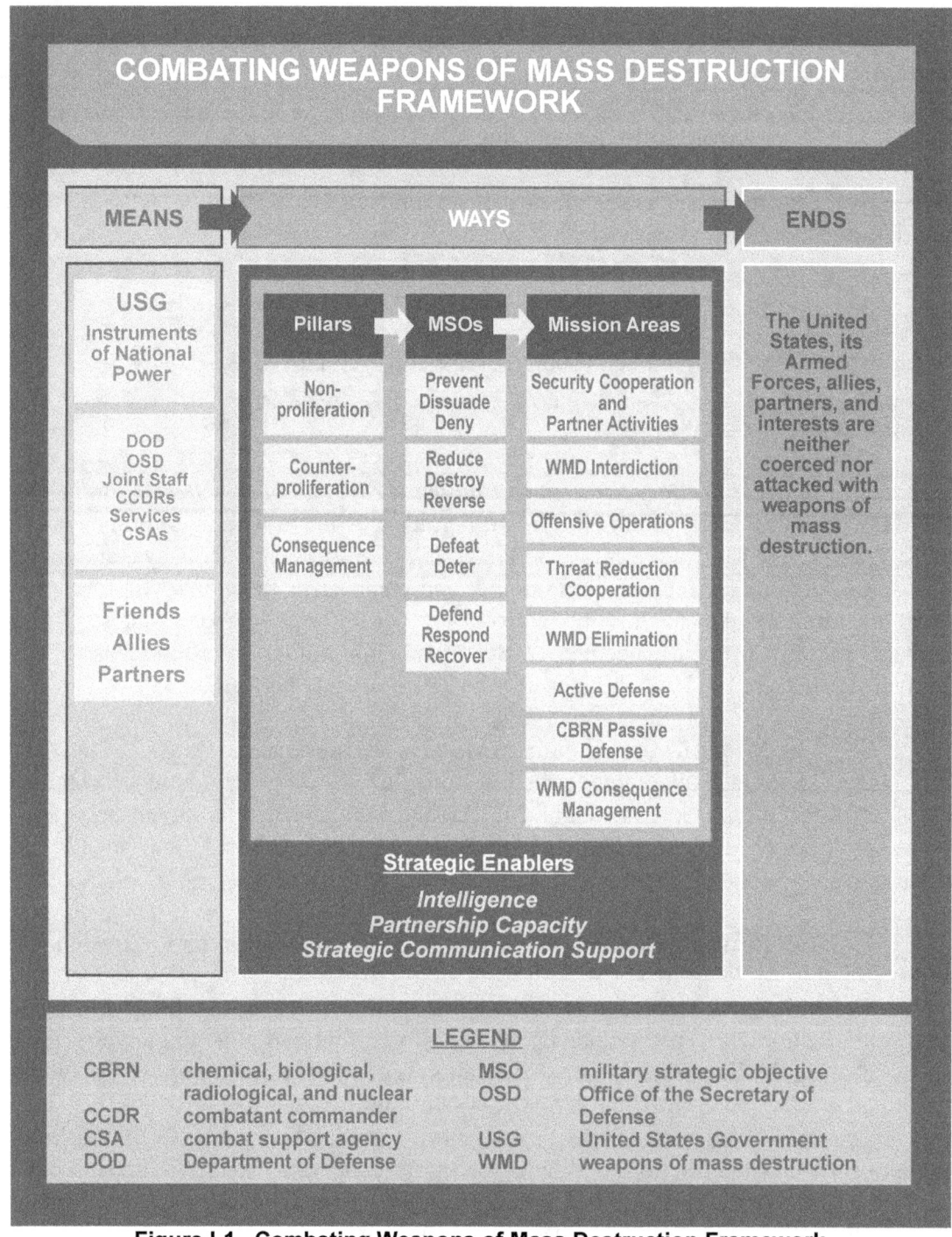

Figure I-1. Combating Weapons of Mass Destruction Framework

(b) **Reduce, Destroy, or Reverse WMD Possession.** The purpose of this MSO is to destroy or secure WMD when there is an agreement to do so. This includes reversing WMD programs and reducing WMD and related material stockpiles. This MSO focuses on threat reduction cooperation while operating in a permissive environment. The activities associated with this MSO predominantly occur in phase 0 (Shape) and phase 1 (Deter) operations. Current and potential allies and partners might desire to give up possession of WMD or associated technology at any point in the development process.

(c) **Defeat and Deter WMD Use and Subsequent Use.** The purpose of this MSO is to counter an adversary's willingness and capability to use WMD. Adversaries must believe they will suffer severe consequences and that their objectives will be denied if they threaten or resort to WMD use. If deterrence fails, the WMD offensive operations, WMD elimination, WMD interdiction, CBRN passive defense, and WMD active defense MMAs could be conducted to support this MSO. The emphasis on deterrence and defeat in this MSO shows that, while phase 0 (Shape) is an especially critical phase for the CWMD mission, CWMD considerations must be integrated into all phases of joint operations.

(d) **Defend, Respond, and Recover from WMD Use.** The purpose of this MSO is to respond to an adversary that has used WMD in an operational area or against US strategic interests. This includes not just minimizing the effects of WMD on military operations but, if directed, supporting the response to a WMD event in the homeland or against multinational partners, as well. The CBRN passive defense, WMD active defense, and weapons of mass destruction consequence management (WMD CM) MMAs are directly linked to this MSO. The execution of these MMAs highlight the importance of interagency coordination in order to effectively combat WMD. The Department of Homeland Security (DHS) and DOS play significant roles in CBRN passive defense and WMD CM. CWMD, from beginning to end, must be a synchronized effort of the USG.

(2) **CWMD MMAs.** The NMS-CWMD outlines eight MMAs for CWMD: offensive operations, WMD elimination, WMD interdiction, active defense, CBRN passive defense, WMD CM, security cooperation and partner activities, and threat reduction cooperation. These eight MMAs provide joint force commanders (JFCs) with a logical grouping of CWMD capabilities. These MMAs are described in greater detail in Chapter IV, "Planning and Execution."

(3) **Strategic Enablers.** The strategic enablers identified in the NMS-CWMD are cross-cutting capabilities that facilitate execution of the military strategy by enhancing the effectiveness and integration of military CWMD mission capabilities. Intelligence, partnership capacity, and strategic communication (SC) support are applicable across the four CWMD MSOs, eight CWMD mission areas and the six phases of joint operations. They also highlight the important role phase 0 (Shape) operations play in the CWMD mission.

(a) **Intelligence, Surveillance, and Reconnaissance (ISR).** This strategic enabler directly supports strategy, planning, and decision making; facilitates improvements in operational capabilities; and informs risk management. Recognizing the limits of combating WMD intelligence, planning and execution decisions will be made using limited or incomplete information. To reduce uncertainty, our intelligence capability must exploit a variety of sources, facilitate information sharing, and improve situational awareness.

(b) **Partnership Capacity.** Building partnership capacity bilaterally and multilaterally enhances US capability to combat WMD. Partnership capacity empowers other nations, increases regional stability, and reduces potential burdens on the United States. Assistance from the international community could be a force multiplier in US efforts to combat WMD effectively. This enabler is linked directly to security cooperation activities within a geographic combatant commander's (GCC's) AOR.

(c) **Strategic Communication Support.** This enabler, a USG-wide effort in which the military plays a significant supporting role, helps shape perceptions at the global, regional, national, and local levels. Synchronized themes, messages, images, and actions reassure multinational partners and underscore to potential adversaries the costs and risks associated with WMD acquisition and use. SC is an especially important enabler and deterrent for achieving deterrence and defeat of WMD use. If an adversary can be convinced of the futility of pursuing WMD prior to developing or acquiring it, then the risk of having to defeat a WMD-armed adversary is decreased.

4. **Combating Weapons of Mass Destruction Construct**

a. CWMD requires a long-term, strategic approach that places heavy emphasis on interagency support and international coordination and cooperation to create an environment inhospitable to the acquisition, development, proliferation, and use of WMD, denying adversaries safe havens, and disrupting WMD-enabling networks. CWMD thus involves execution of a broad global strategy where DOD is often not the lead agency, but military capabilities are essential to reinforce these efforts, and therefore must be integrated and synchronized with a larger USG effort. CWMD operations integrate into their theater campaign plans, particularly security cooperation and shaping activities, with the realization that these actions will produce few immediate results. Combatant commanders' (CCDRs) efforts will consist of a wide variety of CWMD actions across discrete lines of operations (LOOs) being executed in conjunction with other USG efforts and the theater campaign strategy.

(1) **CWMD Operational Environment.** Another aspect of CWMD operations is the global nature of the operational environment. Increasingly, adversaries are pursuing asymmetric approaches, including WMD, to counter US military superiority and as a means to coerce the United States, its friends, and allies. With the growth of transnational extremist movements and the increasing complexity of global proliferation and terrorist networks, threats are no longer confined to states or within a given GCC's AOR. Because potential adversaries with WMD operate globally, the US and its partners must combat WMD globally. CWMD actions are conducted across all instruments of national power. To effectively achieve CWMD-related objectives, these instruments must be applied concurrently, as appropriate.

(2) **Shaping Activities.** Shaping activities are performed to dissuade or deter potential adversaries and to assure or solidify relationships with friends and allies. CWMD shaping activities include security cooperation activities that support a theater campaign and also contribute to a global comprehensive approach to combating WMD

across all three CWMD pillars. Actions in phase 0 (Shape) could preclude the need to employ offensive capabilities by deterring adversarial WMD inclinations with demonstrated US resolve and increased US and multinational partner capabilities to respond to, recover from, and mitigate the effects of WMD use. These activities encourage cooperation in a crisis or WMD event.

(3) **CWMD and Major Contingencies.** CWMD should be integrated throughout major contingency planning and execution to ensure successful prosecution. In any contingency, JFCs should consider the interrelationship of CWMD mission areas with other contingency operations. The global nature of CWMD operations should be considered, as even tactical actions within an operational area may have far-reaching implications and interagency and international considerations may outweigh military considerations.

b. The challenges of CWMD require an integrated approach that leverages the pillars of **NP, CP, and WMD CM.** CWMD success depends on how effectively commanders apply all three pillars against WMD challenges. Since each WMD scenario poses unique challenges, commanders must determine the most effective blend of the three pillars best suited to achieve the CWMD end states. Such activities, while often requiring quick-response measures, should be planned for and integrated into a comprehensive strategy.

(1) **Nonproliferation.** NP activities are those **actions taken to prevent the proliferation of WMD by dissuading or impeding access to, or distribution of, sensitive technologies, material, and expertise.** NP efforts use all instruments of national power to prevent the development and proliferation of WMD. While NP is applied usually to prevent the acquisition of WMD by state or non-state actors during the early stages of WMD development, it may also be employed in latter stages of WMD program dismantlement. NP efforts dissuade or impede the proliferation of WMD, as well as slow and make more costly access to sensitive technologies, material, and expertise. The NP pillar can encompass the MMAs of WMD interdiction, security cooperation and partner activities, and threat reduction cooperation. NP activities include providing inspection, monitoring, verification, and enforcement support for NP treaties and WMD control regimes; supporting cooperative threat reduction (CTR) and export control activities; participating in domestic research activities; conducting military-to-military exchanges; and assisting in the identification of potential proliferators before they decide to acquire or expand their WMD capabilities. WMD proliferation is the transfer of WMD, related materials, technology, and expertise from one actor to another. The actors may be state or non-state. WMD proliferation represents an adversarial intent to either possess WMD, develop WMD programs, or to endorse WMD possession and/or programs to other actors.

(2) **Counterproliferation**. CP activities are those **actions taken to defeat the threat and/or use of WMD against the United States, our forces, allies, and partners.** CP operations are taken in response to proliferation and to stop or roll back current WMD programs, defeat delivery systems, and protect US interests from the threat, or use, of

WMD. CP activities may be applied against adversaries early on in the WMD development and acquisition stages, as well as later after they have developed or acquired WMD, threatened to use it or have used it, and to eliminate any residual WMD capabilities. The CP pillar primarily encompasses the MMAs of WMD offensive operations, WMD interdiction, WMD elimination, WMD active defense, and CBRN passive defense, but may also include WMD security cooperation.

(3) **Weapons of Mass Destruction Consequence Management.** WMD CM activities are those **actions authorized by the President or Secretary of Defense (SecDef) to mitigate the effects of a weapon of mass destruction attack or event and provide temporary essential operations and services at home and abroad.** WMD CM procedures may assist in the restoration of essential operations and services at home and abroad. WMD CM capabilities can also be useful in dissuading adversaries from developing or using WMD and may be necessary in response to certain CP activities. The WMD CM pillar primarily encompasses the MMAs of CBRN passive defense and WMD CM, but may also include the MMA of security cooperation and partner activities.

c. The term **CBRN hazards** is often used in conjunction with the effects of a WMD device, to lend greater fidelity to the hazards encountered from the agent or substance or their dispersal. CBRN hazards are those CBRN elements that could cause adverse affect through their accidental or deliberate release, dissemination, or impacts. These hazards include those created from accidental or intentional releases of CBRN from a weapon, device, or facility, including toxic industrial materials (TIMs), biological pathogens, and radioactive matter. Also included are any hazards resulting from WMD employment. The key distinction between WMD and CBRN hazards is that the former refers to the actual weapon, while the latter refers to the *effects* resulting from the employment of those weapons and from the dispersal of CBRN materials. When DOD capabilities are called upon to conduct WMD CM activities, (i.e., to reduce the effects of a WMD event) they will essentially be responding to CBRN hazards.

For further guidance on CBRN hazards, refer to JP 3-11, Operations in Chemical, Biological, Radiological, and Nuclear (CBRN) Environments.

5. **Combating Weapons of Mass Destruction Outside the United States**

DOD can act as both a supported and a supporting entity during CWMD operations outside of the United States. The broad nature of the task requires DOD, even when acting as the supported entity, to recognize the importance of interagency coordination, as well as working closely with multinational partners. Outside of the United States, DOD activities span the entire CWMD mission and encompass all eight MMAs.

For further guidance on the interagency process, refer to JP 3-08, Interorganizational Coordination During Joint Operations.

6. **Combating Weapons of Mass Destruction, the War on Terrorism, and Homeland Defense**

a. CWMD is not a separate and isolated mission set, but is intertwined with WOT and HD. Therefore, to accomplish the goals of CWMD, a JFC must be prepared to synchronize the efforts of CWMD, WOT, and HD activities during all phases of joint operations. The NSS emphasizes the danger stemming from the crossroads of radicalism and technology. Accordingly, the CWMD mission must be integrated with the WOT to prevent terrorist networks from acquiring finished WMD or precursor technology. Moreover, CWMD must be synchronized with the HD mission to prevent a terrorist group from striking the US homeland with WMD.

b. **Combating WMD and the War on Terrorism.** It is important to understand that not all terrorist incidents are WMD incidents. For a terrorist incident to be categorized as a WMD incident, some element of CBRN that results in a high order of destruction or causes mass casualties from the weapon must be involved. This normally omits HYE weapons as a WMD CM consideration, however, certain domestic response plans include HYE and other weapons.

For further guidance on counterterrorism, refer to JP 3-26, Counterterrorism.

c. **Combating WMD and Homeland Defense.** The homeland is confronted by a variety of threats. These include transnational threats—defined in Title 50, United States Code (USC), Section 402, as "any transnational activity (including international terrorism, narcotics trafficking, the proliferation of weapons of mass destruction and the delivery systems for such weapons, and organized crime) that threatens the national security of the United States." HD operations will be conducted in a complex environment characterized by multiple jurisdictions, and authorities, and therefore require the participation of nontraditional partners, nongovernmental organizations (NGOs), and international partners. Coordination among these various organizations will be imperative to ensure synchronized and integrated operations. CWMD contributes to HD by protecting the United States, multinational partners, and interests through an active, layered defense in depth. DOD plays an essential role in CWMD through a full range of operational capabilities to protect the United States, its military forces, and multinational partners from the threat or actual use of WMD. DOD, as directed by the President, may conduct preemptive HD actions in support of CWMD and in accordance with international and domestic law, national policy, and directives.

For further guidance on HD, refer to JP 3-27, Homeland Defense.

7. **Combating Weapons of Mass Destruction and Civil Support**

DOD provides support to civil authorities for domestic emergencies and for designated law enforcement and other activities. Joint forces supporting civil authorities in response to a domestic WMD incident are part of domestic incident management and operate in accordance with the National Response Framework (NRF). The National

Incident Management System (NIMS) forms the foundation for conducting domestic response operations. When emergency conditions dictate, and when time does not permit approval from higher headquarters (HQ), local military commanders and responsible DOD component officials are authorized to respond to requests from local authorities and to initiate immediate response actions to save lives, prevent human suffering, or mitigate great property damage under imminently serious conditions. For foreign incidents, this is restricted to saving lives as per current memorandums of understanding, memorandums of agreement, and status-of-forces agreements. Within the US, DOD activities are primarily related to the WMD CM MMA.

For further guidance on civil support (CS), refer to JP 3-28, Civil Support.

8. **Combating Weapons of Mass Destruction and Consequence Management**

a. WMD CM is an integral part of CWMD efforts. It is important to note the difference between chemical, biological, radiological, nuclear, and high-yield explosives (CBRNE) CM response to an incident involving the deliberate or inadvertent release of CBRNE materials and WMD CM which deals with the consequences of CBRN weapons and associated materials intentionally used in creating a high order of destruction or causing mass casualties. The WMD CM mission area highlights the complexity of the various lexicons, laws, and agreements for conducting CWMD with interagency, multinational, intergovernmental organization (IGO), and NGO partners. Chapter III, "Organizational and Command Relationships," contains a discussion of interagency and multinational considerations and command and control (C2) for domestic operations.

For further guidance on CBRNE CM, refer to JP 3-41, Chemical, Biological, Radiological, Nuclear, and High-Yield Explosives Consequence Management.

b. **Domestic WMD CM Operations.** DOD will generally be operating in support of another federal agency whenever it conducts CM for a domestic WMD incident. USG coordination in such an event is outlined in the NRF. Therefore, domestic WMD CM response will also include capabilities to perform CBRNE CM response operations. Domestic CM operations include CM activities in Alaska, Hawaii, the Commonwealth of Puerto Rico, the US Virgin Islands, Navassa Island, US Pacific territories of Guam, American Samoa, Jarvis Island, the Commonwealth of the Northern Mariana Islands, Wake Atoll, Midway Atoll, Johnston Atoll, Baker Island, Howland Island, Palmyra Atoll, and Kingman Reef, and the Freely Associated States of Micronesia and the Republic of the Marshall Islands.

For further guidance on domestic CM, refer to Chairman of the Joint Chiefs of Staff Instruction (CJCSI) 3125.01A, Defense Support to Civil Authorities for Domestic Consequence Management Operations in Response to Chemical, Biological, Radiological, Nuclear or High-Yield Explosives Incident.

c. **Foreign CM Operations.** DOS is the lead agency for coordinating USG foreign consequence management (FCM) operations when there is a host nation (HN) request for, or acceptance of, USG assistance unless otherwise directed by the President. In this instance, DOD is a supporting agency for FCM operations. For most FCM operations, DOD will be in support of another government agency, and that organization may be supporting a partner nation or an IGO. Proper coordination of these operations will be very complex, will vary by country and combatant command AOR, and requires considerable effort by all parties. FCM policy more closely aligns with the response limitations of WMD CM and only applies to incidents that involve CBRN materials.

For further guidance on FCM operations, refer to Department of Defense Instruction (DODI) 2000.21, Foreign Consequence Management (FCM) or *CJCSI 3214.01C,* Military Support to Foreign Consequence Management Operations for Chemical, Biological, Radiological, and Nuclear Incidents.

For further guidance on multinational operations, refer to JP 3-16, Multinational Operations.

d. **DOD Led CM Operations.** In both domestic and foreign environments, CM actions are initiated at the national level with DOD providing support as directed by the President or SecDef. DOD forces may, however, be directed to lead CM operations as a direct result of US military operations in a foreign country where DOS does not have an established presence.

For further guidance on CM operations on DOD installations, refer to DODI 2000.18, Department of Defense Installation Chemical, Biological, Radiological, Nuclear, and High-Yield Explosive Emergency Response Guidelines.

Intentionally Blank

CHAPTER II
THE CHALLENGE OF WEAPONS OF MASS DESTRUCTION THREATS

> *"We will not permit the world's most dangerous regimes and terrorists to threaten us with the world's most destructive weapons. We must accord the highest priority to the protection of the United States, our forces, and our friends and allies from the existing and growing WMD [weapons of mass destruction] threat."*
>
> **National Strategy to Combat Weapons of Mass Destruction**
> **December 2002**

1. General

a. This chapter identifies and describes the challenges of WMD threats faced by the JFC and highlights the general characteristics of WMD threats and threat actors. The WMD threat and US perception of that threat has evolved along with the security environment. In the latter half of the 20th century, CWMD strategy was largely based on deterrence of a very small number of nation-states. The threats at the time were characterized by established, effective governments; stringent control and accountability measures for WMD weapons; large conventional militaries with near parity; set geographic areas; substantial economic and industrial bases; and, perhaps most importantly, a relatively clear understanding of adversary motivations and risk calculations. Today's security environment consists of a wide variety of threat actors ranging from state actors, with characteristics similar to earlier threats, to non-state actors, including terrorists, other transnational groups, and even industrial concerns, with vastly different characteristics. These actors may have little to no established government or leadership structure; few controls on weapons or operations; small cells or even no conventional military capability; operate across political and geographic boundaries; no clear economic base that can be held at risk; and differing or even competing agendas, motivations, and objectives.

b. CWMD requires a strong partnership between the United States, its allies, and other friendly nations to assure them and to dissuade, deter, and defeat the potential WMD threat that could result in devastating consequences to all concerned. Because of US overall military superiority, many actors seek asymmetric capabilities, like WMD, due to these weapons' ability to drastically alter any imbalance of conventional force. Such asymmetric capability may allow an actor to give them a strategic advantage and to influence public or political will, and coerce the United States or its friends and allies with the threat of large-scale destruction. To compound this threat, the technology associated with WMD has proliferated globally in the past several decades as information and capabilities have become more accessible. An adversary's threat or use of WMD and the proliferation of these capabilities will continue to challenge commanders at all levels.

c. The evolution of the WMD threat has created new challenges for JFCs beyond dealing with adversary WMD use. The primary challenges facing the JFC are:

(1) The diversity of threat actors, including the emergence of nontraditional WMD threats;

(2) The varied nature of WMD demands a varied approach to deterrence;

(3) A complex WMD proliferation continuum;

(4) The dual-use nature of much of the related technology and expertise;

(5) The increasing complexity and number of WMD proliferation networks.

2. **State Actors and Programs**

a. State actors and their associated WMD programs vary in their level of activity and sophistication and remain a credible threat to the United States. There are strong indications that nuclear weapon capabilities continue to grow and proliferate. New classes of nontraditional biological and chemical agents and threats continue to emerge and challenge our defenses. Advances in delivery systems, both conventional and unconventional, continue to increase. States possessing or seeking WMD see them as a source of strategic leverage, international prestige, regional dominance, local deterrence, or as a means to counter US and western power in areas of potential conflict. A significant challenge lies in assessing the intent and capabilities of the state's leadership. Furthermore, states may intentionally or unintentionally provide WMD resources to non-state actors. In the former case, a state may exploit an all too willing non-state entity as a proxy so that the state can claim plausible deniability of an attack. In the latter case, a state's non-secured WMD may fall into the hands of non-state actors.

b. **Control of State Programs.** Since the fall of the Soviet Union in 1991, and with the possible decline of authority in other states with WMD programs, the US faces an increasingly challenging dilemma involving states that may not be able to control their CBRN weapons, material, technology, or expertise. In such cases, these items can fall into the hands of other states or non-state actors. As government power ebbs and flows in many parts of the world due to local and regional instability, the JFC should plan for the increasing dispersal of state-owned and state-controlled weapons, material, technology, or expertise to rogue factions within states or non-state actors. In some cases, determining the level of security and control of these items will be the source of new challenges.

3. **Non-State Actors and Programs**

a. There is continuing interest by non-state actors in acquiring WMD. **Non-state actors can be categorized as terrorists (including their networks) and other non-state entities. The category of other non-state entities include extremists, insurgents, transnational threats, NGOs, businesses, rogue scientists/technicians, as well as, individuals acting independently of any organization.** The main difference between terrorists and other non-state actors is that of intended use. Whereas terrorists seek to acquire and use WMD, other non-state entities lack the intent to use and may be witting or unwitting participants in WMD proliferation. If they are witting participants, they are likely seeking financial gain. Where efforts against state actors and terrorists can fall within the realm of the JFC, a significant percentage of the effort against other non-state entities may fall outside the purview of the JFC and reside either with the interagency or multinational partners.

    b. **Scale and Complexity.** An additional consideration for the JFC is the scale and/or complexity of non-state actor programs. Traditionally, a state program is vast in resources and physical size. The scale of production from non-state actors (and more specifically terrorists) is typically much smaller in scale and complexity. In fact, many small-scale chemical and biological production facilities for a terrorist organization, such as clandestine laboratories, can occur within a typical bedroom-sized area. Commanders at all levels must be aware of the potential significant threat of these small scale facilities and take appropriate measures. Care must be taken to exploit the intelligence value that can be gained from these production facilities even though they may seem insignificant based on their size and the nondescript nature of much of the equipment. Both scale and complexity of a program is a factor for the JFC in determining the appropriate mix of forces.

4.   **Traditional and Nontraditional Threats**

    Traditional threats are those threats delivered by conventional military delivery means (e.g., aircraft-delivered bombs, rockets, missiles, mortars, and artillery); **nontraditional threats** are those delivered using improvised weapons or material against either conventional or unconventional targets.

    a. Traditional WMD Threats. Advances in conventional delivery means and modern infrastructure construction technology continue to make the traditional WMD threat a concern for national security both regionally and globally. Many of the weapon system advances include increasingly capable cruise missile technology, unmanned aircraft system (UAS) technology, and the continuing development of improved medium- and long-range ballistic missiles. The existence of deeply buried underground facilities has emerged as one of the more difficult operational challenges to confront US military forces. They may be used to manufacture and store WMD delivery systems, as well as used for C2. Because of the nature of their construction, they are difficult to locate and target. As WMD technology and materials advance, the ability to employ WMD technologies and material by our adversaries will become more lethal. Our adversaries possess and will continue to explore unconventional means to employ WMD materials through biological dispersion devices, remote controlled roadside bombs, and improvised explosives devices (IEDs). On the other hand, the following are examples that state sponsored terrorists can use or employ WMD technologies and material by our adversaries: nanotechnology, biotechnology, advanced genetics, space-based capabilities, and advances in computing to allow non-state actors more efficient access to information or production techniques.

    b. Nontraditional WMD Threats. As nontraditional threats are the most open-ended. The JFC must leverage a detailed joint intelligence preparation of the operational environment (JIPOE) and mission analysis to identify potential nontraditional threats within the area of interest. The employment of WMD by nonmilitary means may pose one of the most significant challenges due to detection limitations. Nonmilitary means of delivery may include sprayers (e.g., crop dusters, backpack); existing transportation infrastructure (e.g., air, rail, subway, bus, and ship); private transportation assets (e.g., vehicle, watercraft, or aircraft); IEDs, or UAS technology. Public targets can include, but are not limited to, malls, stadiums, religious gatherings, financial institutions, and industrial facilities.

ADVANCES IN BIOTECHNOLOGY

Advances in biotechnology and life sciences—including the spread of expertise to create modified or novel organisms—present the prospect of new toxins, live agents, and bioregulators that require new detection methods, preventive measures, and treatments. Additionally, the proliferation of biological materials, technologies, and expertise increases the potential for adversaries to design pathogens to evade our existing medical and nonmedical countermeasures.

VARIOUS SOURCES

---

5. Proliferation Continuum

a. The development and employment of WMD capabilities is a complex but identifiable process with several generic activities that together constitute an adversary's proliferation continuum (Figure II-1). This proliferation continuum represents key decision points by an adversary to either possess or proliferate WMD. It also represents a transition in our CWMD activities across the three pillars. Adversaries may, at any point along the proliferation continuum, effectively bypass one of the steps by acquiring (by theft, barter, or purchase) the capability, thereby accelerating the WMD development process. Proactive actions can be taken at every stage of the proliferation continuum to successfully combat the WMD proliferation. However, the JFC should look to combat these threats early in the continuum to minimize risk of further proliferation or use. The generic activities include: a decision to pursue WMD capability; infrastructure and expertise development; production; weaponization; deployment; and employment. In some cases, infrastructure and expertise development, facility preparation, and production may be concealed within industrial or agricultural production (so-called dual use materials), academic institutions, or within underground facilities, making intelligence collection efforts more difficult. Furthermore, JFCs should bear in mind that Article IV of the NPT guarantees its signatories the right to develop nuclear energy for peaceful purposes, which may also mask the development of fissile material for warheads.

b. **Secondary Proliferation.** There is a growing concern that states that were once recipients of WMD related technologies and materials may begin to indigenously produce and export these same technologies to other countries of proliferation concern. The ability and willingness of these states to export WMD-related technologies and materials to other states outside of, or in noncompliance with, international NP rules are a

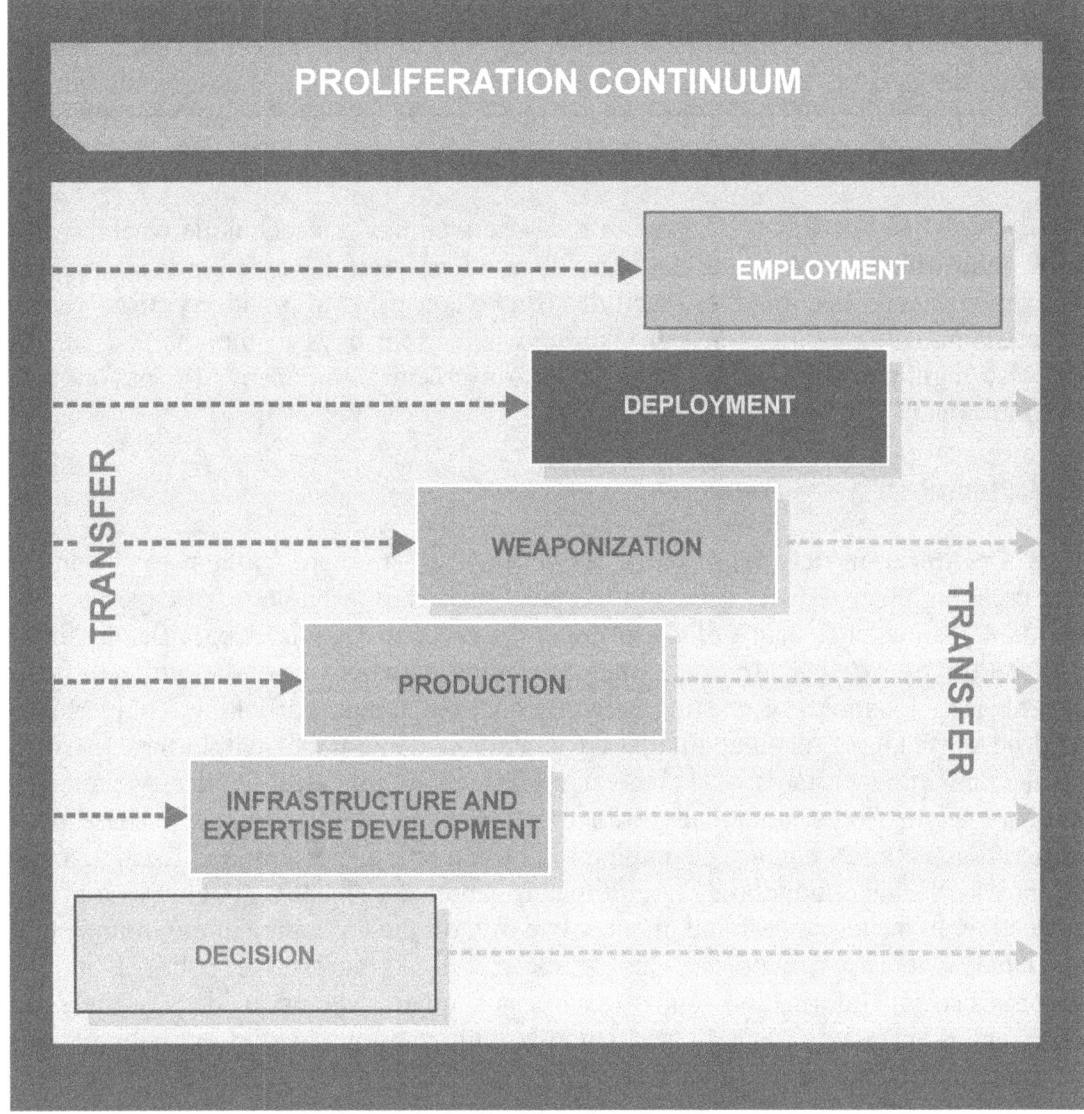

Figure II-1. Proliferation Continuum

serious threat. Furthermore, a secondary proliferation threat exists from non-state actors (e.g., scientists, businesses, and their networks) who proliferate WMD-related technologies and materials. Secondary proliferation compounds the risks of terrorists acquiring WMD. All of this secondary proliferation occurs outside of international controls and, while difficult to detect, must remain a JFC concern.

6. **Dual-Use Technology and Facilities**

a. **Dual-use technology** is technology that can be used for both commercial and military applications and is an area of exploitation by adversaries seeking to develop weapons programs. Furthermore, the dual-use nature of most biological and chemical related technologies makes procurement easier to mask, monitoring efforts more difficult, and enables proliferators to bypass control regimes. The opportunities for WMD acquisition facilitated by dual-use technology will continue to be difficult to detect and track. Even though a number of states follow certain NP agreements, development times for some WMD programs could be shortened because of the relatively advanced research institutes throughout the world; the availability of relevant dual-use studies and information; scientists' enthusiasm for sharing research; and the availability of dual-use training and education.

b. **Dual-Use Facilities.** The use of dual-use facilities is a technique whereby states utilize industrial or agricultural facilities to produce legitimate commercial products; however, with modification, these facilities can be converted to produce CBRN weapons or material. This modification can take anywhere from days to months and can turn otherwise legitimate commercial facilities into a crucial component of a nation-state's WMD program.

7. **Proliferation Networks**

a. **Proliferation networks** are the supporting infrastructure that a state or non-state actor uses to gain or transfer access to weapons, material, technology, or expertise. It is important to note that many of these networks are not organized specifically for the proliferation of WMD. In fact, many existing networks may be utilized out of convenience. Examples of existing networks include human trafficking, counterfeiting, and drug trafficking. As an additional consideration, some nodes within these networks may be unwitting partners. The threat is further complicated by the operations of multinational networks, potentially with the support of state resources. These global proliferation activities employ a combination of secrecy, dispersion, and fiscal resources that must be located, monitored, and ultimately targeted. The JFC should use a systems perspective to better understand the complexity of the operational environment and associated adversary networks. This perspective looks across the political, military, economic, social, information, infrastructure, and other systems to identify the nodes, links, centers of gravity (COGs), and potential vulnerabilities within the network. The JFC must understand that as these networks expand in scope and area, the actions needed to adequately identify and affect them may reside outside DOD influence and may require interagency or IGO efforts. Depending on joint force organization, the JFC may lack a full range of capabilities that can support unity of effort to proactively and comprehensively dissuade, deter, defeat, or deny these networks. To adequately influence all of these networks, the JFC must leverage other instruments of national power.

For further guidance on systems analysis, refer to JP 2-01.3, Joint Intelligence Preparation of the Operational Environment, *and JP 3-0,* Joint Operations.

b. **Characteristics of a Network.** Proliferation networks are multifunctional and multidimensional; consist of state and, increasingly, independent non-state actors; are dynamic, adaptive, and can be transnational; have differing motivations and desired end states; and operate in secrecy to avoid detection and counteraction. They respond to changes in their environment, learn, and acquire new knowledge through study. Many networks are selectively active. They lie dormant when their support is not required and become active when the WMD development process requires (e.g., executing financial activities when buying expertise or knowledge or executing logistic activities when moving or deploying a weapon). Networks may be limited in their duration (days, weeks, months) and may be dissolved once its purpose is achieved.

A.Q. KHAN PROLIFERATION NETWORK

The Khan network was, first and foremost, an elaborate and highly successful illicit procurement network that Khan created in the 1970s to supply Pakistan's gas centrifuge program. The developing program aimed to make highly enriched uranium (HEU) for nuclear weapons. He built his centrifuge procurement network on an extensive collection of sensitive information that he stole or otherwise acquired in Europe in the middle and late 1970s. In addition, he was involved in acquiring overseas nuclear weapon technology for Pakistan and procuring equipment and materials for this endeavor.

Because of Pakistan's weak industrial infrastructure, it was unable to develop gas centrifuges or nuclear weapons without extensive foreign assistance. Khan relied on the support of many foreign businessmen and experts and on the supply of goods and technologies from foreign countries, especially in Europe. Pakistan's nuclear weapons program is still dependent on the foreign supply of spare parts, special materials, and instruments.

Khan and his associates slowly expanded their import operation into a transnational illegal network that exported whole gas centrifuges and production capabilities, as well as designs for nuclear weapons, mostly to Muslim countries. By the late 1990s, the Khan network had evolved into an organization that could provide "one-stop shopping," both for the wherewithal to produce weapons-grade uranium and for nuclear weapons designs and instructions. The motive was to turn a profit while providing additional business for their international collaborators. In addition to money, Khan was also motivated by pan-Islamism and its hostility to Western controls on nuclear technology.

Khan has admitted that his main customers were Iran, Libya, and North Korea. Reports indicate that other countries, including Egypt, Iraq, and Syria, were offered assistance, but they purportedly turned down the offers. However, investigators are still trying to verify these claims and determine exactly what assistance each country accepted or refused. In addition, questions remain as to whether members of the Khan network, including Khan himself, offered nuclear weapon assistance to terrorists in Afghanistan prior to the fall of the Taliban.

SOURCE: The A.Q. Khan Illicit Nuclear Trade Network and Implications for Nonproliferation Efforts, Strategic Insights, Volume V, Issue 6 (July 2006) by David Albright and Corey Hinderstein

c. Many of these networks, whether focused solely on WMD proliferation or not, are comprised of several common functions. While this list is not all-inclusive, these networks can include:

(1) **Leadership.** Activities to provide motivation and the physical means to control activities of the WMD program. This includes providing strategic direction, coordinating the activities of other networks, facilitating the flow of information and resources throughout the networks, and providing the motivation to acquire WMD. This function may be state-directed or may reflect ideological, financial, business, or other concerns that motivate WMD proliferation.

(2) **Finance.** Activities to secure and transfer the financial resources to fund all aspects of a WMD program. These activities can include brokers, middlemen, financial institutions, banking systems, and charities.

(3) **Scientific and Technical Expertise.** Activities to provide the knowledge and expertise necessary to produce WMD and related infrastructure (e.g., designing, producing, machining, testing, storing). This function harnesses information and expertise from scientists, researchers, engineers, and technicians necessary to support capability development.

(4) **Communications.** Activities to provide the necessary information throughout the network. Because of the importance of these programs, great effort will be taken to protect communication channels.

(5) **Logistics.** Activities to acquire, produce, and transport the raw material, people, production materiel, and finished products. This function acquires missing components or technology; trains and recruits needed expertise, as required; and may support the theft of WMD technology, components, and fully-weaponized WMD. This facet includes a significant portion of the network, such as front companies (clandestine or legitimate), shipping companies, producers, import/export companies, and other means of conveyance.

(6) **Intelligence, Surveillance and Reconnaissance.** Activities to acquire detailed target data and determine potential sources of WMD components, technology, and expertise.

(7) **Weapon Delivery.** Activities to deliver the WMD to the target and direct its firing. These activities can be both conventional and unconventional.

(8) **Security.** Activities to protect the identity of the leadership or the operations being conducted (e.g., finance, production of WMD, acquisition, and logistics). This action allows the organization the ability to operate undetected while preparing for future operations.

8. Role of Deterrence

a. The JFC must consider the changing role of deterrence against state actors and, more importantly, the role of deterrence against non-state actors. WMD deterrence has shifted from a Cold War focus on a very small number of actors to a wide perspective on multiple and varied actors. Traditional economic, diplomatic, informational, and military deterrent measures, including the threat of overwhelming response, remain key aspects of deterrence, especially against state actors and state-sponsored WMD threats. However, the difficulty of definitively attributing use, as well as the emergence of non-state actors whose values and decision making may be difficult to analyze, makes the capability to deny adversaries' objectives an increasingly important element of WMD deterrence. Finally, the diversity of the types of threats and number of threat actors requires a broader deterrence construct and themes and messages tailored to each adversary.

b. The general principles of deterrence against a state actor have not significantly changed. An established state would carefully consider US defense capabilities, the potential US response against its use of WMD, and the political will of the US to react. Deterrent measures, in close coordination with SC, have proven effective against states. However, the current security environment has two new aspects with regard to state actors. The first is an increased number of state actors possessing or developing WMD and the second is the rise of state-sponsored terrorist groups.

(1) During the Cold War, the "nuclear umbrella" of the superpowers provided a measure of security to their allies and client states. Also, the major powers wielded considerable influence over the development of military capabilities of their allies and clients. The superpowers had a strong incentive to maintain the balance of power and to prevent WMD development by countries under their influence. With the end of the Cold War, the foundation of many of the security guarantees shifted and economic and military support to some states was withdrawn. This increased the desire of certain states to obtain WMD to enhance their own security, while simultaneously reducing the influence of the major powers in the decision-making process of these nations. Thus, some nations that had not shown interest in WMD began programs to obtain them. State actors are generally driven to obtain WMD to enhance state or regime security, to gain influence, or to enhance national prestige. Additionally, states with WMD capabilities may desire to proliferate those capabilities to gain influence and enhance prestige for economic gain or for ideological reasons.

(2) The end of the Cold War also saw an increase in state sponsored terrorists, which states use as a means to mask hostile activities, gain influence, or increase internal political support. While the desire of a terrorist group itself to obtain or use WMD may not be directly influenced, an element of WMD deterrence may be achieved by applying pressure on the state sponsor to control the group's activity or reduce the state's support to that actor. While not generally thought of as deterrent measures, many NP activities and capabilities provide a deterrent effect by creating an environment hostile to proliferators. The "guilt by association" may influence states to withhold support to groups that are attempting to obtain or use WMD. Furthermore, US nuclear forensics

capabilities, which tie nuclear and radiological devices to their point of origin, could also deter states from employing or proliferating such devices.

c. Deterring non-state actors is a difficult challenge because it may not be possible to deter the most devoted violent extremists. However, a measure of WMD deterrence may be achieved by demonstrating capabilities such as robust WMD active defense and CBRN passive defense, as well as exercising WMD CM, to deny adversaries accomplishment of their objective. A strong SC program could create an environment unfavorable to WMD use. The actor may not only fail to achieve its goals, but may risk erosion of popular and political support by using or attempting to use WMD. For example, the conduct of direct action operations against locations and key personnel suspected of WMD-related activities may compel surviving leadership to abandon efforts to obtain WMD capabilities. While non-state actors' values, decision making, and risk calculations may be dramatically different from those of state actors, each actor desires to accomplish some goal or objective by obtaining or using WMD. By determining those goals and demonstrating the ability to deny success the JFC can limit the options available to the adversary.

d. An effective WMD deterrence capability rests on understanding the adversary. To be effective, deterrent measures must consider factors such as values, motivation, objectives, leadership and decision making, risk calculations, and tolerance. The increasing number of WMD actors and the diversity of their characteristics require the JFC to develop an understanding of each of the actors and to tailor specific operations to deter each one. The nuances involved do not permit a "one size fits all approach" to WMD deterrence in today's strategic environment.

CHAPTER III
ORGANIZATIONAL AND COMMAND RELATIONSHIPS

> *"...The United States, through a concerted interagency and partner nation effort, must be prepared to detect, tag and track, intercept, and destroy WMD [weapons of mass destruction] and related materials. We must also be prepared to act quickly to secure those weapons and materials in cases where a state loses control of its weapons, especially nuclear devices. Should the worst happen, and we are attacked, we must be able to sustain operations during that attack and help mitigate the consequences of WMD attacks at home and overseas."*
>
> **National Defense Strategy 2008**

1. **Organizations and Functions**

    a. **Office of the Secretary of Defense.** The Office of the Secretary of Defense (OSD) develops, coordinates, and oversees implementation and integration of DOD CWMD policy. OSD coordinates with the interagency for the transition or transfer of responsibility of CWMD operations from the Armed Forces of the United States to other government agencies (OGAs), international agencies, or other countries, as appropriate. OSD coordinates with both DOS and the Joint Staff (JS) to obtain international CWMD legal authorities, protocols, standards, and agreements; multinational support for CWMD operations; and, when required, HN support. They coordinate with DOS to notify the Organization for the Prohibition of Chemical Weapons of discoveries or destruction of chemical weapons materials and former production facilities. They coordinate with the National Counterproliferation Center to enhance intelligence support regarding WMD capabilities of all state and non-state actors. They coordinate with partner agencies and organizations of the USG in support to the homeland in the conduct of CS operations, such as domestic CBRNE CM or nuclear forensics. They also will coordinate DOD processes and procedures within the USG National Technical Nuclear Forensics interagency community.

    b. **Chairman of the Joint Chiefs of Staff (CJCS).** The CJCS serves as the principal military advisor to the President, National Security Council, and SecDef regarding CWMD activities and apportions CWMD resources for planning and execution of the mission. The JS coordinates with combatant commands and Services to ensure CWMD operations are executed in compliance with domestic, international, and foreign laws, policies, treaties, and agreements. They assist with interagency support for CWMD operations and assist in planning and exercising CWMD activities within the interagency process. They also coordinate and provide intelligence support to the CCDRs for target identification and prioritization. When required after SecDef approval, CJCS will publish appropriate execution orders for CWMD activities.

    c. **Geographic Combatant Commanders.** GCCs plan and execute CWMD operations within their AORs. They develop regional CWMD plans for their AORs and incorporate CWMD operations into their other plans. CCDR planning includes preparing strategic estimates, priorities, and joint operation plans for CWMD; incorporating

CWMD-related activities in theater security cooperation planning; and planning for minimizing or mitigating potential WMD collateral effects from WMD offensive operations and WMD active defense. GCCs also provide for intratheater movement of specialized CWMD personnel and equipment and coordinate transition of suspect or confirmed WMD-related material, to include weapons, agents, delivery systems, and infrastructure for short- to long-term storage, protection, dismantlement, destruction, or disposal. This includes tracking, documenting, accounting, and reporting WMD weapons, material, facilities, and personnel discovered, stored, or destroyed in the AOR. In support of phase IV (Stabilize) and phase V (Enable Civil Authority) operations, CCDRs coordinate with OSD and JS to plan for transition or transfer of responsibility of CWMD operations to or from the Armed Forces of the United States from or to other multinational forces or nation-states. When applicable, they develop threat reduction and cooperation plans to allow for transfer and termination of CWMD missions. Finally, they coordinate with OSD and JS to ensure CWMD operations are in compliance with US obligations under international laws, policies, treaties, and agreements.

(1) **Commander, United States Northern Command** is responsible for conducting HD and CS operations (including WMD CM and CP operations) within the United States Northern Command (USNORTHCOM) AOR. USNORTHCOM organizes and executes its missions through assigned Service components, designated functional components, and subordinate standing joint task forces (JTFs). The standing subordinate JTFs have specific missions to prevent transnational threats to the homeland or to plan and integrate DOD domestic CBRN response to WMD incidents or accidents.

(2) **Commander, United States Pacific Command (CDRUSPACOM).** When directed by the President or SecDef, CDRUSPACOM conducts domestic CM and defense support of civil authorities (DSCA) in support of the lead agency to mitigate the effects of, and assist in the recovery from, CBRNE events, natural or man-made disasters situation in the US states and territories within its AOR.

d. **Functional Combatant Commanders.** Each functional CCDR has a specific role in CWMD as described below:

(1) **United States Strategic Command (USSTRATCOM). Commander, United States Strategic Command (CDRUSSTRATCOM).** USSTRATCOM is responsible for synchronizing DOD CWMD planning and advocating for CWMD capabilities.

(2) **United States Joint Forces Command (USJFCOM). Commander, United States Joint Forces Command (CDRUSJFCOM)** in coordination with USSTRATCOM, develops and makes recommendations to the CJCS regarding joint force integration for CWMD. As the joint force provider, USJFCOM provides forces, resources, and capabilities, as directed, to the supported CCDR's CWMD operations. As the designated establishing authority for joint task force - elimination (JTF-E), CDRUSJFCOM is responsible for those activities outlined in JP 3-33, *Joint Task Force*

Headquarters. CDRUSJFCOM exercises combatant command (command authority) over JTF-E.

(3) **United States Transportation Command (USTRANSCOM). Commander, United States Transportation Command (CDRUSTRANSCOM).** USTRANSCOM plans and executes the common user transportation aspects of global CWMD operations. As the mobility force provider, USTRANSCOM supports intertheater and intratheater transportation of CWMD forces, equipment, and material, including specialized WMD shipments or certified containers provided by the appropriate agency. USTRANSCOM is prepared to expeditiously conduct retrograde movements of samples and specialized WMD tools for identification and attribution, providing in-transit visibility for positive control of CWMD shipments. In a contaminated environment, USTRANSCOM may restrict the retrograde of contaminated cargo to "mission critical" equipment (as determined by the GCC and authorized by SecDef.) Transportation of contagious and contaminated casualties is also very limited and requires GCC and CDRUSTRANSCOM coordination and endorsement, as well as SecDef approval. Logistics planners must be cognizant of the potential effects of large-frame aircraft or ship contamination on international mobility operations and implement contamination avoidance and control measures to preserve mobility capabilities. **If unable to avoid contaminated areas, then planners must obtain the appropriate transit country clearances for contaminated vessels and equipment.**

(4) **United States Special Operations Command (USSOCOM). Commander, United States Special Operations Command.** USSOCOM is the lead combatant command for planning, synchronizing, and, as directed, executing global operations against terrorist networks. CWMD planning and operations must be closely coordinated with USSOCOM. USSTRATCOM and USSOCOM integrate and synchronize their global campaigns. USSOCOM provides the following CWMD capabilities:

(a) Expertise, material, and teams to supported combatant command teams to locate, tag, and track WMD, as required.

(b) Capabilities to conduct direct action operations in limited access areas, as required.

(c) Other specialized CWMD capabilities.

e. **Services.** The Services organize, train, equip, and otherwise prepare their respective forces to combat WMD, means of delivery, and related materials. Services play a vital role in contributing to shaping an international environment hostile to proliferation and strengthening deterrence through building partners' CWMD-related capabilities and capacities. Specifically, the Services provide forces with the capability to conduct WMD interdiction, WMD elimination, WMD offensive operations, WMD active defense, CBRN passive defense, and WMD CM operations.

f. **National Guard Bureau (NGB).** NGB is responsible for formulating, developing, and coordinating all policies, programs, and plans affecting CWMD assets within the National Guard.

g. **Combat Support Agencies (CSAs).** There are two principal CSAs with significant responsibilities related to CWMD: the Defense Threat Reduction Agency (DTRA) and the Defense Intelligence Agency (DIA).

(1) **Defense Threat Reduction Agency.** DTRA's mission is to provide capabilities to reduce, eliminate, and counter the WMD threat, and mitigate its effects. The Director, DTRA, also serves as the Director, United States Strategic Command Center for Combating Weapons of Mass Destruction (SCC-WMD). In these roles, DTRA provides the following:

(a) Provides planning support, real-time technical reachback for the GCCs, technical development, and capabilities analysis.

(b) Manages and oversees research, development, testing, and evaluation needed to counter the threat and use of WMD; supports CCDR CWMD planning; and assists in the development and integration of capabilities to support DOD CWMD efforts and activities.

(c) Supports the construction, operation, and maintenance of a central destruction or offshore facility for the destruction and demilitarization of WMD agents, weapons, and material, if required, in support of WMD elimination operations and/or threat reduction cooperation requirements.

(d) Leads the development of the Interagency Combating Weapons of Mass Destruction Database of Responsibilities, Authorities, and Capabilities (INDRAC). INDRAC provides the CWMD community a web-based reference resource for understanding DOD and other USG departments and agencies' CWMD roles, authorities, and capabilities. INDRAC is designed to be a reference tool to inform and assist government departments and agencies tasked with integrating and synchronizing applicable interagency-wide CWMD efforts. INDRAC is not designed or intended to be a Global Force Management tool to assess readiness levels or for units to be tasked outside existing processes.

(2) **Defense Intelligence Agency.** DIA advises SecDef, CJCS, and CCDRs on WMD intelligence and provides military intelligence support for CWMD planning. They support CCDR preparation of strategic estimates, priorities, and joint operation plans for CWMD operations. This includes threat prioritization data on WMD actors; development of dynamic threat assessments; network analysis and interdiction planning data; WMD facility and program assessments and projections; and database support for WMD facilities, individuals, and organizations. DIA assesses the importance of a current or pending movement or transfer of WMD-related materials, precursors, funding, information, or personnel and coordinates with the supported commander to exploit

personnel, data, information, and materials obtained during CWMD operations. DIA provides capabilities, as directed, to the supported CCDR's CWMD operations using established policies and procedures and provides expertise, if required, for identifying WMD materials.

h. **Interagency and Intergovernmental Considerations.** Coordination between DOD and OGAs, NGOs, and IGOs is critical to the success of CWMD operations. In many cases, the JFC will be supporting an OGA and that organization may be supporting a partner nation or IGO. In particular, security cooperation and partner activities; threat reduction cooperation; and WMD elimination, WMD interdiction, and WMD CM missions require significant interagency and intergovernmental coordination.

(1) CWMD operations may be subject to monitoring by various government agencies or IGOs; therefore, planning should anticipate specific national level guidance. CWMD operations must be coordinated and authorized at the appropriate level in accordance with approved WMD specific rules of engagement (ROE) and rules for the use of force (RUF). Commanders must also determine legal and policy authorities and requirements, to include a review of applicable laws, policies, treaties, and agreements. When CWMD operations involve significant or complex interactions with foreign civil authorities or IGOs, the commander should consider forming a civil-military operations center (CMOC) or supplementing an existing CMOC with CWMD expertise.

For further guidance on CMOCs, refer to JP 3-57, Civil-Military Operations.

(2) In addition to IGO participation, CWMD operations often involve multinational partners since they also possess unique military CWMD capabilities. In many cases, the JFC will be part of a multinational force or be supporting a multinational operation.

For further guidance on multinational operations, refer to JP 3-16, Multinational Operations.

(3) CWMD operations require commanders and their staffs to coordinate and integrate with all instruments of national power and recognize which agencies bring the best capabilities to meet the objective(s). The combatant command's joint interagency coordination group (JIACG) is an important tool to assist in this effort by promoting interaction and cooperation among diverse agencies. The JIACG is an interagency staff group that can synchronize, while promoting working relationships with OGA (e.g., Central Intelligence Agency, DOS, Federal Bureau of Investigation (FBI), and US Department of the Treasury) representatives and military operational planners at the combatant commands. The JIACGs complement the interagency coordination that takes place at the national level through DOD and the National Security Council System and provide a conduit back to their parent organizations to help synchronize joint operations with OGA efforts.

For further guidance on interagency coordination and JIACGs, refer to JP 3-08, Interorganizational Coordination During Joint Operations, and JP 3-0, Joint Operations.

(4) As soon as practical, JFCs must begin planning and close coordination with OGAs and/or IGOs for the transition of CWMD operations to civilian entities. Military forces may transition to a supporting role with support not ceasing until the activity is complete.

2. Command Relationships

a. **General.** GCCs plan and execute CWMD operations in accordance with their Unified Command Plan responsibilities and as directed by SecDef. USSTRATCOM is responsible for synchronizing DOD CWMD planning. Specific command relationships for CWMD operations are established by SecDef tasking orders or CCDR plans and operation orders, as appropriate. Because of the interagency aspects of CWMD operations, agencies other than DOD may lead effort with DOD providing support; however, US military forces, other than National Guard forces due to their unique status when operating under Title 32, USC authority, will remain under the DOD command structure while supporting other agencies.

b. **Command and Control**

(1) **Day-to-Day Operations.** Many critical CWMD activities take place as phase 0 (Shape) activities. These operations should be included in regional CWMD plans and supporting plans; integrated into theater campaign plans and executed as part of the theater security cooperation strategy. The day-to-day integration of these activities is particularly important as successful application of integrated, balanced CWMD strategies across the three pillars of CWMD: NP, CP, and WMD CM help deter adversarial WMD acquisition, use, or threat of use. They also may produce an environment that prevents an actor from obtaining or successfully employing WMD and may prevent the necessity of dealing with a WMD armed adversary or responding to a WMD attack.

(2) **Contingency Operations.** C2 arrangements for CWMD operations are tailored for the requirements of each contingency and are determined by the supported commander. The size and scope, as well as preplanned integration, of CWMD operations determine the requirements for specific CWMD C2 functions. Small-scale CWMD operations may not require formation of a separate C2 structure. A combatant command's preexisting command structure, with limited technical augmentation, may suffice. This could take the form of a small task force using the combatant command's standing joint force HQ, or a component HQ. For a large-scale effort, CWMD operations may be integrated into overall JTF operations or a functional JTF for CWMD operations could be formed. The following discussion can apply to the formation of a JTF to execute a single CWMD mission or to the consolidation of several CWMD operations or functions under a single functional JTF for CWMD.

(a) **Functional JTF Considerations.** SecDef, a CCDR, a subordinate unified command commander, or an existing commander, JTF (CJTF) can establish a JTF to execute a specific CWMD mission or when CWMD operations require joint resources on a significant scale. Examples of functional CWMD JTFs are JTF-CM as described in JP 3-41, *Chemical, Biological, Radiological, Nuclear, and High-Yield Explosives Consequence Management*, and JTF-E, as described in Appendix A, "Weapons of Mass Destruction Elimination Operations."

For further guidance on the responsibilities and formation of a functional JTF HQ, refer to JP 3-33, Joint Task Force Headquarters.

<u>1</u>. Functional JTFs are created by an establishing authority, usually a CCDR, and are dissolved when the mission is complete or transitioned to another agency or government. Functional JTF activities are generally coordinated and integrated by the supported combatant command with its own intelligence, planning, and operations as well as the activities of other tasked agencies (e.g., Department of Energy (DOE), DOS, and the intelligence community).

<u>2</u>. **Subordinate Commands and Forces**. Forces conducting CWMD operations are often highly technical in nature and drawn from a limited resource pool. These forces may be a combination of conventional forces and functional or technical experts from the Services or CSAs, augmented by non-DOD or non-US personnel, as appropriate. These forces often require real-time reachback capability to national level technical experts.

<u>3</u>. **Command and Control Relationships**. Specific C2 relationships are determined by the supported commander. Figures III-1 through III-3 provide notional C2 relationships for a functional CWMD JTF.

<u>a</u>. Figure III-1 is an option to establish a separate JTF at the combatant command level, with the CJTF reporting directly to the CCDR. This option supports a situation in which the CCDR requires a direct command link to the activities of the CWMD JTF. This option maximizes coordination between the CWMD JTF and interagency support without having to coordinate through additional intermediate HQ. This option also assumes that the CWMD JTF can operate independently.

<u>b</u>. Figure III-2 is an option to establish the CWMD JTF as a JTF under an existing JFC. This option best suits operational environments in which the CWMD JTF must be better synchronized with other JTF operations. It provides flexibility for inter-service support to the CWMD JTF from other components when such support is only needed for specific periods of time or specific missions.

<u>c</u>. Figure III-3 is an option to establish a CWMD task force under a component commander. This option provides a CWMD task force capability when joint interdependency is not critical for mission success. This option may apply when a

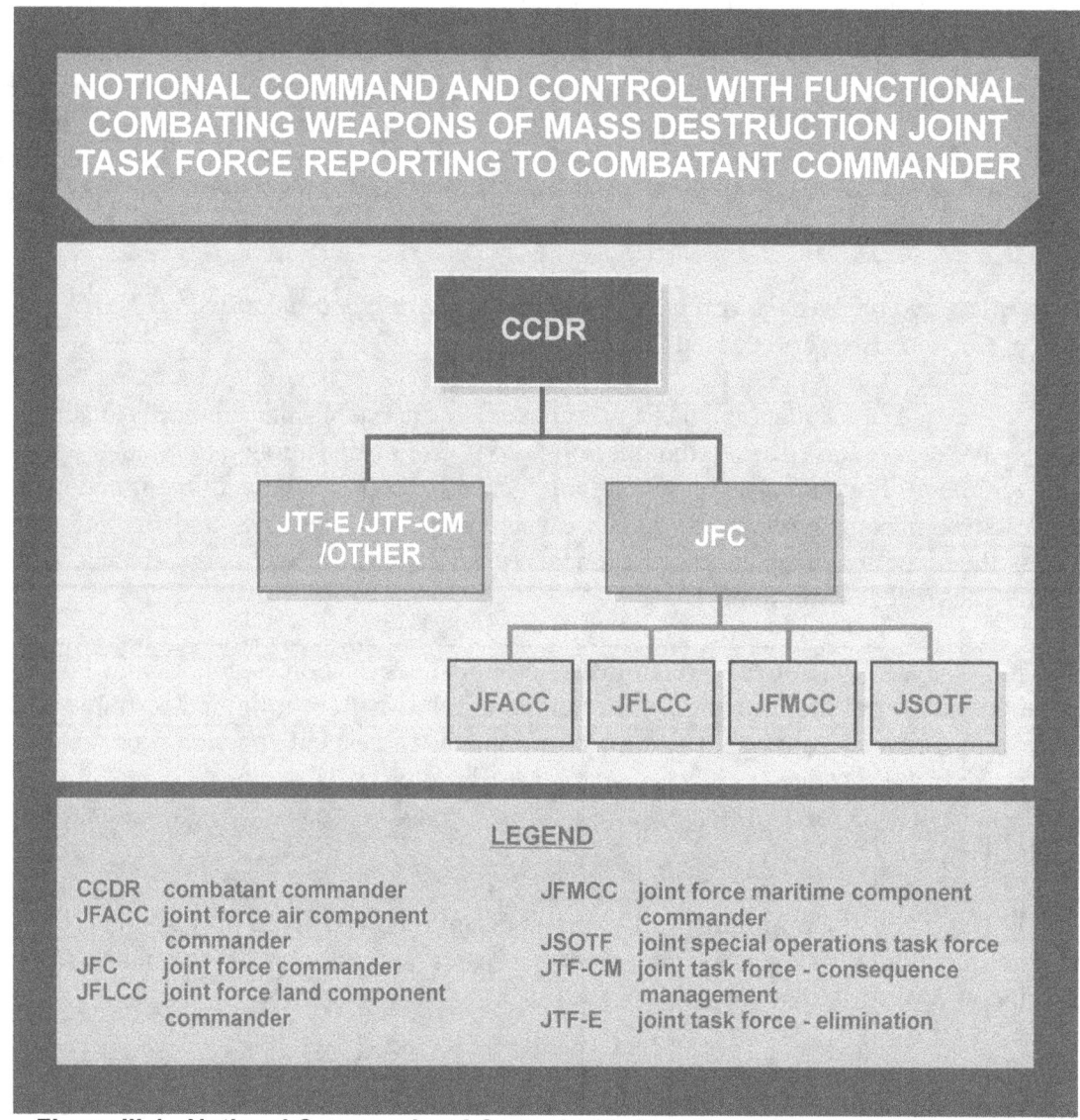

Figure III-1. Notional Command and Control with Functional Combating Weapons of Mass Destruction Joint Task Force Reporting to Combatant Commander

WMD program is not sufficiently large scale or complex, but still requires a higher level organization with multiple organizational capabilities to achieve CWMD objectives.

(b) JTF Headquarters. At a minimum, and as required by the supported commander to conduct a specific CWMD operation, the functional JTF HQ should possess the capabilities to:

1. Conduct the assigned CWMD mission, C2, and coordinate operations of assigned forces.

2. Coordinate with US forces, OGAs, foreign governments, IGOs, and HNs.

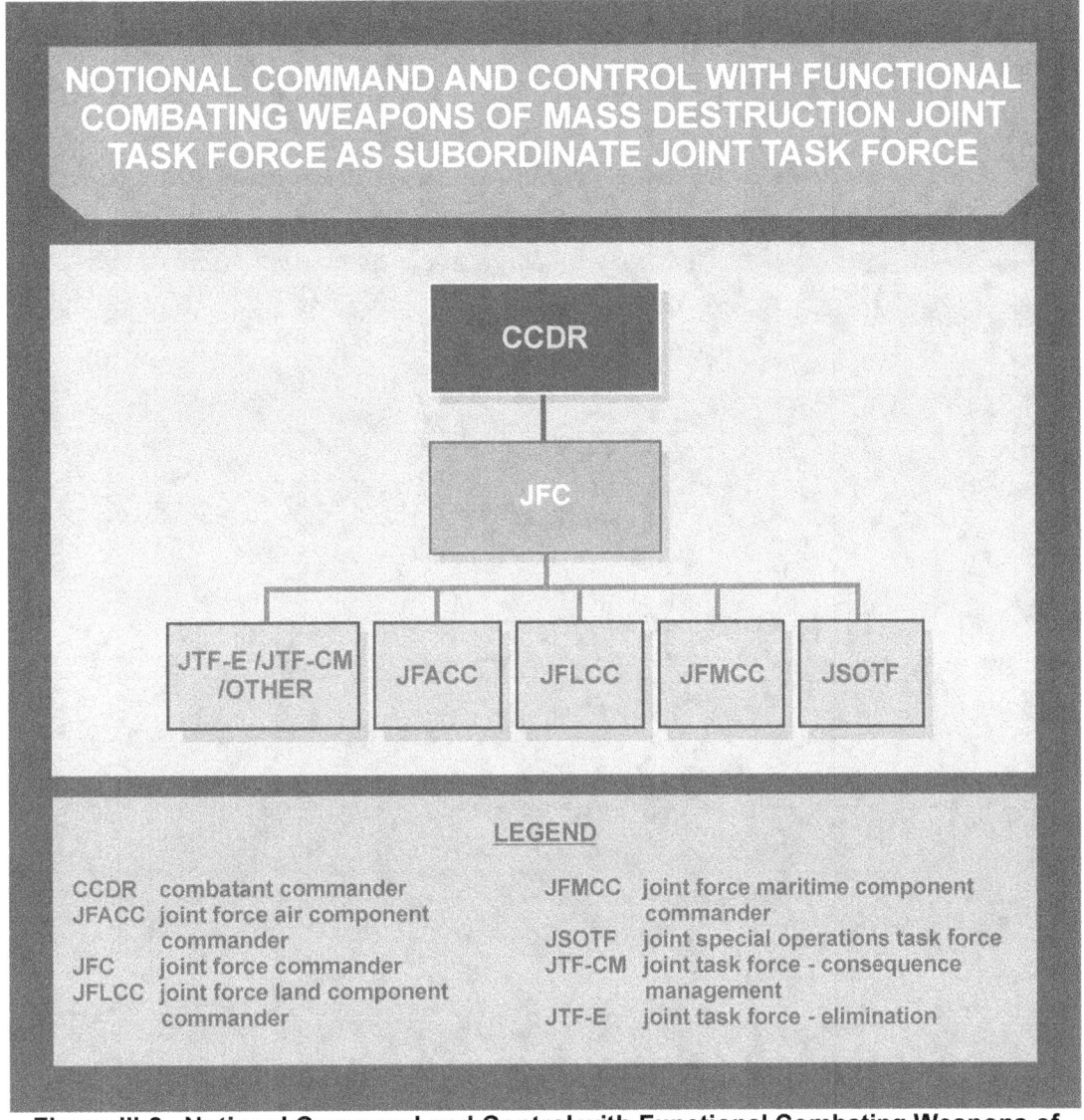

Figure III-2. Notional Command and Control with Functional Combating Weapons of Mass Destruction Joint Task Force as Subordinate Joint Task Force

<u>3.</u> Provide overall assessment, analysis, and planning for CWMD operations.

<u>4.</u> Coordinate CWMD planning activities with other commands.

<u>5.</u> Plan for JTF deployment, employment, and redeployment.

<u>6.</u> Plan for transfer of responsibility of CWMD operations to or from the CCDR and from or to OGAs, IGOs, and HNs, as appropriate.

<u>7.</u> Plan for minimizing or mitigating potential CWMD collateral effects.

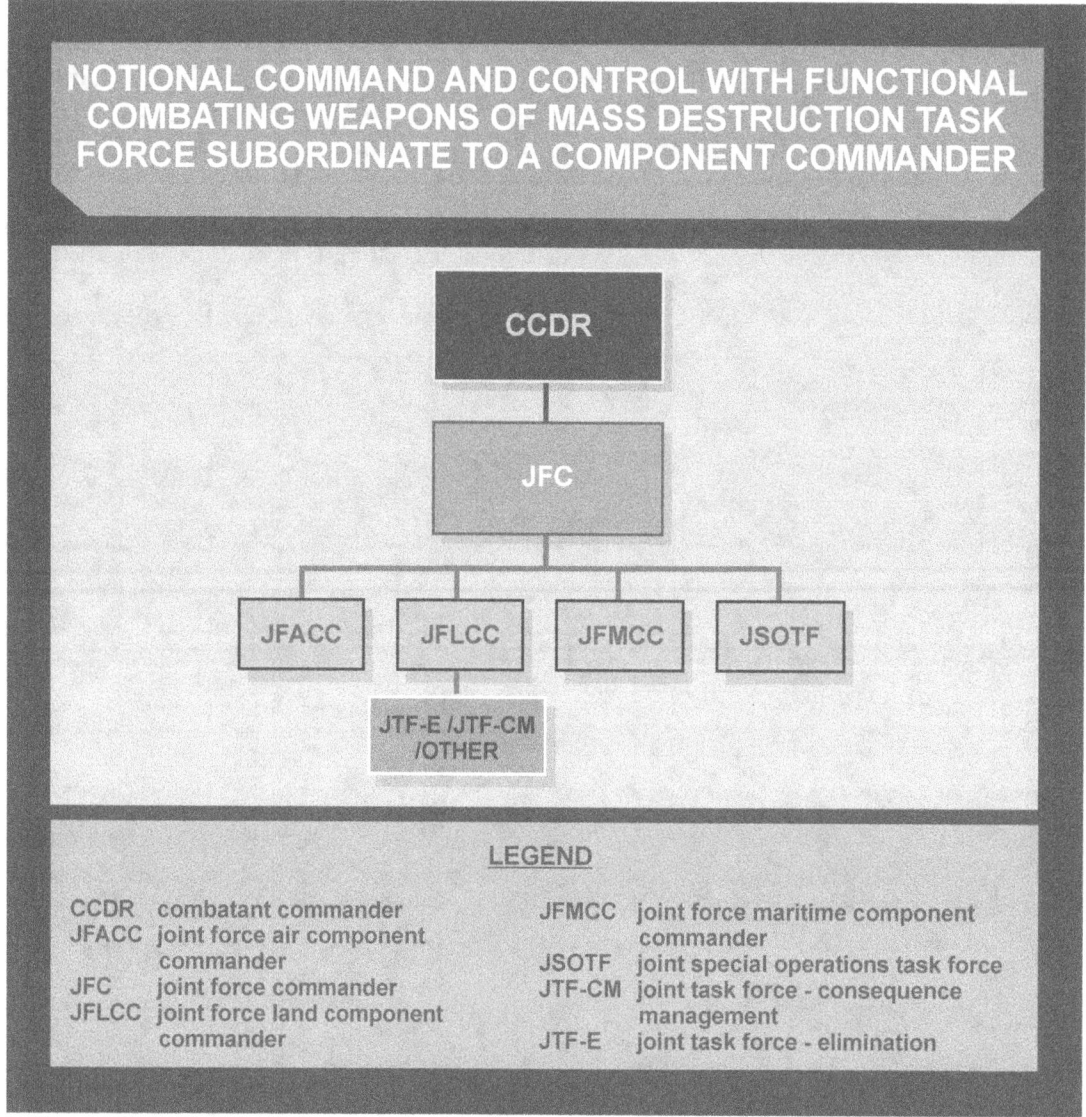

Figure III-3. Notional Command and Control with Functional Combating Weapons of Mass Destruction Task Force Subordinate to a Component Commander

8. Maintain situational awareness of CWMD activities and operations, both friendly and adversary.

9. Recommend prioritization of CWMD resources and forces.

10. Integrate into the supported combatant command's C2 and coordination processes (e.g., joint targeting coordination board).

(3) **Domestic Operations.** Domestic CWMD operations involve complex command relationships; in most cases, DOD will act in a supporting role to another USG department or agency. DOD will support civil authorities in minimizing the damage and recovering from domestic WMD incidents or attacks. USNORTHCOM is the DOD designated planning agent and the supported commander for CS missions in the

USNORTHCOM AOR. United States Pacific Command (USPACOM) is the DOD planning agent and supported commander for CS missions in the USPACOM AOR.

(a) DOD protects the homeland through two distinct but interrelated missions: HD and CS. While these missions are separate, they have areas where roles and responsibilities may overlap or lead and supporting roles may transition between organizations. DOD serves as the lead for HD, which may be executed by DOD alone or include support by OGAs. CS is the overarching term for DOD support to civil authorities for domestic emergencies; designated law enforcement; and other activities. HD and CS operations may occur in parallel and require extensive integration and coordination. In addition, operations may transition from HD to CS and vice versa with the lead agency dependant on the situation. When emergency conditions dictate, and when time does not permit approval from higher HQ, local military commanders and responsible DOD component officials are authorized to respond to requests from local authorities and to initiate immediate response actions to save lives, prevent human suffering, or mitigate great property damage under imminently serious conditions. Domestic WMD CM operations generally are CS operations, whereas WMD active defense and CBRN passive defense generally fall under HD operations.

(b) **National Response Framework.** The NRF is the USG's comprehensive approach to domestic incident management built on the template of the NIMS. As part of a comprehensive national response, DOD supports a primary federal agency to prevent or to respond to an emergency. The NRF provides the structure and mechanisms for national-level policy and operational direction for managing this national response. The NRF identifies how federal departments and agencies will respond to state, tribal, or local requests for assistance. The NRF provides the framework for most DOD support to civil authorities. The NRF is designed to encompass all hazards including high-yield explosives incidents.

For further guidance on CS operations and responsibilities, refer to JP 3-28, Civil Support.

Intentionally Blank

CHAPTER IV
PLANNING AND EXECUTION

> *"The strategy uses an "ends, ways, means" approach to planning, executing and resourcing that emphasizes those combating WMD [weapons of mass destruction], missions in which the military plays a prominent role."*
>
> **National Military Strategy for Combating Weapons of Mass Destruction, 13 February 2006**

1. General

a. This chapter translates strategic CWMD guidance into an operational approach leveraging capabilities from the six joint functions across campaign phases and across the range of military operations. This chapter will discuss the types of operations for which CWMD activities will be planned and conducted; joint operation and campaign planning; and the integration of CWMD actions and activities into operations and campaigns supporting the other instruments of national power in the accomplishment of USG strategic objectives.

For further guidance on the six joint functions refer to JP 3-0, Joint Operations.

b. **CWMD Military Mission Areas.** The eight CWMD MMAs provide JFCs with a logical grouping of CWMD activities. It should be noted that the following definitions differ from those previously introduced in the NMS-CWMD. These enhanced descriptions offer the JFC a more precise and operational perspective to combat WMD:

(1) **Weapons of Mass Destruction Security Cooperation and Partner Activities.** Activities to improve or promote defense relationships and capacity of allied and partner nations to execute or support the other MMAs to combat WMD through military-to-military contact, burden sharing arrangements, combined military activities, and support to international activities.

(2) **Threat Reduction Cooperation.** Activities undertaken with the consent and cooperation of HN authorities in a permissive environment to enhance physical security, and to reduce, dismantle, redirect, and/or improve protection of a state's existing weapons of mass destruction program, stockpiles, and capabilities.

(3) **Weapons of Mass Destruction Interdiction.** Operations to track, intercept, search, divert, seize, or otherwise stop the transit of WMD, its delivery systems, or related materials, technologies, and expertise. In peacetime, WMD interdiction operations are planned and executed in order to intercept dual-use materials and expertise in transit aboard nonmilitary transports.

(4) **Weapons of Mass Destruction Offensive Operations.** Actions to disrupt, neutralize, or destroy a WMD threat before it can be used, or to deter subsequent use of such weapons.

(5) **Weapons of Mass Destruction Elimination.** Actions undertaken in a hostile or uncertain environment to systematically locate, characterize, secure, and disable, or destroy WMD programs and related capabilities.

(6) **Weapons of Mass Destruction Active Defense.** Active measures to defeat an attack with chemical, biological, radiological, or nuclear weapons by employing actions to divert, neutralize, or destroy those weapons or their means of delivery while en route to their target.

(7) **Chemical, Biological, Radiological, and Nuclear Passive Defense.** Passive measures taken to minimize or negate the vulnerability to, and effects of, chemical, biological, radiological, or nuclear attacks causing a high order of destruction or mass casualties. This mission area focuses on maintaining the joint force's ability to continue military operations in CBRN environments.

(8) **Weapons of Mass Destruction Consequence Management.** Actions authorized by the SecDef to mitigate the effects of a WMD attack or event and restore essential operations and services.

c. **Operational Construct for CWMD.** The CWMD MMAs are useful to the JFC as logical groupings of capabilities and in order to relate them to the strategic pillars. However, the distinctions and subtleties between several CWMD MMAs are also important in determining the operational tasks and related activities to a successful CWMD program. In doing so, the JFC uses logical flow of simultaneous or sequential military activities that determine whether or not his CWMD program is successful. It also informs JFC decisions for future actions, some of which may have diplomatic implications. And finally, it provides an architecture within which to frame, organize, mass, and optimize friendly capabilities necessary for the CWMD program.

(1) **WMD Interdiction and WMD Offensive Operations. WMD interdiction operations include a broad spectrum of military and USG activities, short of WMD offensive operations, to detect and disrupt potential proliferation networks.** Examples of WMD interdiction can include maritime surveillance, intercept, search, and seizure of WMD materials carried by merchant vessels. These operations can be executed unilaterally, in cooperation with other agencies, or in concert with foreign partners. WMD interdiction can also include cooperation with interagency or foreign partners in the sea and airport surveillance activities. WMD interdiction operations support the non-proliferation and counter-proliferation pillar of CWMD and are an important activity in phase 0 shaping activities with a GCC's AOR. **WMD offensive operations are military activities to destroy WMD, WMD-related installations, or other supporting infrastructure.** WMD offensive operations likely involve the use of force. WMD offensive operations support the counter-proliferation pillar of CWMD.

(2) **WMD Interdiction, WMD Offensive Operations and WMD Elimination.** All three of these MMAs represent failure in cooperative actions associated with NP, but in which an adversary has not employed weapons. WMD

interdiction is aimed at early defeat of an adversary WMD program before it matures and focuses primarily on moving targets. The operational distinctions between WMD offensive operations and WMD elimination operations lie in the overall end state of the actions associated with the MMA. While WMD elimination operations focus on systematic elimination of the entire WMD program, WMD offensive operations focus only on distinct targets or nodes of the WMD program or capabilities. WMD offensive operations therefore support achieving the objectives of WMD elimination operations. The following vignette, entitled Operation OPERA, is an example of a WMD offensive operation.

OPERATION OPERA

At 1255 Greenwich Mean Time on Sunday June 7, 1981, eight Israeli F-16 fighter-bombers take off along with two F-15 interceptors from Etzion air force base in Egypt's Sinai Desert (occupied at the time by Israel). A number of other F-15s head elsewhere in Iraq as back-up. The 10 planes fly about 1,000 kilometers (km) (600 miles) through Jordanian and Saudi airspace unchallenged, hugging the desert. Entering Iraqi airspace, the planes descend to 30meters (m) to avoid radar detection. At 1735, the bombers are about 20km east of the Tammuz 1 nuclear reactor - better known as Osirak - just south of Baghdad. The reactor has still to load its first nuclear fuel. The F-16 pilots ignite their afterburners and climb for the attack run. They dive towards the reactor dome and release eight pairs of 1,000 kilogram (kg) bombs at 5-second intervals. All 16, each fitted with a time-delay fuse, hit Osirak, though two fail to explode. As Iraqi anti-aircraft fire goes up, the planes climb for the trip home. Fears of Iraqi interceptors appearing on the Israeli planes' tails prove unfounded. By dusk, all 10 planes are back at base unscathed. They have an average of just 450kg (1,000 pounds) of fuel left - enough for about 270km in the air. At Osirak, a French-designed reactor, the death toll is 10 Iraqi soldiers and a French civilian researcher. The reactor lies in ruins, having never entered operation. On 19 June, the United Nations Security Council condemns the attack in a resolution. Israel ignores the condemnation, insisting it was acting to preempt a nuclear threat.

Following this attack, Iraq restarted the program as a clandestine nuclear weapons program distributed at multiple sites across the country. The program continued at an accelerated rate until 1991. Following the 1991 Gulf War, United Nations inspectors undertook an effort to characterize and reduce the threat from this program. They were surprised at both the progress and size of the nuclear program. Over seven years of extensive effort to defeat Iraqi cover, concealment, and deception, United Nations Special Commission dismantled most of the remnants of the program but it is not certain that they uncovered the full range of activities.

VARIOUS SOURCES

For further guidance on WMD elimination operations, refer to Appendix A, "Weapons of Mass Destruction Elimination Operations."

(3) **WMD Elimination and Threat Reduction Cooperation.** These two MMAs are habitually linked, but very different. The difference comes down to consent and cooperation of the HN and the operational environment in which they take place. While the ultimate goal may be the same—to characterize and reduce or eliminate the threat of WMD—the operational aspects are very different. Threat reduction cooperation activities occur in a permissive environment. WMD elimination operations may ultimately transition to threat reduction cooperation activities as the operational environment changes.

(4) **WMD Interdiction and WMD Active Defense.** The focus of WMD interdiction and WMD active defense operations differ. While WMD active defense focuses on weapons on their means of delivery en route to a target, WMD interdiction focuses on stopping the transit of WMD capabilities. The distinction can be illustrated by an example involving a nuclear weapon being shipped to a given port. In the case of nuclear weapon pieces and/or parts being shipped to a buyer, only interdiction is applicable. If a complete nuclear weapon was being delivered to a buyer, both mission areas could be applicable. However, if the port was the target for the employment of the nuclear weapon, then it would be an active defense mission.

For further guidance on WMD interdiction operations, refer to Appendix B, "Weapons of Mass Destruction Interdiction Operations."

(5) **CBRN Passive Defense and WMD CM.** These two MMAs have a strong relation when an adversary employs CBRN weapons that are not defeated, and subsequently produce adverse effects, such as casualties and/or contamination. CBRN passive defense measures may preclude the need to implement WMD CM measures if the magnitude of the effects are mitigated by immediate response.

For further guidance on CBRNE CM, refer to JP 3-41, Chemical, Biological, Radiological, Nuclear, and High-Yield Explosives Consequence Management.

d. **Range of Military Operations.** Joint CWMD actions and activities span the range of military operations. CWMD actions and activities are a part of military engagement, security cooperation, and deterrence; crisis response and limited contingency operations; and major operations and campaigns. **CWMD actions and activities must not be planned or executed in isolation but must be integrated throughout the range of military operations.** CWMD actions and activities can take place in permissive, uncertain, or hostile environments.

For further guidance on range of military operations and types of military operations see JP 3-0, Joint Operations.

e. **Types of Military Operations.** CWMD must be integrated into all types of military operations. Three key aspects of CWMD actions include the execution of regional campaigns to shape the environment into one inhospitable to proliferators; specific, limited CWMD actions to respond to an emerging event (e.g., WMD interdiction or WMD offensive operations); and CWMD actions conducted as part of a major operation or campaign (e.g., WMD elimination) to deter an opponent, preempt adversary use of WMD, protect against WMD attack and, if required, recover from WMD effects within the operational area. Examples of how the eight CWMD MMAs support the types of military operations are outlined in Figure IV-1 and are discussed throughout this chapter.

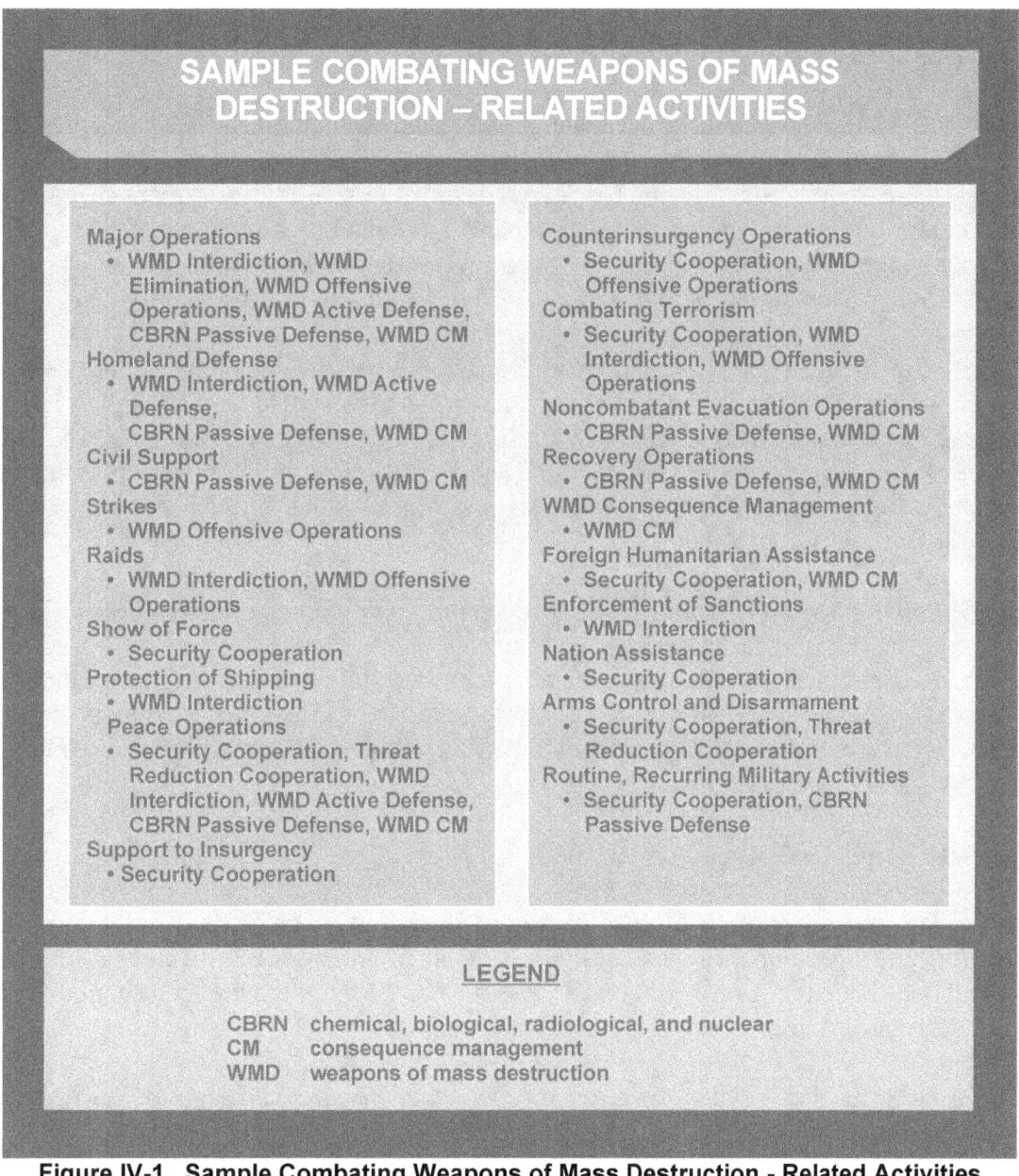

Figure IV-1. Sample Combating Weapons of Mass Destruction - Related Activities

(1) While understanding and planning the integration of CWMD operations into major campaigns and the interrelationship of CWMD mission areas with other contingency operations is critical when joint forces are faced with an adversary possessing WMD it is just as important to focus CWMD planning and activities at a strategic level. As noted earlier, CWMD is a global, continuous campaign that crosses AOR boundaries and requires close coordination and cooperation with interagency and multinational partners. The importance of effectively planning and conducting activities along the WMD security cooperation, threat reduction cooperation, CBRN passive defense, and WMD CM MMAs cannot be emphasized enough—the former two MMAs for reducing the existence of the WMD threat, and the latter two MMAs for deterring the use of WMD once they are developed. Even during major contingency operations, the global effects of CWMD operations must be considered when executing actions at the tactical or operational level.

(2) The global reach of networks and technology enabling WMD proliferation requires an interagency approach to effectively meet these challenges. The JFC may desire to create effects that cannot be created with the military instrument of national power alone and require interagency support and coordination. In many operations, DOD may not be the lead agency and military programs and activities must be integrated with a larger USG or international action.

(3) In the best case, successful execution of CWMD shaping activities may prevent or disrupt adversary acquisition or employment of WMD, alleviating the need for more aggressive and costly CWMD action later or in combat operations. Even if these actions do not have the desired effect on the adversary, they build partner capabilities and stronger security relationships with friends and allies, which will enhance the JFC's response to a crisis.

f. **Joint CWMD Operations.** CWMD could require either CWMD-specific forces or assets, or the unique application of conventional forces. To this end, a JFC can leverage capabilities from the six joint functions as required and during any campaign phase to accomplish CWMD-related tasks, generate the effects to precipitate desired behavior or circumstances, and achieve objectives. Figure IV-2 illustrates how CWMD is integrated into joint operations.

2. **Operation and Campaign Planning**

a. This section presents a broad overview of the CWMD aspects of joint operation planning and operational art and design. Chapter V, "Combating Weapons of Mass Destruction Planning Considerations," describes CWMD planning considerations of particular concern to JFCs and operational planners.

For further guidance on joint operation planning and operational design, refer to JP 5-0, Joint Operation Planning.

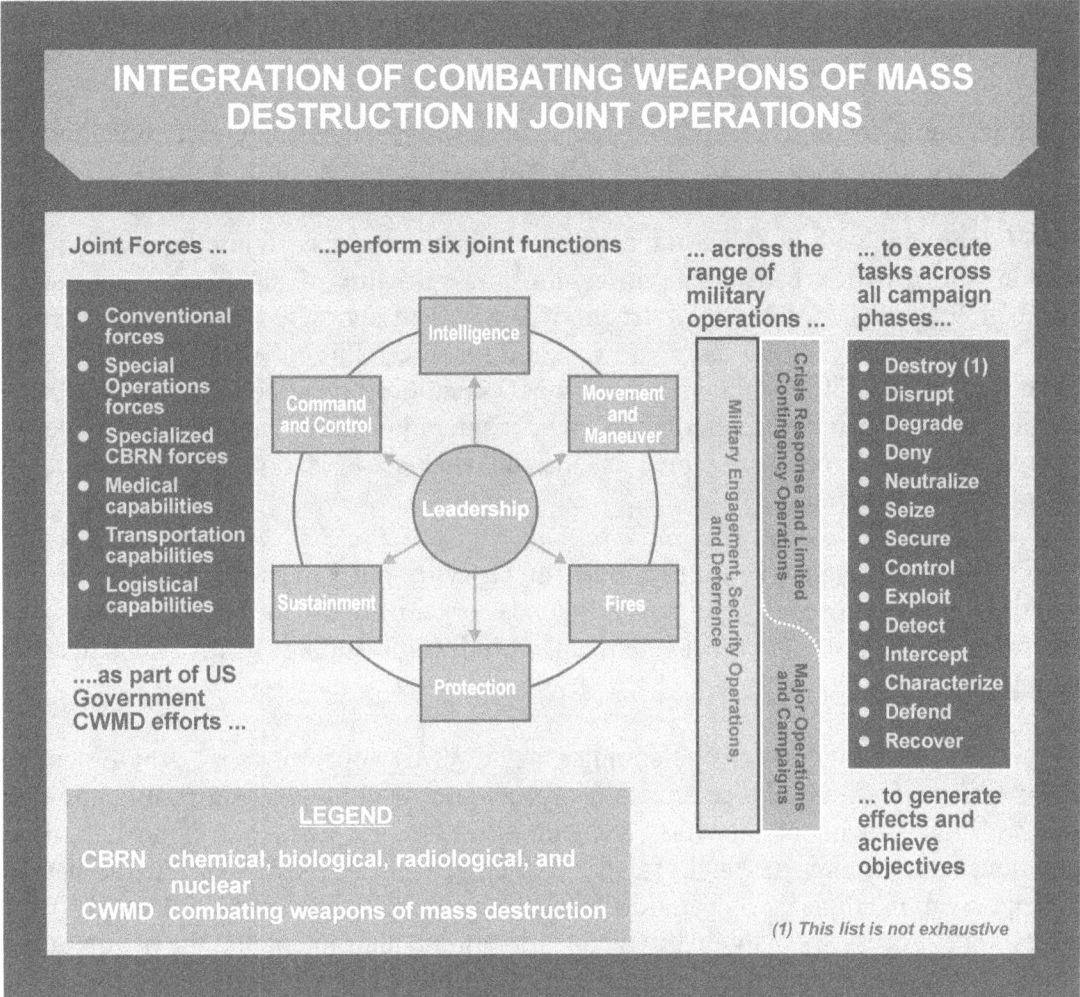

Figure IV-2. Integration of Combating Weapons of Mass Destruction in Joint Operations

b. Joint strategic planning has three subsets: security cooperation planning, force planning, and joint operation planning. This section touches on all three but focuses on joint operation planning. **CWMD planning is not a separate process; it is the integration of WMD-specific knowledge, experience, and capabilities into the existing joint operation planning process (JOPP).** Like planning for any other campaign or operation, the process is meant to guide JFCs in developing plans to combat WMD and employ conventional or specialized CBRN units to shape events, respond to crises, and meet contingencies. This planning is an adaptive, collaborative process between superior and subordinate levels within the context of strategic guidance and end states.

c. **Levels of War.** The three levels of war help clarify the links between national strategic objectives and tactical actions and are not unique or different for CWMD. Commanders at every level must be aware that in a world of constant, immediate communications, any single action may have consequences at all levels. Nowhere is this more evident than in joint operations involving WMD, where action or inaction at the tactical level can have profound strategic repercussions. Commanders must consider this as part of their campaign and operation planning.

d. Planning for joint operations uses two closely related, integrated, collaborative, and adaptive processes – the **Joint Operation Planning and Execution System (JOPES)** and the **JOPP.** The majority of JOPES activities and products occur prior to SecDef approving and the CJCS transmitting the execute order. While there is a distinct location for CWMD considerations within the structure of a plan - appendix 2 (Combating Weapons of Mass Destruction [WMD]) to annex C (Operations), planners must fully integrate CWMD tasks and required resources throughout the remainder of a plan or order. In addition, planning for CWMD operations must be integrated in the less formal, but proven, JOPP. Including WMD considerations throughout the seven steps of JOPP – the most crucial of which is mission analysis – is critical for a successful operation or campaign.

e. **Joint Intelligence Preparation of the Operational Environment.** JIPOE is the analytical process used by joint intelligence organizations to produce intelligence assessments, estimates, and other intelligence products in support of the JFC's decision-making process.

(1) JIPOE underpins planning for CWMD operations. JIPOE enables identification of actors, characterization of networks enabling WMD proliferation and use, and assessment of network vulnerabilities to facilitate development of the operational design elements and effective targeting (see Figure IV-3). At the national strategic level, intelligence preparation focuses on strategic assessment of existing WMD threats. The process seeks to identify actors, determine their intent and the nature of their activities, and assess the methods those actors use to proliferate, acquire, or use WMD. Analysis of potential transformational events, such as the rise of new actors and the impact of technology breakthroughs, facilitates national-level determination of end states, objectives, and priorities. JIPOE supports CWMD planning efforts by identifying potential threat streams, resource allocation, and the development of friendly and threat courses of action (COAs). The JFC and their staff must view CWMD challenges as network-based. The approach must be holistic in its methodology – identifying state and non-state actors (individuals, terrorist groups, and nongovernmental entities) in a comprehensive fashion, not as singular entities operating independent from one another.

(2) **Systems Perspective.** A JFC must understand the system (i.e., proliferation network or state WMD program) to be able to influence that system in a way that achieves and does not hinder CWMD-related objectives and end states. As identified in Chapter II, "The Challenge of Weapons of Mass Destruction Threats," one of the primary challenges facing the JFC is the proliferation of WMD technology and products. This proliferation takes place through systems. The JFC must understand the continuous and complex interaction of friendly, adversary, and neutral systems.

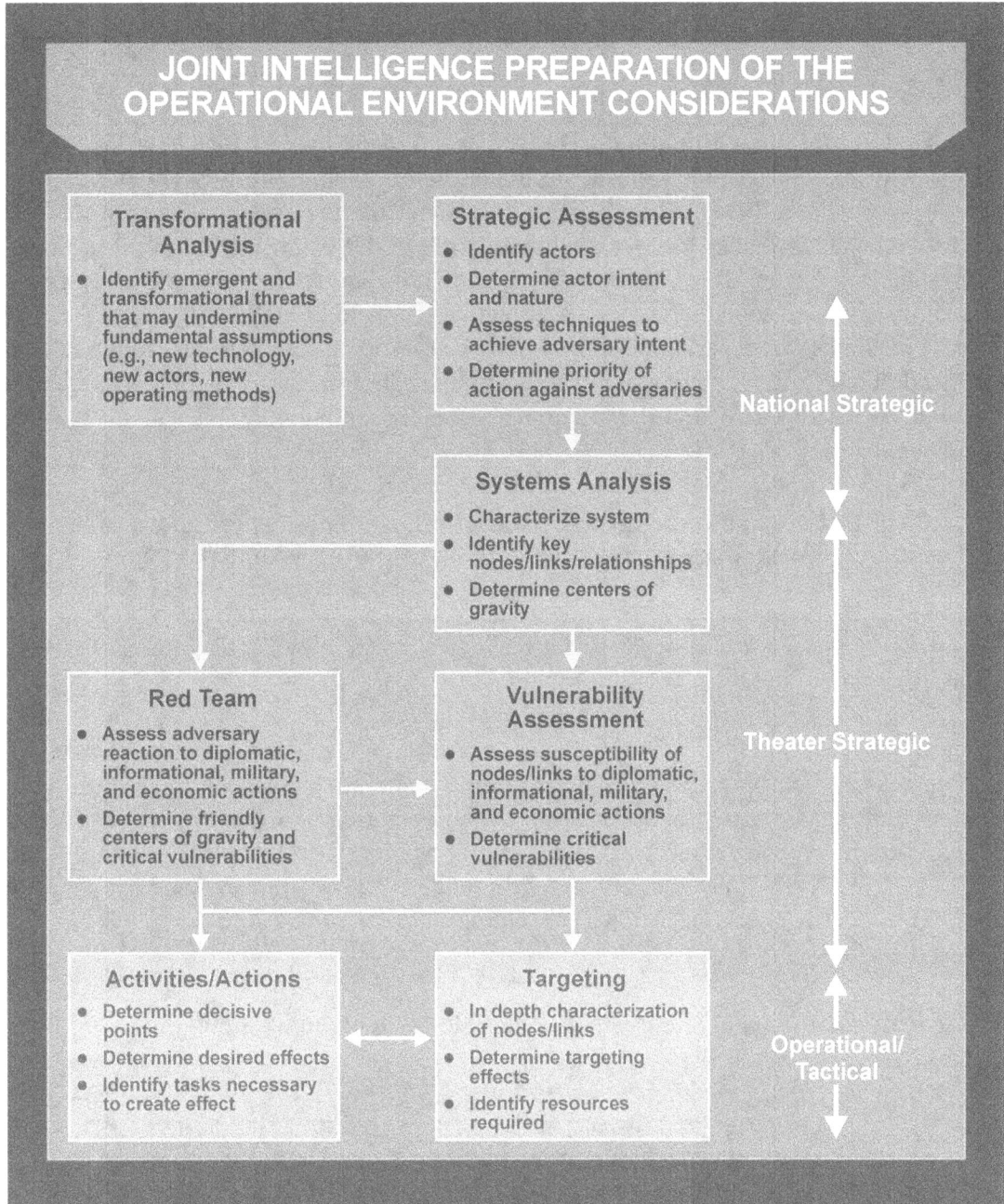

Figure IV-3. Joint Intelligence Preparation of the Operational Environment Considerations

(3) Examining and planning appropriate responses to adversary counter-actions is essential to mitigate potentially undesirable effects of a set of actions. For example, an offensive operation to destroy a WMD capability may result in the adversary undertaking additional camouflage, concealment, and deception (CCD) activities to protect that capability. These CCD activities will potentially complicate follow-on WMD elimination and WMD offensive operations.

For further guidance on intelligence support to joint operations, refer to the JP 2-0 series. For further guidance on JIPOE, refer to JP 2-01.3, Joint Intelligence Preparation of the Operational Environment.

f. **End State and Objectives.** Due to its strategic implications, the President or SecDef will provide criteria for the termination of most CWMD operations. JFCs approve **strategic military objectives** which comprise the **military end state.** The military end state (whether focused specifically on WMD or not) is the point in time, or circumstances, beyond which the President does not require the military instrument of national power to achieve the remaining objectives of the national strategic end state. An example of this is the transition of WMD site security to an international body for which DOS leads the effort. Commanders should include the military end state or objectives related to CWMD early in their planning guidance and commander's intent during mission analysis.

> **NOTE: In the case of security cooperation, termination criteria may be associated with long-term strategic goals requiring years to achieve.**

For further guidance on end states and objectives, refer to JP 5-0, Joint Operation Planning.

g. **Effects.** The identification of desired and undesired effects clarifies the relationship between objectives and tasks and helps commanders and their staffs gain a common picture and shared understanding of the operational environment that promotes unified action. When campaigns or operations include CWMD operations, the commander and staff must identify CWMD-related desired and undesired effects that support the commander's objectives. Effects must be observable and measurable to support the assessment process.

For further guidance on effects, refer to JP 5-0, Joint Operation Planning.

NOTIONAL COMBATING WEAPONS OF MASS DESTRUCTION END STATE-OBJECTIVE-EFFECT LINKAGE

End State: US, the Armed Forces of the United States, multinational partners, and interests are neither coerced nor attacked by enemies using weapons of mass destruction (WMD) *(strategic goal).*

Objective: Proliferation of WMD technology from Country X is contained.

Effect: Decrease in WMD technology leaving Country X.

VARIOUS SOURCES

---

h. **Targeting.** CWMD considerations must be taken into account during the entire targeting process. **WMD-related targets should not be considered in a separate targeting board; they must be integrated into the existing JFC targeting process or board.**

(1) **WMD Targets.** WMD-related targets represent highly sensitive and critical capabilities of many states and non-states and carry unique targeting considerations. In many cases, hard and deeply buried facilities and extensive CCD measures protect critical WMD capabilities. Many WMD delivery systems are highly mobile and, once detected, become time-sensitive targets. Adversary CCD measures may complicate target identification and selection. An extensive ISR effort may be necessary to identify, characterize, and assess the vulnerabilities of these targets. Holding these targets at risk is a priority for the JFC and requires a wide array of capabilities—both lethal and nonlethal.

(2) **Collateral Damage and Consequence of Execution Considerations.** Although the initial impact of a conventional munition on a WMD-related target may cause little collateral damage, secondary effects could include a release or dispersal of chemical, biological, or radiological material or even an imperfect detonation of a nuclear device. For this reason, WMD-related targets are usually placed on a restricted target list; however, CWMD mission priorities or military necessity may require engagement of WMD-related targets. A detailed analysis to determine the potential release of hazards when targeting adversary WMD storage sites, weapon systems, or production facilities is required; the utility of employing agent defeat weapons to minimize the dispersal and collateral effects of CBRN hazards should be considered. Joint forces throughout the operational area must be advised of the predicted hazard area and must be given enough time to take appropriate force protection measures. Effects on local civilians and critical infrastructure must be anticipated and planned for as well. This planning must be done not only for WMD sites, but also for targets known or suspected to contain toxic industrial chemicals or materials. JFCs should seek to minimize collateral damage consistent with higher-level guidance as well as plan for follow-on WMD CM operations, as appropriate.

For further guidance on mitigating collateral damage, refer to JP 3-60, Joint Targeting, *and the methodology contained within Chairman of the Joint Chiefs of Staff Manual (CJCSM) 3160.01,* Joint Methodology for Estimating Collateral Damage and Casualties for Conventional Weapons: Precision, Unguided, and Cluster.

i. **Line of Operations. Logical LOOs are often the most appropriate for CWMD operations or campaigns.** A LOO depiction at this level can help the commander and staff discuss the relationship and status of decisive points or key tasks, as required.

j. **Phases.** CWMD operations can occur throughout all phases of a campaign or operation. Phasing is most directly related to arranging of operations and LOOs during operational design. Figure IV-4 illustrates the integrated nature of CWMD-related activities throughout the phasing model of a campaign or operation, but is not meant to be all inclusive. Planning for CWMD must consider operations or actions that must be completed within or throughout the various phases.

For further guidance on LOOs and phases, refer to JP 5-0, Joint Operation Planning.

k. **Branches and Sequels.** Many plans require adjustment beyond the initial stages of the operation. Consequently, JFCs build flexibility into their plans by developing branches and sequels to preserve freedom of action in rapidly changing conditions. Branches and sequels directly relate to phasing.

(1) **Branches are contingency options built into the basic plan.** Examples of CWMD-related branches could include adversary use of WMD against the HN civilian population; adversary threat of use of WMD against multinational partners; adversary use of WMD against multinational partners; adversary transfer of WMD to a terrorist

Figure IV-4. Sample Combating Weapons of Mass Destruction-Related Activities Across the Phasing Model

organization; or alternate areas of embarkation for scenarios involving contaminated sites.

(2) **Sequels are major operations that follow the current operation.** Examples of CWMD-related sequels could include transition of WMD elimination operations to threat reduction cooperation activities within Country X, or operations to secure WMD-related sites based on the collapse of a country's leadership and control.

For further guidance on branches and sequels, refer to JP 5-0, Joint Operation Planning.

l. **Flexible deterrent options (FDOs)** are preplanned, deterrence-oriented actions carefully tailored to bring an issue to early resolution without armed conflict. Figure IV-5 provides examples of CWMD-related FDOs across all instruments of national power.

For further guidance on FDOs, refer to JP 5-0, Joint Operations Planning.

m. **Strategic Communication.** SC planning is critical to CWMD and must create a responsive and agile whole-of-government effort to synchronize crucial themes, messages, images, and actions (see Figure IV-6). JFC planning must consider public diplomacy, public affairs (PA), and information operations (IO) requirements when confronting the WMD threat or use. Public interest in WMD-related developments may be intense and may affect US and multinational partner decision making. Therefore, the JFC must be a source of timely, accurate information, with particular emphasis on the explanation of actions taken in response to WMD threats or use. Establishing productive relationships with diplomatic channels and media organizations is an inherent element of JFC planning.

n. **CWMD Force Planning.** Force planning for CWMD encompasses all those activities performed by the supported CCDR, subordinate component commanders, and OGAs to select (source and tailor), prepare, integrate, and deploy forces and capabilities required to accomplish CWMD-related missions. Force packaging must provide a range of CWMD-related capabilities tied to the six phases of an operation. It should provide an active, layered defense against WMD and prepare for the possibility of rapid escalation to counter or respond to WMD use by an adversary. **Many of the tasks necessary for CWMD can be accomplished by conventional forces or OGAs.** However, force planning also encompasses activities performed by force providers to develop forces with unique CBRN-related capabilities and integrate them with conventional forces. It is important to note there are few CBRN-specific units and capabilities, but this does not exhaust the potential forces that can conduct CWMD operations. A challenge for the JFC is in managing expectations for employing CBRN-specific forces. An additional, yet related, challenge is balancing the use of low-density, CBRN-specific units with assigned forces that can accomplish many of the CWMD related tasks.

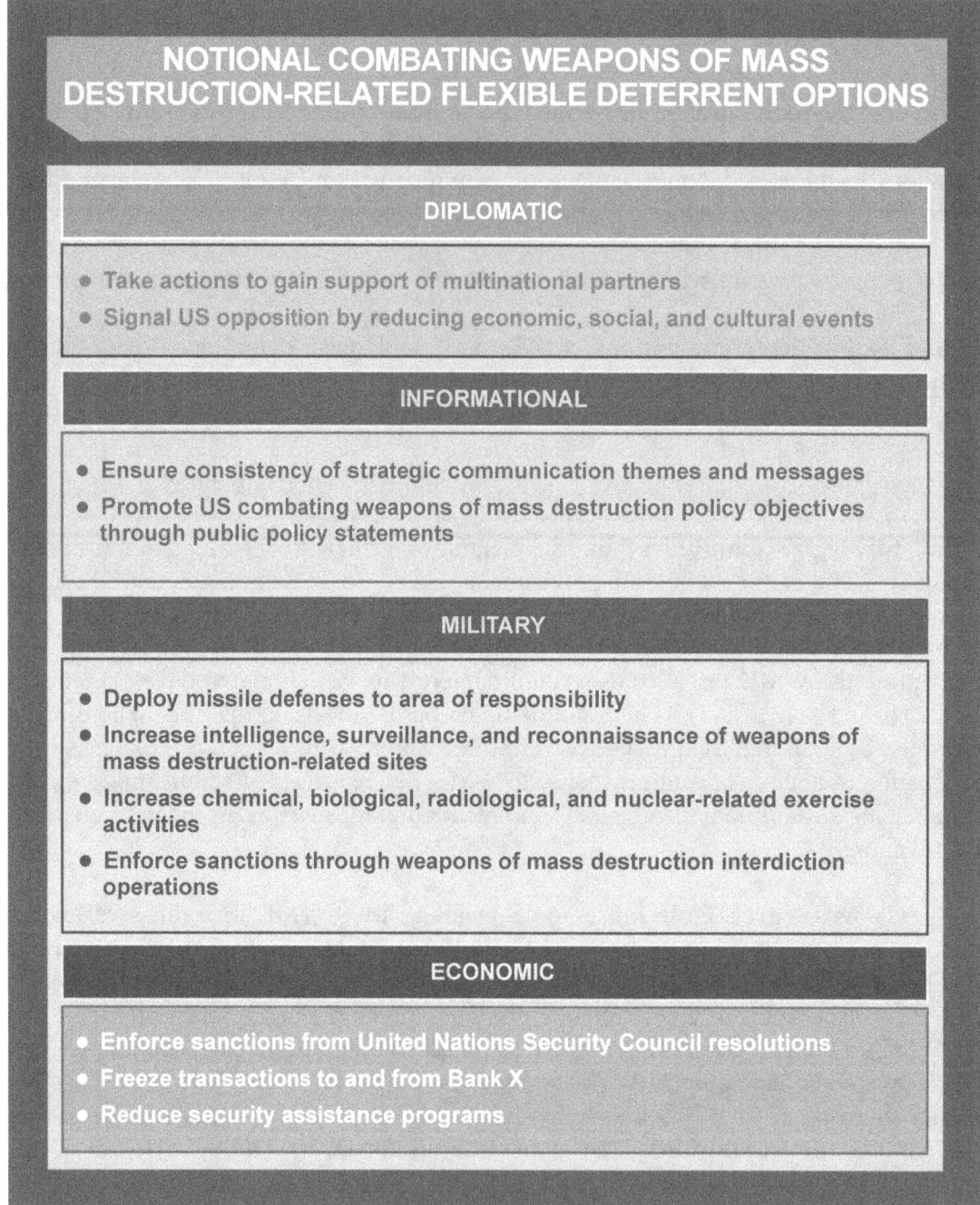

Figure IV-5. Notional Combating Weapons of Mass Destruction-Related Flexible Deterrent Options

o. Health service support (HSS) planning is an important aspect in CWMD operations. HSS is related to three joint functions: sustainment, movement and maneuver, and protection. Organization of the HSS system is determined by the joint force's mission, the threat, intelligence, anticipated number of patients, duration of the operation, the theater patient movement policy, available lift, and hospitalization and movement requirements. HSS considerations include, but are not limited to, **health threat, medical intelligence, patient movement, clinical capabilities and health**

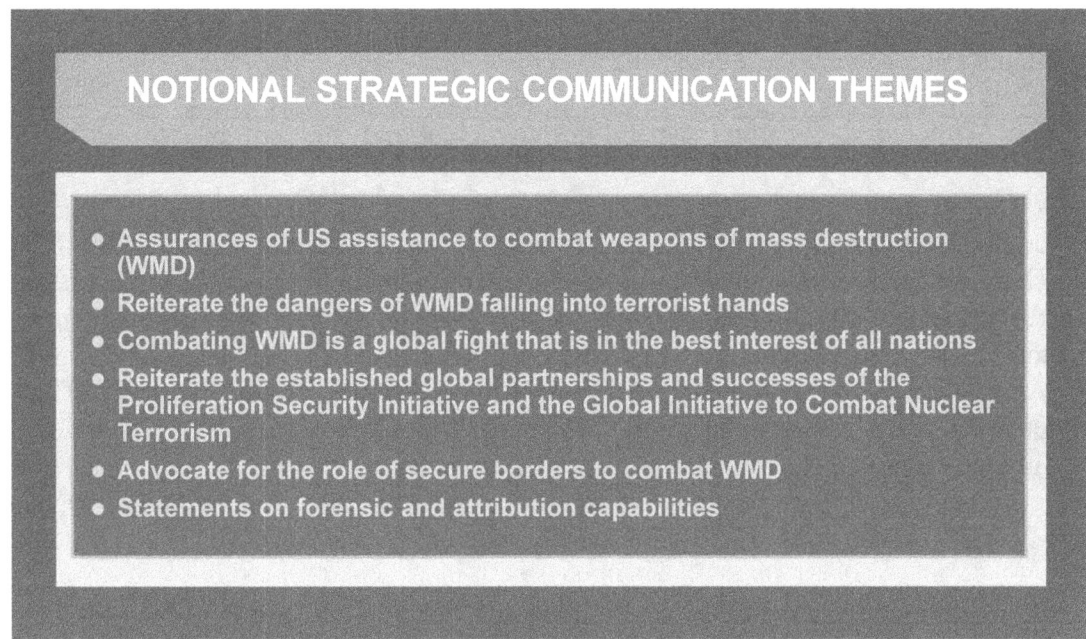

Figure IV-6. Notional Strategic Communication Themes

service logistics, preventive medicine and health surveillance, to include force health protection (FHP) products, and mass casualty situations.

For further guidance, see JP 4-02, Health Service Support, *and DOD Instruction 6490.03,* Deployment Health.

3.   **Military Engagement, Security Cooperation, and Deterrence Execution**

a. This section begins the execution portion of this chapter. Up until now, this chapter focused on defining the operation environment and the unique CWMD considerations for campaign and operational planning. The remaining sections discuss the integration of CWMD into the range of military operations (execution).

b. This section discusses the JFC's ability to shape the environment through military engagement, security cooperation, and deterrence, underpinned by situational awareness and SC, to create an environment hostile to the development, proliferation, or use of WMD. Shaping activities establish the conditions to combat WMD across the range of military operations. Shaping focuses on building multinational partner capacity and will, as well as creating the relationships required to undertake crisis response or combat operations. These actions support many of the goals of the National Defense Strategy and NMS-CWMD:

(1) Assuring friends and allies by demonstrating US resolve and capabilities for mutual defense;

(2) Dissuading actors from developing WMD by creating an environment hostile to proliferation;

(3) Deterring use of WMD by demonstrating capabilities to deny adversary objectives and respond to an attack; and

(4) Increasing partner capabilities to defeat use and mitigate the effects of WMD.

c. Successful shaping activities can be a very cost effective approach to combating WMD by investing relatively few resources in engagement versus costly responses to adversary use of WMD. CWMD MMAs that support shaping the environment can include security cooperation, threat reduction cooperation, and WMD interdiction. These MMAs tend to be NP in nature. As previously discussed, security cooperation is a unique MMA that supports the other MMAs and is extremely useful in shaping the operational environment. This section also identifies other existing military engagement and security cooperation programs available to the JFC that, with minimal input or modifications, could shape the operational environment for CWMD.

d. **Military engagement** is the routine contact and interaction between individuals or elements of the Armed Forces of the United States and those of another nation's armed forces, or foreign and domestic civilian authorities or agencies to build trust and confidence, share information, coordinate mutual activities, and maintain influence. **Success in CWMD relies heavily on military engagement opportunities.** Activities and initiatives could involve developing CBRN contacts; establishing programs for regular senior official visits; visits to foreign military CBRN sites; counterpart staff exchange visits and military-to-military talks (on a regular or ad hoc basis); and sponsorship of, or attendance at, WMD-related conferences; and bilateral exercise program that establishes and develops military to military contacts with targeted nations.

e. **Security cooperation** involves all DOD interactions with foreign defense establishments to build defense relationships that promote specific US security interests, develop allied and friendly military capabilities for self-defense and multinational operations, and provide US forces with peacetime and contingency access to a HN. Security cooperation is a key element of global and theater shaping operations and the WMD security cooperation MMA. Security cooperation requires close coordination and integration with DOS's country plans, USSOCOM and USSTRATCOM global plans. Combatant command and component command planning should complement DOS country plans and link security cooperation and partner capacity improvement activities to national CWMD objectives by identifying, prioritizing, and integrating efforts within and across AORs. Security cooperation activities could include, but are not limited to, multinational planning, security assistance, or multilateral assistance aimed at:

**COMBATING WEAPONS OF MASS DESTRUCTION (CWMD)
EXERCISES IN AZERBAIJAN**

Since 1999, the Defense Threat Reduction Agency has conducted CWMD classes in Azerbaijan, providing the former Soviet Union state with a strong foundation to deter, detect, identify, and investigate situations involving chemical, biological, radiological, and nuclear (CBRN) agents. These courses included crime scene investigation, criminal investigation, radiation detection and response, and other CBRN related subjects. The classes culminated on June 8, 2006 when a Department of Defense (DOD)-led interagency team conducted a three-day field exercise in Baku as part of the International Counterproliferation Program (ICP), designed to combat the spread of weapons of mass destruction (WMD). Forty representatives from DOD, the US Federal Bureau of Investigation, the US Customs and Border Protection Service and their contractors served as instructors for over 100 personnel from numerous Azerbaijan military and law enforcement agencies.

The exercise was designed for Azerbaijan participants to practice and assess their capability for WMD material detection and multiagency coordination and problem solving. It also presented Azerbaijan authorities the opportunity to integrate the ICP training in a realistic, no-fault environment. The overall scenario focused on WMD response procedures, crime scene management, use of an incident command system, and interagency coordination.

These exercises led to continuing security cooperation activities with Azerbaijan ministries to further develop CMWD and related capabilities.

VARIOUS SOURCES

(1) Improving the defense relationships with and capacity of allied and partner nations to combat WMD.

(2) Education, training, and exercises focused on WMD-related activities (e.g., WMD elimination and interdiction, response to mitigate effects of a CBRN incident).

(3) Initiatives aimed at building cooperation and support for WMD-related arms control and treaty monitoring activities.

(4) Building regional alliances or regional capabilities for mutual support.

(5) **WMD Security Cooperation and All Other MMAs.** The security cooperation MMA supports all other MMAs and the strategic enabler of building partner capacity. The GCC must tie this CWMD MMA in with all other ongoing security cooperation activities in the AOR. As an example, equipping and training border guards

with radiological detectors is security cooperation supporting WMD interdiction activities.

f. **Deterrence** prevents an action by an adversary through the perception of cost imposition, benefit denial, or the consequences of restraint. As discussed in Chapter II, "The Challenge of Weapons of Mass Destruction Threats," the role of deterrence for both state and non-state actors is varied. Threats (including terrorism involving WMD) directed against the United States, multinational partners, or other friendly nations require the maintenance of a full array of response capabilities. Effective deterrence requires security cooperation plans that emphasize the willingness of the United States to employ forces in defense of its interests. Various joint operations (e.g., show of force and enforcement of sanctions) support deterrence by demonstrating national resolve and willingness to use force when necessary. Others (e.g., nation assistance and foreign humanitarian assistance) support deterrence by enhancing a climate of peaceful cooperation, thus promoting stability. Having a credible threat of response in the form of WMD interdiction, WMD elimination, WMD offensive operations, WMD active defense, CBRN passive defense, and WMD CM capabilities supports the overall USG deterrence goals.

g. **Joint actions** that support military engagement, security cooperation, and deterrence objectives include emergency preparedness (EP); enforcement of sanctions; nation assistance (to include security assistance and foreign internal defense [FID]); show of force operations; joint and combined exercises and training; and arms control and disarmament activities.

(1) **Emergency preparedness** encompasses those measures taken in advance of an emergency to reduce the loss of life and property and to protect a nation's institutions from all types of hazards through a comprehensive emergency management program of preparedness, mitigation, response, and recovery. Activities may include continuity of operations (COOP) and continuity of government. National security emergencies, as a result of domestic WMD incidents, will have unique activities and must be considered as part of COOP and continuity of government plans. **EP is not a stand-alone activity, but an integral part of training, mitigation, and response for both HD and CS.** EP actions largely fall within CBRN passive defense and WMD CM.

(2) **Enforcement of sanctions** are operations that employ coercive measures to interdict the movement of certain types of designated items (including WMD and dual-use equipment) into or out of a nation or specified area. Many of the activities and actions the JFC can employ to support these efforts support larger interagency goals and end states. These operations are multinational and interagency dependent. These operations are military in nature and serve both political and military purposes. The **political objective** is to compel a country or group to conform to the objectives of the initiating body, while the military objective focuses on establishing a barrier that is selective, allowing only authorized goods to enter or exit. Depending on the geography, **sanction enforcement normally involves some combination of air and surface forces.** Assigned forces should be capable of **complementary mutual support** and

communications interoperability. The JFC may also be asked to support the enforcement of CWMD-related sanctions as part of United Nations Security Council resolutions.

(a) **WMD interdiction** operations can support the enforcement of sanctions. For example, DOD is one of many USG departments or agencies that support the multinational Proliferation Security Initiative (PSI). This activity, supported by the United Nations Convention for the Suppression of Unlawful Acts at Sea, is designed specifically to prevent and, if required, counter the proliferation of WMD capabilities. The following vignette, entitled "Maritime Interdiction Operations: So San (December 2002)", exemplifies the type of efforts required to support the task of offensive operations and both its associated subtasks: specifically, the interception and/or diversion of shipments of WMD-related technologies and the seizing of WMD and related technologies.

MARITIME INTERDICTION OPERATIONS: SO SAN (DECEMBER 2002)

The North Korean (Democratic People's Republic of Korea) marine vessel *So San*, an 83-meter long cargo carrier, was interdicted via a noncompliant boarding on 9 December 2002, in waters south of Yemen. United States Pacific Command and United States Central Command tracked the *So San* throughout its voyage. Spanish forces conducted a noncompliant boarding of the *So San* and discovered 16 Scud missiles and containers of related parts and fuel that were eventually released for delivery to Yemen. The operation was the first implementation of the latest weapons of mass destruction interdiction strategy (13 November 2002).

The interdiction of the *So San* was accomplished using a standing combined task force, with existing tactics, techniques, and procedures (TTP) for maritime interdiction operations. The existing TTP significantly reduced the amount of time needed to plan, coordinate, and execute the *So San* interdiction operation. The intercept force was augmented by technical expertise from the US to assist in the characterization of the suspected cargo.

VARIOUS SOURCES

For further guidance on WMD interdiction, refer to Appendix B, "Weapons of Mass Destruction Interdiction Operations."

(b) To execute the WMD interdiction MMA, a JFC would plan actions to interdict WMD and WMD enablers in order to prevent their proliferation. This includes operations that track, divert, disrupt, intercept, delay, and/or deny enemy use or transfer of CBRN knowledge and materials. WMD interdiction operations could include the use of forces in the physical domains of air, land, maritime, and space as well as the cyberspace portion of the information environment. WMD interdiction operations may complement, support, or be supported by other joint operations.

(3) **Nation assistance is civil or military assistance.** A JFC can use nation assistance programs to support their CWMD goals and objectives, and integrate them into the US ambassador's country plan goals and objectives.

(4) **Foreign Internal Defense. DOS is generally the lead government agency in executing US FID programs.** Threats posed through illegal drug trafficking, terrorism, acquisition of WMD, and civil unrest affect all aspects of a nation's defense and development. The military plays an important supporting role in the FID program. FID provides an existing structure to support the internal defense and development of a nation against the proliferation of WMD and commanders should integrate CWMD considerations into FID programs and activities.

For further guidance on FID, refer to JP 3-22, Foreign Internal Defense.

(5) **Show of force operations** are designed to demonstrate US resolve.

(6) **Arms control and disarmament** is the identification, verification, inspection, limitation, control, or reduction of armed forces and armaments of all kinds under international agreement. This includes the steps taken under such an agreement to establish an effective system of international control, or to create and strengthen IGOs, for the maintenance of peace. **Although it may be viewed as a diplomatic mission, the military plays an important role.** For example, US military personnel may be involved in monitoring an arms control treaty; seizing WMD; escorting authorized deliveries of weapons and other materials (i.e., enriched uranium) to preclude loss or unauthorized use of these assets; or dismantling, destroying, or disposing of weapons and hazardous materials. Additionally, the JFC may have responsibility to help establish and enforce the initial stages of WMD disarmament, inspection, or monitoring regimes mandated by a ceasefire or peace accord. This responsibility may transition, in full, to an IGO (e.g., the United Nations [UN]) within a relatively short period of time.

(7) To support the WMD security cooperation, a JFC would engage with partner nations to help them develop an indigenous CWMD capacity; this independent capability could subsequently reduce the US forces' deployment and resource allocation to support regional stability. This effort could include multinational training events and exercises, joint combined exchange training, and state partnership programs. Security cooperation and partner activities could include joint activities that enable partner countries to secure, reduce, reverse, or eliminate CBRN materials, and respond to their potential effects in the case of dispersal.

(8) To support the WMD threat reduction cooperation MMA, a JFC could conduct activities to help eliminate the WMD threat and ensure nations are following international treaties and agreements. Missions could include recovery operations, nation assistance by enhancing the security of existing WMD programs, assuming the

responsibility for residual, long-term tasks transferred from a WMD elimination operation, removing and consequently eliminating some or all of a state's WMD capabilities in a permissive environment, and implementing arms control agreements. The joint force may provide intelligence, security, transportation, and operational and technical support to other government agencies or HNs for the implementation of treaties, agreements, sanctions, and export-control procedures.

4. Crisis Response and Limited Contingency Operations

a. CWMD MMAs that support crisis response and limited contingency operations include WMD interdiction, WMD offensive operations, WMD active defense, CBRN passive defense, and WMD CM.

b. CWMD in Crisis Response and Limited Contingency Operations

(1) **Peace operations (PO).** CWMD in PO can vary in duration and scope, but primarily falls in one of three types of PO: peacekeeping operations (PKO), peace enforcement operations (PEO), and peace building (PB). The JFC must understand that even during PO, CWMD can play a critical role.

(a) **PKO** can include the verification or supervision of the storage or destruction of certain categories of WMD or dual-use equipment specified in relevant agreements.

(b) **PEO.** Due to their increased threat postures, commanders should consider the requirement for CBRN defense forces during PEO if there is evidence belligerent forces may employ such capabilities. A mix of different units (decontamination units or CBRN reconnaissance elements) is often necessary to achieve the proper balance. These capabilities may include local security, spray, storage, personnel shower, and firefighting capability. CBRN staff officers may advise on commercial CBRN threats, as well as on the collection, packaging, storage, disposal, and clean-up of hazardous materials or wastes. Additionally, commanders may be tasked to secure specific WMD technology sites as part of these operations.

(c) **PB** tasks may include assisting a HN with decontamination of residual effects from WMD use; reducing the WMD threat within the HN by helping to enhance the physical security; and reducing, dismantling, or redirecting their WMD programs.

For further guidance on PO, refer to JP 3-07.3, Peace Operations. *For further guidance on CBRN defense and decontamination, refer to JP 3-11,* Operations in Chemical, Biological, Radiological, and Nuclear (CBRN) Environments.

(2) **CM** operations involve actions taken to maintain or restore essential services and manage and mitigate problems resulting from disasters and catastrophes, including natural, man-made, or terrorist incidents. WMD CM is a specific type of CM. WMD CM operations/missions respond to the effects of a WMD attack or effects

resulting from the deliberate or inadvertent release of CBRN materials and to help restore essential operations and services. Within WMD CM, there are three types the JFC must consider – foreign, domestic, and WMD CM conducted as part of a major operation or campaign. This section will briefly discuss the basics of both domestic and FCM. WMD CM conducted as part of a major campaign or operation is discussed in paragraph 5, "Major Operations and Campaigns." Additionally, the JFC and staff must understand the effects on the populace and infrastructure to apply the right resources at the right time.

For further guidance on CM, refer to JP 3-41, Chemical, Biological, Radiological, Nuclear, and High-Yield Explosives Consequence Management, *JP 3-27,* Homeland Defense, *and JP 3-28,* Civil Support. *For medical FHP aspects refer to JP 4-02,* Health Service Support.

(a) **Immediate Response Authority.** DOD policy on immediate response addresses the authority delegated to military commanders to provide immediate assistance to civil authorities to save lives, prevent human suffering, or mitigate great property damage in the event of imminently serious conditions resulting from any civil emergency or attack. Immediate response is situation-specific and may or may not be associated with a declared or undeclared disaster. The potentially catastrophic nature of WMD incidents would most likely lead to DOD forces initially conducting WMD CM under immediate response authority, but there are no policy exceptions or special authorities for WMD CM.

(b) **Foreign Consequence Management.** FCM refers to assistance provided by the USG to a HN to mitigate the effects of a deliberate or inadvertent chemical, biological, radiological, nuclear, or high-yield explosives attack or event and restore essential government services. When authorized, the GCC is responsible for supporting DOS, through the US ambassador, by planning, coordinating, and assisting DOD's CM activities within the AOR to support approved FCM operations.

For further guidance on FCM operations, refer to JP 3-41, Chemical, Biological, Radiological, Nuclear, and High-Yield Explosives Consequence Management, *DODI 2000.21,* Foreign Consequence Management (FCM), *or CJCSI 3214.01C,* Military Support to Foreign Consequence Management Operations for Chemical, Biological, Radiological, and Nuclear Incidents*.*

(c) **Domestic Consequence Management.** Normally, domestic CM is managed at the USG-level by DHS or Department of Justice (DOJ), with DOD providing support as directed. When conducting domestic WMD CM operations in accordance with the NRF, DOD supports a lead or other primary agency. The domestic operational environment presents many challenges to the JFC. It is imperative that commanders and staffs at all levels understand the statutory and operational relationships among US states and federal agencies involved in the operation. Therefore, commanders and staffs at all levels must be knowledgeable about the NRF and the NIMS and know how their commands fit in to the overall NIMS framework. They must also understand the distinctive roles, responsibilities, capabilities, and limitations of Titles 10, 14, and 32

USC, and state active duty personnel. Upon request by the appropriate authority and approval by SecDef, DOD provides assistance to the lead or other primary agency. The NRF contains a number of incident annexes that apply to WMD situations. Domestic CM operations are closely related CS operations discussed in the following section. Note: The geographical boundaries for domestic CM are the continental US, territories, possessions, Hawaii, and Alaska.

For further guidance on domestic CM operations, refer to JP 3-41, Chemical, Biological, Radiological, Nuclear, and High-Yield Explosives Consequence Management.

For further guidance on domestic CM, refer to CJCSI 3125.01A, Military assistance to Domestic Consequence Management Operations in response to Chemical, Biological, Radiological, Nuclear or High-Yield Explosive Situation.

(3) **Defense Support of Civil Authorities.** DSCA activities follow the NRF, which includes specifics on support to WMD incidents, and the requirements of other US interagency agreements and guidelines.

For further guidance on DSCA, refer to JP 3-28, Civil Support.

(4) **Homeland Defense.** The HD and CS missions are separate, but have areas where roles and responsibilities may overlap or transition between organizations. The purpose of HD is to protect against, and mitigate the impact of, incursions or attacks on sovereign territory, the domestic population, and critical defense infrastructure. DOD is the federal agency with lead responsibility, supported by other agencies, in defending against external threats or aggression. DOD must be prepared to operate, in concert with OGAs or law enforcement agencies conducting homeland security, to counter threats to the homeland. The overlap in departmental roles, responsibilities, authorities, and capabilities forced the USG to review its approach to coordination during operations. The current approach promotes early identification of the desired USG outcome and required collaboration. The Maritime Operational Threat Response (MOTR) plan is an example of this new approach to operations.

For further guidance on interagency roles, responsibilities, and required coordination protocols for conduct of air defense and maritime operations to counter threats to the US, refer to the Aviation Operational Threat Response *and* Maritime Operational Threat Response *plans. For further guidance on HD, refer to JP 3-27,* Homeland Defense. *For further guidance on CS, refer to JP 3-28,* Civil Support.

(5) **Strikes** are attacks conducted to damage or destroy an objective or capability. Strikes in support of the WMD offensive operations MMA take place in both crisis response or limited contingency operations and major operations or campaigns. A strike focused on a CWMD objective could involve an air and missile strike on WMD-related facilities.

(6) **Raids** are operations to temporarily seize an area, usually through forcible entry, to secure information, confuse an adversary, capture personnel or equipment, or destroy an objective or capability. Raids in support of the WMD interdiction and WMD offensive operation MMAs take place in both crisis response or limited contingency operations and major operations or campaigns. Raids end with a planned withdrawal upon completion of the assigned mission. A CWMD-related raid could include the seizure of a WMD production facility or the capture of critical expertise.

5. Major Operations and Campaigns

a. When required to achieve national strategic objectives or protect national interests, US national leadership may decide to conduct a major operation or campaign. In such cases, the goal is to prevail against the adversary as quickly as possible, conclude hostilities, and establish conditions favorable to the HN, United States, and multinational partners. Establishing these conditions often requires CWMD considerations for termination objectives and end states. Major operations and campaigns are the most complex and require the greatest diligence in planning and execution due to the time, effort, and national resources committed. This chapter discusses those CWMD areas that must be considered and addressed when conducting major operations and campaigns. Many of the factors from previous sections must be considered since they may be precursors to major operations or, if successfully resolved, may forestall escalation to that level. Major operation and campaign plans must feature an appropriate balance between **offensive, defensive, and stability operations.** All eight CWMD MMAs could be part of a major operation or campaign. A key consideration for conducting CWMD activities in support of joint operations is in the translation of unique CWMD language into language common to the JFC. The following sections discuss this translation for offensive, defensive, and stability operations.

b. **CWMD Supporting Actions.** Figure IV-7 cross-references supporting actions for CWMD MMAs. Figure IV-7 identifies commonly used terms that may be useful to staffs to accurately convey actions associated with these MMAs. This figure is not exhaustive.

c. **Offensive Operations.** Offensive operations are designed to locate and take action against the threat of WMD use. The JFC can create desired effects on the adversary's WMD system that support CWMD-related objectives by drawing upon actions from the following CWMD MMAs: WMD interdiction, WMD offensive operations, WMD elimination, WMD active defense, CBRN passive defense, and WMD CM.

(1) Destroy. To destroy is to ensure a WMD capability cannot perform its intended function or be restored to a useable condition. Destruction can be achieved by lethal means. Nonlethal means can be used in conjunction with lethal means to enhance lethal effectiveness. Destroying WMD capabilities requires a significant amount of pre-strike considerations and authorizations at the appropriate levels of command. Destruction and elimination are not synonymous terms in regard to CWMD, they are

linked. Destruction is one of four operational tasks under WMD elimination although it may take place outside the scope of elimination as defined by the NMS-CWMD. While destruction refers to a specific target, elimination refers to an operation against an entire WMD program. The JFC must consider national and strategic objectives for the

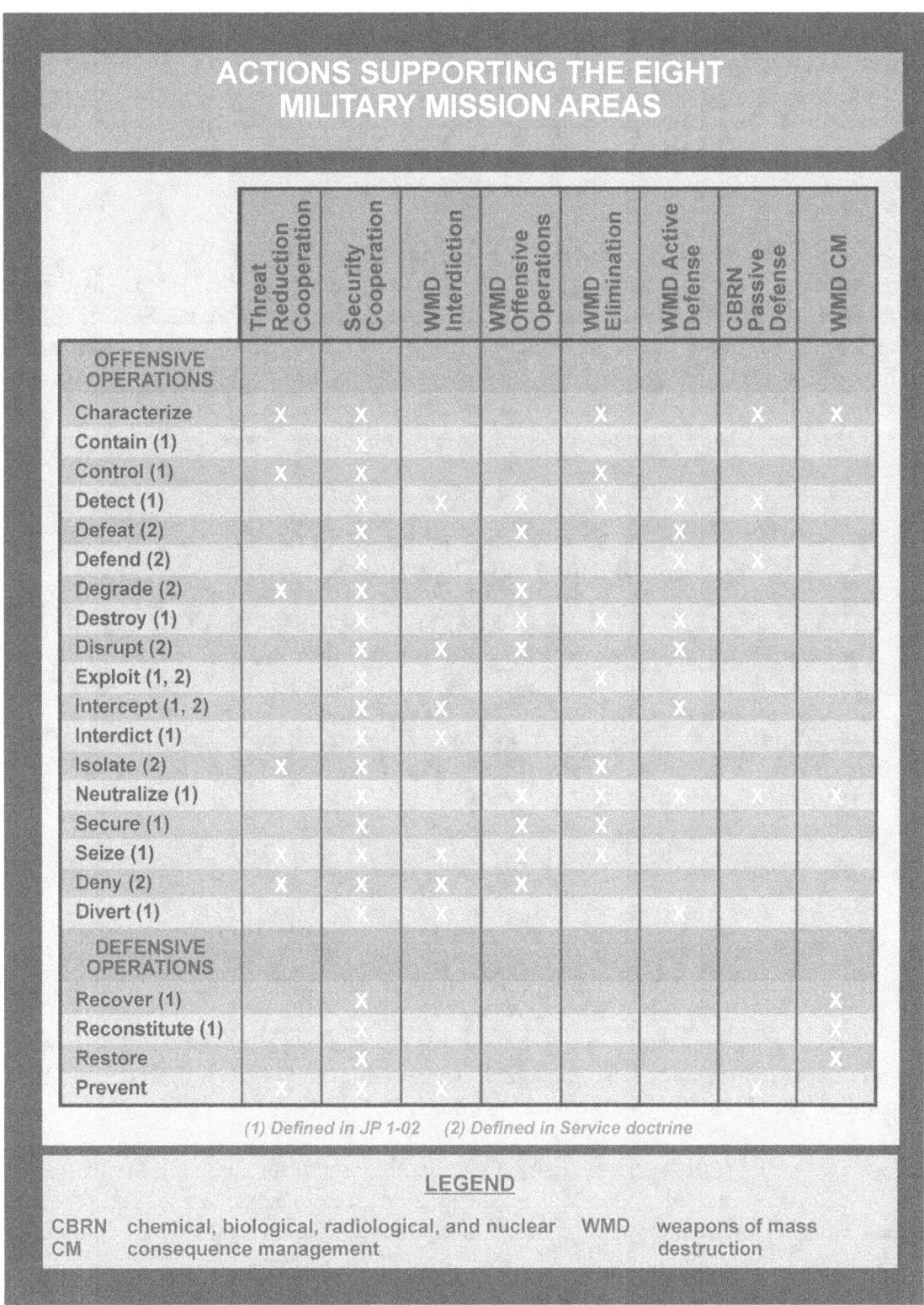

ACTIONS SUPPORTING THE EIGHT MILITARY MISSION AREAS

	Threat Reduction Cooperation	Security Cooperation	WMD Interdiction	WMD Offensive Operations	WMD Elimination	WMD Active Defense	CBRN Passive Defense	WMD CM
OFFENSIVE OPERATIONS								
Characterize	X	X			X		X	X
Contain (1)		X						
Control (1)	X	X			X			
Detect (1)		X	X	X	X			
Defeat (2)		X		X		X		
Defend (2)		X				X	X	
Degrade (2)	X	X		X				
Destroy (1)		X		X	X	X		
Disrupt (2)		X	X	X		X		
Exploit (1, 2)		X			X			
Intercept (1, 2)		X	X			X		
Interdict (1)		X	X					
Isolate (2)	X	X			X			
Neutralize (1)		X		X	X	X	X	X
Secure (1)		X		X	X			
Seize (1)	X	X	X	X	X			
Deny (2)	X	X	X	X				
Divert (1)		X	X			X		
DEFENSIVE OPERATIONS								
Recover (1)		X						X
Reconstitute (1)		X						X
Restore		X						X
Prevent	X	X	X				X	

(1) Defined in JP 1-02   (2) Defined in Service doctrine

LEGEND

CBRN	chemical, biological, radiological, and nuclear	WMD	weapons of mass destruction
CM	consequence management		

Figure IV-7. Actions Supporting the Eight Military Mission Areas

operation or campaign before deciding to destroy a WMD-related target. Many of these targets are necessary for intelligence exploitation or may cause damage to the surrounding area if destroyed. Refer to the targeting section in paragraph 2h, "Targeting," for more information about consequences of execution and collateral damage considerations. Actions to destroy WMD capabilities within a major operation or campaign often require capabilities from the following CWMD MMAs: WMD offensive operations, WMD active defense, or WMD elimination.

(a) The WMD elimination MMA is conducive for a long-term, systematic approach to ensure those elements of a WMD program designated for destruction are destroyed and monitored so they are not reconstituted.

(b) **Friendly Nuclear Weapons Employment.** One of the key considerations when conducting major operations and campaigns in a WMD environment is friendly use of nuclear weapons. When directed by the President and SecDef, CCDRs plan for the US employment of nuclear weapons in a manner consistent with national policy and strategic guidance. The employment of nuclear weapons is a Presidential decision. USSTRATCOM will assist in the collaborative planning of all nuclear missions. If directed to plan for the employment of nuclear weapons, JFCs typically have two escalating objectives.

NOTIONAL EXAMPLE OF A NONLETHAL OPERATION TO NEUTRALIZE A WEAPONS OF MASS DESTRUCTION-RELATED TARGET

An attack on a nuclear power plant could cause irreversible damage but would not affect the reactor core or any other radiological material thereby reducing the consequences of the attack. The attack would also keep key areas of the nuclear power plant unharmed for further exploitation, as required. The attack could shut down the plant resulting in an inability to further produce plutonium as part of a nuclear weapon program.

VARIOUS SOURCES

<u>1</u>. The first is to deter or prevent an adversary attack that employs WMD. To make opponents understand that friendly forces possess and will use such weapons, JFCs may simply communicate that to the adversary, using IO or other means. Regardless, JFCs must implement measures to increase readiness and preserve the option to respond, including the alert and forward positioning of appropriate systems, if required. Prevention or denial may include targeting and attacking adversary WMD capability by conventional and special operations forces (SOF).

<u>2</u>. If deterrence is not an effective option or fails, JFCs will respond, consistent with national policy and strategic guidance, to adversary aggression while seeking to control the intensity and scope of conflict and destruction. This response may include employment of conventional, special operations, or nuclear forces.

(2) **Disrupt.** Disruption seeks to interrupt or interfere with an adversary's actions. This can entail breaking or interrupting the command and/or enabling processes needed to proliferate or employ WMD. This action may be desired when offensive resources are limited; to comply with ROE or RUF; or to create certain effects. IO can enable the commander to disrupt adversary WMD proliferation or employment. Actions to disrupt WMD proliferation or employment during a major campaign or operation often require capabilities from the following CWMD MMAs: WMD security cooperation and partner activities, WMD interdiction, WMD offensive operations, or WMD active defense.

(3) **Degrade.** Degrade can include the use of lethal and nonlethal means to reduce the effectiveness or efficiency of adversary WMD capabilities. Examples of nonlethal actions include IO which can degrade the morale of a unit, reduce the perception of a target's worth or value, or reduce the opportunities for adversaries to achieve their objectives. Nonlethal weapons can include weapons, munitions, and devices explicitly designed to incapacitate personnel and materiel, which can degrade operations by denying individuals and materiel access to or exit from WMD facilities. Actions to degrade WMD capabilities within a major operation or campaign often require capabilities from the following CWMD MMAs: WMD interdiction, WMD offensive operations, CBRN passive defense, and WMD CM.

(4) **Deny.** Deny, in CWMD operations, entails preventing an adversary from having C2 over, or access to, their WMD capabilities. Effective denial provides commanders freedom of action and freedom from the effects of WMD use. Actions to deny WMD proliferation or employment within a major operation or campaign often require capabilities from the following CWMD MMAs: WMD interdiction, WMD offensive operations, threat reduction cooperation, or WMD security cooperation and partner activities.

(5) **Exploit.** Due to the inherently strategic nature of WMD, the exploitation of any WMD-related information must be integrated into the JFC's operations. Most of the exploitation of WMD-related material will come from WMD elimination operations (if conducted) or SOF operations. This information must be collected and fused to increase the commander's operational picture and drive future exploitation actions. Actions to exploit WMD capabilities within a major operation or campaign often require capabilities from the WMD elimination MMA.

For further guidance on exploitation as a part of sensitive site operations, refer to Army Field Manual (FM) 3-90.15, Sensitive Site Operations.

(6) **Neutralize.** Neutralize includes actions to render WMD capabilities ineffective or unusable against US or multinational partners. Examples of CWMD-related actions include making CBRN agents and materials harmless or making delivery systems unusable. When assigning a task to neutralize, commanders must specify the adversary or material and the duration. The commander normally uses a combination of lethal and nonlethal effects to neutralize adversary personnel or material. Assets required

OPERATION ALSOS

During WWII, the United States created an organization under the Manhattan Project called Operation ALSOS. The mission was to collect and exploit all people, places, and things associated with German atomic research and development, and to ensure the capability was not passed on to the Soviet Union. ALSOS was the code name for the Allied special intelligence forces' mission to collect information about German nuclear fission developments. Actual raids were carried out by subordinate teams designated by a letter, such as "S Force" in Italy and "T Force" in France, Holland, and Germany. These units traveled rapidly and were minimally armed. However, because they traveled with accomplished linguists, scientists, and police specialists, they were able to rapidly identify, capture, and exploit experts and materials.

T-Force was the technical intelligence effort by the Americans and British to exploit German capabilities. Originally incorporated as part of the Office of Strategic Services in Italy under 15th Army group, it became a part of the 12th and 6th Army Groups in Germany and France.

During the war, technical intelligence teams often combined with other intelligence and counterintelligence personnel in ad hoc task forces to exploit newly liberated areas of intelligence interest. The task force of 20 to 25 members (including 4-5 scientists) arrived after the site was secured. They were able to fully exploit the site between one day and several weeks depending on the amount of material and personnel.

By the end of the war, the group had a full and complete understanding of the breadth and scope of the German atomic effort; located all key scientists and interviewed them; visited most laboratories used to conduct research; acquired most documents, and recovered quantities of test equipment, uranium, and heavy water.

VARIOUS SOURCES

to neutralize a target vary according to the type and size of the target and the desired effects. Actions to neutralize WMD capabilities within a major operation or campaign often require capabilities from the following CWMD MMAs: WMD interdiction, WMD offensive operations, WMD elimination, or WMD active defense.

(7) **Secure.** Securing WMD-related sites is often necessary to prevent use, proliferation, or looting. The requirement to secure these sites is a crucial mission analysis consideration due to the potentially large force requirements and the balance of other competing missions. A prioritized list of WMD-related sites is recommended and should be deconflicted with national level objectives, exploitation objectives, and other operations within the AOR. Actions to secure WMD capabilities within a major

operation or campaign often require capabilities from the following CWMD MMAs: WMD offensive operations or WMD elimination.

(8) **Seize.** These actions can involve taking possession of WMD capabilities (e.g., a designated area, building, transport, material, or personnel) using combat force. As a result of these actions, an adversary force can no longer access the WMD capabilities that have been seized. Seizing differs from securing because it requires offensive action to obtain control of the designated area or objective. Once a force seizes a WMD-related objective, it secures the objective and prepares it for potential follow-on actions such as exploitation or destruction. Actions to seize WMD capabilities within a major operation or campaign often require capabilities from the following CWMD MMAs: WMD interdiction, WMD offensive operations, or WMD elimination.

OPERATION DESERT FOX

Operation DESERT FOX launched following a 14-month pattern of Iraqi obstruction of United Nations Special Commission inspections. The four day air strike was designed "to attack Iraq's nuclear, chemical, and biological weapons programs and its military capacity to threaten its neighbors" while demonstrating the consequences of flouting international obligations. The original list of potential targets was extensive, including over 100 chemical-related facilities and 90 biological-related facilities across Iraq. The final list of 100 targets narrowed the focus to weapons of mass destruction (WMD) delivery systems as the surest way to degrade and diminish Saddam Hussein's WMD capabilities using airpower. United States Central Command (USCENTCOM) Commander General Anthony Zinni, United States Marine Corps, and his planners concentrated chiefly on Iraq's missile production programs and command and control systems. USCENTCOM and administration officials stated that "air strikes would not target known WMD storage sites or stockpiles in order to reduce collateral damage." Dual use facilities were also avoided to minimize civilian casualties.

Strikes commenced the night of December 16, 1998 and included more than 600 sorties flown by more than 300 combat and support aircraft. Aircraft employed 600 pieces of air-dropped ordnance, 90 air-launched cruise missiles, and 325 Tomahawk land-attack missiles. Although the operation was considered an air strike, forty naval vessels supported DESERT FOX in some capacity and thousands of ground troops deployed to protect Kuwait against a potential counterattack from Iraq. DESERT FOX inflicted serious damage on Iraq's missile program, destroying potential WMD delivery systems that could not be easily replaced due to existing United Nations sanctions.

VARIOUS SOURCES

---

(9) To execute the WMD offensive operations MMA, a JFC would conduct missions to seize, secure, and/or engage WMD and WMD capabilities. This would entail operations to detect, deny, degrade, or destroy adversarial WMD program-related weapon systems, material and facilities, and critical enablers (e.g., technical expertise, associated networks, and C2), through the maneuver and engagement of combat forces. The choice of which resources or systems to employ is driven by the threat, operational environment, available intelligence, and most importantly, the desired effects. The range of joint capabilities that may be leveraged to successfully achieve this mission includes aircraft, naval vessels, missiles, unmanned systems, SOF, IO, communications system support, and ISR, ground forces, and agent defeat weapons to limit dispersal or collateral effects of chemical agents. The JFC could also use the threat of seizure or destruction of an adversary's WMD capabilities to deter adversarial employment against friendly targets.

e. **Defensive Operations.** CWMD aspects of defensive operations are the integration and coordination of operations, personnel, and technology to protect and defend friendly forces from the effects of WMD. The purpose of these operations is to ensure adversary WMD attacks are defeated and, if required, provide the means to rapidly recover; operate, as necessary, in a CBRN environment; and when directed support US and the HN's civil population and governments to reconstitute essential operations and services. Defensive operations support efforts to maintain effective combat power and essential capabilities. Timely, accurate intelligence – some of which is based on information collected during offensive operations – is essential to defensive operations.

(1) **Adversary Employment of WMD.** An adversary's use of WMD can quickly change an operation or campaign. The use or threat of use of these weapons can cause large-scale shifts in strategic and operational objectives, phases, and COAs. Multinational operations become more complicated with the threat of WMD employment. An adversary may use WMD against multinational partners, especially those with little or no defense against these weapons, to disintegrate the alliance or coalition.

(2) **Defend.** WMD defense is the capability to effectively respond to, and defend against, WMD attacks. Sustaining operations in CBRN environments requires forewarning and properly trained and equipped forces. US forces must be prepared to conduct and sustain operations in CBRN environments with minimal degradation. In order to sustain operations, US forces must assess the environment for CBRN hazards and prepare for WMD defense, when appropriate. WMD defense includes both CBRN passive defense and WMD active defense.

For further guidance on CBRN defense, refer to JP 3-11, Operations in Chemical, Biological, Radiological, and Nuclear (CBRN) Environments.

(3) **Recovery and Reconstitution.** Recovery and reconstitution are those actions taken by one nation prior to, during, and following an attack by an adversary nation to minimize the effects of the attack, rehabilitate the national economy, provide for

the welfare of the populace, and maximize the combat potential of remaining forces and supporting activities. This also includes those actions taken by a military force during, or after, operational employment to restore its combat capability to full operational readiness. Reconstitution is the mission to repair and replace assets or capabilities damaged by, or lost to, CBRN weapons or effects. Actions to recover and reconstitute from WMD attacks require capabilities from the CBRN passive defense and WMD CM CWMD MMAs.

(4) **Force Protection.** JFCs and their subordinate commanders must implement force protection measures appropriate to all anticipated threats, to include terrorists and the use of WMD or other CBRN hazards. Force protection often requires capabilities from WMD active defense and CBRN passive defense.

For further guidance on recovery and reconstitution following a WMD attack, refer to JP 3-11, Operations in Chemical, Biological, Radiological, and Nuclear (CBRN) Environments.

(5) **Force Health Protection.** JFCs and their subordinate commanders implement FHP measures appropriate to all anticipated threats, to include the use of WMD or other CBRN hazards.

For further guidance on force health protection see JP 4-02, Health Service Support.

(6) To implement the CBRN passive defense MMA, a JFC would plan operations in such a way as to ensure the ability to survive, operate, and recover friendly forces affected by WMD. This includes measures taken in a hostile or uncertain environment to reduce vulnerability and minimize the effects of WMD employed against US and HN installations and facilities, interests, points of embarkation and debarkation, and critical infrastructure. They assist the joint force to continue operations despite the use or presence of CBRN agents through neutralizing, containing, and/or managing the effects of WMD attacks. These include operations associated with sensing the hazard, shaping the environment, shielding combat power from CBRN hazards, and sustaining operations through and after CBRN releases.

f. **Relationship Between Offensive and Defensive Operations.** Commanders synchronize offensive and defensive operations to produce complementary and reinforcing effects. While offensive CWMD operations support the decisive operation, defensive CWMD operations protect friendly force critical assets and COGs. Conducting offensive and defensive operations independently detracts from the efficient employment of CWMD assets. At best, independent operations expend more resources than would be required if done in concert. At worst, uncoordinated efforts increase conflicts and mutual interference. In the extreme, they may compromise friendly intentions or result in loss of operational momentum. Fully integrating CWMD offensive and defensive operations requires JFCs and their staffs to treat CWMD as a single, integrated function.

g. **Stability Operations.** CWMD-related capabilities and expertise support stability operations by providing unique capabilities that directly support the commander's objectives. **Many of the CWMD considerations that are a part of PO are the same for stability operations.** This unique support can be in the form of CBRN material identification, security, and or collection to ensure public health and safety. Additionally, these resources support the execution of security cooperation activities to assist in the shaping of interagency and HN success. CWMD operations also provide specific expertise to interagency elements to transition a former adversary's WMD program towards peace-time applications.

For further guidance on stability, security, transition, and reconstruction, refer to Department of Defense Directive (DODD) 3000.05, Military Support for Stability, Security, Transition, and Reconstruction Operations.

h. To implement the WMD CM MMA, a JFC could leverage capabilities and assets to support US and/or friendly nations' restoration of essential operations and services. In response to or when recovering from attacks or disasters associated with WMD and their effects, to include planning for the disposition of hazardous materials, sites, and remains. Disposing of CBRN and CBRN-contaminated material and casualties entails unique challenges and coordination with HN and interagency entities.

PALOMARES, SPAIN (JANUARY 1966)

On January 17, 1966 a B-52G heavy bomber collided with a KC-135 tanker during a mid-air refueling operation off the coast of Spain and broke-up. The conventional explosion of two of its nuclear bombs, which fell on land, detonated causing radioactive contamination of approximately two square kilometers of land. In response to the effects of the accident, the US excavated approximately 1,750 tons of contaminated material and sent for disposal at the Savannah River Plant in South Carolina. Subsequently, the US settled claims by Palomares residents and the town received a desalination plant.

VARIOUS SOURCES

CHAPTER V
COMBATING WEAPONS OF MASS DESTRUCTION PLANNING CONSIDERATIONS

> *"Capabilities-based plans for resourcing should focus on development of tools that have broad-spectrum application. For example, our planning and capability development should not be focused on one biological warfare threat agent, one threat country, or one non-State actor. We must plan for and develop capabilities that could be employed against a range of threats and associated capabilities while balancing the requirements for targeted strategies against known proliferators."*
>
> **National Military Strategy to Combat Weapons of Mass Destruction**
> **February 2006**

1. General

This chapter describes CWMD planning considerations of particular concern to JFCs and operational planners. For additional information on the CWMD aspects of joint operation planning and operational art and design, review paragraph 2, "Operation and Campaign Planning," of Chapter IV, "Planning and Execution." CWMD operations are a component of a comprehensive USG effort requiring a coordinated interagency approach and the cooperation of the international community. Many DOD CWMD activities occur during phase 0 (Shape) operations. In many cases, DOD CWMD activities will support OGAs. Alternatively, when DOD is the lead agency, these same entities will provide essential support to DOD CWMD missions. These activities require early coordination with these OGAs and often require the participation of multinational partners during planning.

2. Strategic Considerations

a. **Legal Guidance.** The complexity of CWMD and associated laws, policies, treaties, and agreements requires continuous involvement of the staff judge advocate (SJA), or appropriate legal advisor with the planning, control, and assessment of operations. Because of the global nature of CWMD, this will also include continuous consultation with OGAs, multinational partners, HN governments, and IGOs to establish the legal authorities, capabilities, and limitations associated with their organizations.

(1) The SJA should be involved throughout the planning process, including mission analysis and COA development, to ensure the JFC is aware of potential CWMD-related legal issues. For instance, multinational partners, allies, and HNs will have their own treaty obligations and laws that may significantly differ from our own and restrict or prohibit their participation in CWMD operations. SJA involvement in WMD targeting and RUF or ROE development is essential. The SJA can advise the JFC and his staff of potential associated issues, such as consequences of execution and harmful environmental impacts, collateral damage, or other WMD-related legal issues that should be considered in the targeting process.

(2) The SJA should develop a legal staff estimate during mission analysis that accounts for WMD-related legal issues associated with joint operations. The legal staff estimate is contained in appendix 4 (Legal) to annex E (Personnel) and should reflect the description of legal support required to support the mission as developed during the planning process. For example, protecting enemy prisoners of war and third country nationals from CBRN agents must be considered.

For further guidance on legal support, refer to JP 1-04, Legal Support to Military Operations.

b. **International Law and Agreements.** International law, policies, treaties, and agreements to which the United States is a signatory identify certain rights and obligations that may impact joint operations. These legal requirements may pose constraints and restraints. They will shape the design of operations and campaigns that deal with the WMD threat or hazards associated with WMD-related targets.

(1) **Arms Control and NP Treaties.** Arms control and NP treaties and regimes establish global norms against the proliferation of WMD precursors, weapons, their means of delivery, and weapons manufacturing equipment. **Treaties provide international standards to gauge and address the activities of potential proliferators.** International treaties may also provide diplomatic tools and legal recourse to isolate and punish violators.

(2) **Security Assistance.** Through security assistance activities, the Armed Forces of the United States can help multinational partners develop the ability to cope with a WMD attack as well as reduce their vulnerability to armed aggression.

(3) **Technology Security. An important aspect of NP is preventing the spread of WMD technology through physical security and export controls.** Export control regimes work to inhibit the proliferation of WMD technologies and deny access to potential suppliers. Protecting sensitive technologies includes guarding US technological information through information security programs and limits on foreign disclosure to ensure military compliance with federal legislation and regulations implementing the export control regime. **In addition, protecting sensitive technologies includes assisting other countries monitor and control sensitive technologies and equipment.**

(4) **Nonproliferation and Counterproliferation Initiatives.** Various international cooperation programs have been initiated to defeat the proliferation of WMD and the materiel, technology, and expertise necessary to create and sustain a WMD program. These initiatives have varied levels of DOD participation and are usually part of phase 0 (Shape) activities. Three examples are listed below:

(a) **Cooperative Threat Reduction.** The CTR program helps deny rogue states and terrorist access to WMD and related materials, technologies, and expertise from former Soviet Union (FSU) states. This includes providing for the safe destruction of Soviet era WMD, associated delivery systems and related infrastructure, and consolidating and securing FSU WMD and related technology and materials. DTRA implements the CTR program.

(b) **The Proliferation Security Initiative.** PSI is designed to enhance and expand international efforts to impede and interdict the flow of WMD, their means of delivery, and related materials to and from state and non-state actors of concern. Interdiction of WMD shipments by air, sea, or land is the foundation of the initiative. PSI activities include all the instruments of national power, and are consistent with national laws and international legal frameworks. Overall, the PSI expands the range of interdiction options in an effort to combat WMD. PSI leverages proactive measures found in both NP and CP activities. The detection and monitoring of potential WMD transshipment activities and the actual interdiction of WMD transshipments are accomplished through the cooperation of PSI nations under the PSI Statement of Interdiction Principles.

(c) Missile Technology Control Regime (MTCR). MTCR is an informal and voluntary association of countries which share the goal of NP of unmanned delivery systems capable of delivering WMD. MTCR was initiated in response to the increasing proliferation of WMD, recognizing that one way to counter the threat is to maintain vigilance over the transfer of missile equipment, materiel, and related technologies usable for systems capable of delivering WMD. The partner countries also seek to coordinate national export licensing efforts aimed at CP.

3. **Operational Considerations**

Operational planning considerations of particular importance to the JFC are listed below.

a. **Task Organization.** The JFC organizes forces and phases their arrival in support of his concept of operations (CONOPS) while maintaining the flexibility to exploit unforeseen opportunities or adjust to evolving events (including adversary actions and environmental impacts). Shortfalls in CWMD capabilities across the eight MMAs should be identified and additional CWMD specific capabilities should be requested as early as feasible, via the request for forces process.

b. **Intelligence, Surveillance, and Reconnaissance.**

(1) Intelligence planning must support the CONOPS for each of the CWMD MMAs. Summaries of enemy capabilities must include descriptions of CBRN conventional and unconventional delivery means and possession/previous use of CBRN by non-state actors.

(2) ISR tasks in support of CWMD missions must be clearly defined and designed.

(3) Procedures for the handling, processing, and exploitation of WMD weapons and materiel will be situation dependent and should carefully consider operations security (OPSEC) requirements. Intelligence support also considers the requirement for identification, tracking, and handling of key leadership and scientific personnel associated with the adversary's WMD programs or proliferation networks.

c. **Operations**

(1) **Flexible Deterrent Options.** DOD supports USG NP efforts and preventive diplomacy by **providing FDOs that can be readily implemented to deter or forestall a crisis.** FDOs can be used individually, in packages, sequentially, or concurrently. FDOs are designed to be used in groups that maximize integrated results from all instruments of national power. As such, it is imperative that extensive, continuous coordination occur with interagency and multinational partners to maximize their impact. Examples of FDOs that involve the military instrument of national power include:

(a) **Establish and Maintain Military-to-Military Contacts with Multinational Partners.** These relationships can be utilized to build and sustain their capacity for NP and CP activities and operations against WMD threats.

(b) **Forward Deploy Military Forces.** The forward deployment of forces capable of conducting WMD interdiction, WMD elimination, and WMD offensive operations against WMD threats contributes to the maintenance of regional security and stability. The forward deployment of military forces demonstrates readiness and resolve to defend US interests against WMD threats.

(c) **Exercise CWMD Capabilities with Multinational Partners.** These activities contribute to the deterrence of the use, or threat of use, of WMD against multinational partners by demonstrating the capability of US forces and multinational partners to respond to a WMD attack, operate in a contaminated environment, and mitigate the effects of WMD use.

(2) **Deployment.** Operations in areas potentially targeted by a WMD threat must incorporate WMD active defense and CBRN defense considerations as part of force protection measures. Vulnerability analyses of key aerial port of debarkation (APOD), seaport of debarkation (SPOD), and joint reception, staging, onward movement, and integration sites, to include proximity of TIM storage facilities/sites, must be conducted to ensure adequate defensive and WMD CM assets are available for these areas during all phases of operations. To ensure the continuation of deployment, sustainment, and redeployment support following WMD attack, planners must designate alternate APODs/SPODs and exchange zone locations, identify and resource decontamination sites for strategic transportation assets, and coordinate diplomatic clearances for the international movement of formerly contaminated airlift aircraft, ships, and cargo.

For additional guidance, see JP 3-11, Operations in Chemical, Biological, Radiological, and Nuclear (CBRN) Environments.

For further guidance on WMD CM assets, refer to CJCSI 3525.01A, Defense Support of Civil Authorities (DSCA) for Domestic Consequence Management Operations in response to Chemical, Biological, Radiological, Nuclear, or High-Yield Explosives Incidents.

(3) Employment

(a) CWMD operations, whether undertaken in support of an OGA or in conjunction with other joint operations, must be carefully coordinated with all participants to be effective. Consideration should be given to interagency coordination during all phases of planning. Interagency coordination is a continuous process that should be established and emphasized prior to an event occurring, as well as during and after an event. The JIACG, a fully integrated participant on the staff at each combatant command, is composed of liaison members from OGAs with a daily focus on planning. While JIACG members are not necessarily CWMD subject matter experts, they represent their parent organizations and provide a capability specifically organized to enhance situational awareness of interagency activities to prevent undesired consequences and uncoordinated activity.

For further guidance on interagency coordination, refer to JP 3-08, Interorganizational Coordination During Joint Operations.

(b) **Prosecution of WMD Targets.** The engagement of targets involved with the production, storage, and delivery of WMD present the JFC with significant challenges. The risks of catastrophic, long term, human and environmental impact as a consequence of engaging these targets must be carefully considered. Options the JFC has available to overcome the challenges associated with this target set include careful construction of RUF or ROE; lethal and nonlethal engagement options; and nodal analysis of the target to exploit vulnerabilities that minimize the potential for contaminant release into the atmosphere.

<u>1</u>. **One of the Operational Decisions is the Type of Attack.** Course of action analysis should consider both covert and overt operations. Since covert and overt planning incorporate different planning criteria, this decision must be made early in the planning cycle.

<u>2</u>. **Target Selection.** Planners and targeting experts will recommend whether to strike the primary WMD facility or a separate support facility. If the actual WMD facility is to be struck, the target will be further refined to determine what portions of the facility to strike, and with what weapons and tactics, in order to accomplish the mission while avoiding or minimizing collateral contamination. In some instances, a commander may want to destroy supporting infrastructure without attacking the portion

that actually stores the agent or nuclear material so as to either deny the adversary access to WMD or immobilize it.

3. **Ordnance Selection.** Understanding the commander's intent for the target is critical. **What effects are being sought? What are the agent defeat criteria?** In some cases, the intent is to consume the entire agent with the effects of the ordnance. Too little ordnance may release some of the agent or nuclear material into the atmosphere. In other cases, evidence must be preserved to prove WMD was being produced. Too much ordnance may destroy residual evidence.

4. **Consequences of Execution and Collateral Damage.** At a minimum the early analysis of consequences of attacks against WMD and WMD-related targets should identify the worst case local, as well as downwind, hazards. Effects modeling will help refine targeting. Modeling may also assist in determining acceptable risk and requirements for prior notification of a pending strike.

a. **Minimizing Collateral Damage.** WMD-related targets carry unique targeting considerations. Although the initial effect of conventional munitions on a WMD-related target may cause little collateral damage, secondary effects could include a release or dispersal of chemical, biological, or radiological material or even an imperfect detonation of a nuclear device. For this reason, WMD-related targets are usually placed on a restricted target list; however, mission priorities to combat WMD or military necessity may require JFCs to engage WMD-related targets. JFCs should seek to minimize collateral damage consistent with the law of armed conflict and higher-level guidance, and plan for follow-on WMD CM operations to mitigate the potential WMD effects, as necessary.

b. **Consequences of Execution Planning.** Planners must complete a detailed consequence of execution analysis to determine the potential release of hazards when targeting enemy WMD storage sites, weapon systems, or production facilities. Joint and friendly forces throughout the operational area need to be advised of the predicted hazard area and given enough warning time to take appropriate force protection and FHP measures. Effects on local civilians and critical infrastructure must be anticipated and planned for as well. This planning must be done not only for WMD sites, but also for targets known or suspected to contain toxic industrial chemicals or materials. To protect forces and civilian populations, WMD CM planning should include both immediate and long term effects of dispersed CBRN hazards.

For further guidance on mitigating collateral damage, refer to JP 3-60, Joint Targeting, and the methodology contained within CJCSM 3160.01, Joint Methodology for Estimating Collateral Damage and Casualties for Conventional Weapons: Precision, Unguided, and Cluster.

(c) **SOF-Conventional Force Integration.** The JFC, using SOF independently or integrated with conventional forces, gains an additional and specialized capability to achieve CWMD objectives that might not otherwise be attainable.

Integration of these forces and their specialized capabilities enables the JFC to take full advantage of conventional and SOF core CWMD competencies. SOF provide unique capabilities to monitor and support arms control treaties. SOF are tasked with organizing, training, equipping, and otherwise preparing to conduct operations in support of USG CWMD objectives. SOF CWMD missions include:

<u>1</u>. **Direct Action.** Actions can include raids, ambushes, direct assaults, precision destruction operations, standoff attacks, terminal attack control and terminal guidance operations, and anti-surface operations.

<u>2</u>. **Special Reconnaissance.** Special reconnaissance can include assessment of CBRN or environmental hazards in denied areas.

<u>3</u>. **Foreign Internal Defense.** FID may involve training countries on use of CBRN detection equipment.

<u>4</u>. **Combating WMD Terrorism.** Combating WMD terrorism consists of efforts to prevent the acquisition, development, proliferation, or use of CBRN by a terrorist network.

For further guidance on integration of SOF and conventional forces, refer to USSOCOM Publication 3-33, Conventional Forces and Special Operations Forces Integration and Interoperability Handbook and Checklist, *Version 2, September 2006.*

(d) **Storage and Security.** Initial efforts should focus on securing suspected WMD sites to prevent unintended destruction, looting (with its associated danger to the civilian population), or transfer of WMD-related materials. Guidelines for storage and security of confiscated and/or captured materiel may be subject to international treaties or agreements. It may be more cost- and manpower-effective to consolidate suspect materiel into one or a limited number of centralized sites. Proximity of storage to demilitarization (destruction) facilities will reduce the risk of losing control of suspect materiel and facilitate the demilitarization process. The risks to non-CWMD missions due to the attrition of combat power as units are tasked with securing WMD-related sites must be considered at the earliest stages of planning.

(e) **Information Operations.** IO includes electronic warfare, computer network operations, psychological operations, military deception, and operational security, each useful and necessary in CWMD. Prior to the initiation of combat operations, psychological operations and military deception can reinforce a deliberate CS campaign targeting government and military leadership and technical experts associated with WMD programs. IO would include dissuading adversary use or proliferation of WMD to cooperation with multinational forces. While OPSEC is essential to prevent tipping the adversary to the specific timing and method of the blue force operation, a WMD target could be neutralized by a psychological operations leaflet/media warning local populace of the potential targeting causing the workers to evacuate the area for fear of being contaminated.

For further guidance on integrating IO, refer to JP 3-13, Information Operations.

(f) **Multinational Operations.** Many of the technical skills required to support CWMD operations are low density and very costly to establish and maintain. The large demand for explosive ordnance disposal, technical escort, intelligence, and scientific support may preclude some states from actively participating in the effort. **There are, however, a number of supporting roles for which multinational partners are perfectly suited.** They can include site and team security, transportation, medical and veterinary/animal support, language support, and intelligence. The presence of international members increases the legitimacy of CWMD efforts and fosters greater cooperation in the overarching CWMD challenge. Special consideration must be given to the classification level of intelligence supporting WMD elimination operations. The United States has standing agreements with some states that allow for the sharing of high-level intelligence (e.g., special category). Others are denied access by the 'not releasable to foreign nationals' and 'originator controlled' caveats. A systematic process must be implemented to determine classification and releasability guidance for multinational partners. Additionally, during the integration of multinational partners into operations, commanders and planners must identify operational restrictions due to WMD-related laws, policies, treaties, and agreements specific to those forces.

(4) **Forensics and Evidence Collection.** In planning the intelligence tasks for a WMD offensive operation, commanders determine the forensic evidentiary requirements for collecting/retaining adversary WMD warhead residuals, agents, nuclear material, and remnants of delivery means after the attack for post-mortem analysis, intelligence purposes, or the enforcement or prosecution of international law. Commanders and their staffs should know, prior to developing the plan, if there is a requirement because this will affect the means of attack, agent defeat criteria, type of ordnance, and additional forces required. Considerations may include sample collection, packaging, change of custody, and hazardous material transportation requirements. Agent defeat criteria are efforts to neutralize, destroy or deny access to or immobilize WMD and their delivery systems while causing low-to-no collateral damage. For prompt operations in support of national technical nuclear forensics, commanders will determine in coordination with the lead agency the forensic evidentiary requirements following an adversary's radiological or nuclear attack.

d. **Logistics.** Logisticians must be fully engaged for both feasibility and responsiveness to any changes in plans.

(1) **Mission Specific Equipment.** Much of the equipment associated with CWMD operations is unique and low density. Some items may require specialized logistic support for sustainment throughout the mission. Many logistic requirements for CWMD specialized capabilities will be shared between competing mission requirements. For example, while it is highly desirable for forces conducting WMD elimination, WMD interdiction, and WMD CM operations in an area to each have their own organic decontamination capability, it may not be feasible due to the limited number of these assets available.

(2) Consideration should be given to WMD-specific transportation requirements during all phases of planning. WMD samples often have specialized packaging, handling, and storage requirements. Additionally, to preserve the opportunity for exploitation and future prosecution, storage and handling procedures must comply with evidentiary chain of custody requirements. Logistics planners must be aware of airframe size limitations, ship decontamination constraints, and the effects of CBRN contamination on transportation assets and international mobility operations. Due to the threat of cross contamination of defense transportation assets, operations into contaminated APOD, SPOD, and transportation nodes that could be significantly degraded. The retrograde of contaminated cargo will be restricted to "mission critical cargo" (as designated by the CCDR, in consultation with the CDRUSTRANSCOM). Planners must ensure proper transient/overflight country clearances are obtained when transporting contaminated materials and equipment, including the contaminated transporting vessel.

For further guidance, refer to JP 3-11, Operations in Chemical, Biological, Radiological, and Nuclear (CBRN) Environments.

(3) The CWMD-related logistic requirements of the HN and all multinational partners must be addressed. Additionally, the respective logistic burden to be assumed by them in support of CWMD operations must be considered with respect to their unique requirements and capabilities.

(4) **Contaminated Facilities, Equipment, and Remains.** The impact of CBRN contamination on logistics is substantial. Procedures for the temporary or permanent disposition of equipment and materiel that cannot be decontaminated, or that do not meet agreed upon cleanliness standards, must be addressed during planning. Similarly, the disposition of contaminated human remains requires logistic planning to meet health-based clearance requirements for decontamination, safety requirements for transportation, and environmental/diplomatic requirements for temporary interment in theater. It may be more cost-effective to abandon contaminated facilities than decontaminate and rebuild. To preserve inter theater mobility capabilities, limit the movement of contaminated cargo to "mission critical" items (as determined by the CCDR, in consultation with the CDRUSTRANSCOM).

For further guidance, refer to JP 3-41, Chemical, Biological, Radiological, Nuclear, and High-Yield Explosives Consequence Management, *JP 3-11,* Operations in Chemical, Biological, Radiological, and Nuclear (CBRN) Environments, and *JP 4-06,* Mortuary Affairs in Joint Operations.

e. **Public Affairs**

(1) PA is integral to the success of any operation. The United States can win the battle but lose the war of public opinion. A proactive PA plan will address CWMD events, incorporate the media strategy into all phases of the plan, and keep everyone on message. PA products and themes should be synchronized with SC themes and support

US policy objectives. PA should work with USG agencies and NGOs to quickly and effectively communicate risk and response information to the public in order to avoid confusion and hysteria. The JFC's PA officer plays a major role in coordinating public information activities to ensure consistency of messages, and also in keeping USG agencies and NGOs informed on the capability and intent of the joint force.

(2) The chain of command for PA activities must be clearly defined and in consonance with higher level guidance. This is especially true regarding the release of internal and external WMD-related information. The release of WMD information may require non-DOD lines of communications and authority such as DOS and other diplomatic points of contact.

(3) The pursuit of WMD attracts national and international media attention. An essential component of a successful PA plan includes provisions for delivering updates on the progress of CWMD efforts in a way that will not interfere with intelligence gathering and other tasks. Regular media events can provide timely and accurate information to address the progress of CWMD events.

(4) Prearranged news information materials (e.g., fact sheets, background papers, general news release on CWMD operations) can be made available for immediate release, as necessary.

(5) Because of their multimedia capabilities, PA assets can often be utilized to support CWMD missions. If appropriately tasked, units like combat camera can provide valuable support for the documentation of WMD sites and CWMD activities.

f. **Civil-Military Operations**

(1) The assistance of the local indigenous population is imperative in CWMD operations. The local populace can assist in determining the location and function of WMD facilities; identification and location of key personnel employed at WMD or dual use sites; identification of local environmental hazards; identification and location of individuals that are not part of the local populace; and assistance in characterization of potential WMD sites.

(2) The Civil-military operations annex should address actions necessary to minimize HN or civilian populace interference in CWMD operations; synchronization of IO and PA messages relating to CWMD operations; and integration of the various OGAs, NGOs, and HN agencies into operations where their support is necessary.

(3) The civil affairs operation concept of support should address the unique aspects of the CWMD mission including:

(a) Identification of "dual-use" facilities and assets;

(b) Determination of CM requirements (accidental or deliberate release);

(c) Evidence collection;

(d) Legal considerations, ROE, and RUF;

(e) Identification and disposition of scientists, experts, and technocrats (use of HN WMD experts);

(f) Policies toward "third parties" (i.e., other nations, tribes, organizations, or enterprises);

(g) Identification, prioritization, and characterization of targets and sites for WMD elimination operations; and

(h) Assistance available to the civilian populace in the event of a WMD-related event or CBRN contamination.

g. **Meteorological and Oceanographic Operations**

(1) Meteorological and oceanographic (METOC) products and information are key components of modeling and simulation analysis used to accurately predict WMD effects. METOC products are integral to target planning during WMD offensive operations, and to predict hazard areas and estimate casualties during CM operations.

(2) Provisions should be made to ensure METOC support is available. This support should include the capability to disseminate required METOC products to users via classified transmission means (i.e., SECRET Internet Protocol Router Network).

h. **Environmental Considerations**

(1) Environmental recovery actions will address contamination and clean up measures from a CBRN event. Associated environmental plans will consider and ensure compliance with all applicable domestic obligations, international treaties and agreements, and foreign laws which the United States is a signatory.

(2) One of the key environmental issues that must be addressed is the determination of the standard to which the environment must be decontaminated or "cleaned." This standard will be a key planning factor in both WMD elimination and WMD CM operations. Identify the appropriate organizations to be involved in determining appropriate clean-up criteria (e.g., clean standards) in the event of a CBRN release and incorporate into plans for WMD CM and WMD elimination operations. Where available/appropriate, identify and incorporate the specific clean-up criteria including technical assets/resources (e.g., laboratories) necessary to verify.

(3) Another environmental consideration is the necessity to address the transportation of WMD materiel within, or outside, the AOR. This includes operations to transition forces out of theater. International health regulations require the identification

of potential health risks (such as the movement of contaminated/contagious personnel, cargo, or conveyances) to transited and destination countries.

i. **Health Service Support.** Medical and health issues have an operational impact on many other areas regardless of whether CWMD is the JFC's primary mission or operations are conducted in a potentially CBRN-contaminated area. Key planning factors include:

(1) HSS planning should address CWMD mission objectives by phase for each MMA.

(2) **Requirements for a comprehensive health surveillance program.** Personnel conducting CWMD operations must have appropriate prophylaxis available for probable WMD threats.

(3) **Medical intelligence, logistics, and FHP considerations must be assessed for the impact of likely WMD threats in the AOR.** Considerations include availability of adequate supplies, personnel, and equipment in theater to deal with contamination of patients resulting from a WMD event. Supplies, including pharmaceuticals, for use on the affected civilian population may be obtained locally or regionally. Coordination with the National Center for Medical Intelligence, United Nations Joint Logistics Center, World Food Programme, or World Health Organization may be desirable. Health service logistic personnel can assist IGOs, NGOs, and the HN by conducting an assessment of the military or civilian medical supply infrastructure and industry.

(4) Immunization requirements and prophylaxis against CBRN should be identified and stocked, as necessary.

(5) Establishment of policies for contaminated mass casualty decontamination resulting from the deliberate or accidental use of WMD (to include contamination from toxic industrial chemicals or TIMs.) Policies and procedures should include provisions for casualty decontamination and evacuation both in and out of the area of operations. Due to the limited capability to airlift contaminated/contagious patients, DOD may elect to move medical treatment forward following a mass-casualty WMD event. Medical planners must be cognizant of the restrictions imposed on the aeromedical evacuation of contaminated or contagious persons.

(6) **Medical assistance to be provided to indigenous populations, multinational forces, USG employees, contractors, and, as appropriate, IGOs and NGOs in the event of a WMD incident.** Medical obligations under international law will be particularly crucial to the management of nonmilitary personnel. US military forces should be prepared to lead activities necessary to accomplish this medical task when indigenous capacity does not exist or is incapable of assuming responsibility. The JFC and joint force surgeon must plan to address these obligations. Once legitimate civil authority is prepared to conduct and sustain this medical support, US military forces may provide support, as required or necessary.

(7) **Requirements for public HSS to indigenous populations, multinational forces, USG employees, contractors, and, as appropriate, IGOs and NGOs in the event of a WMD incident.** Considerations include availability of adequate supplies, personnel, and equipment in theater to deal with animal and food contamination from a WMD incident. Coordination with the World Food Programme, Food and Agriculture Organization, World Organization for Animal Health, or World Health Organization may be desirable. Veterinary service personnel can assist IGOs, NGOs, and the HN by conducting an assessment of the military or civilian veterinary and animal infrastructure and industry.

For further guidance, refer to JP 4-02, Health Service Support.

j. **Weapons of Mass Destruction Consequence Management.** WMD CM planning must address the JTF response to an accidental or deliberate release of CBRN hazards or contaminants into the operational environment or resulting from possible collateral damage and consequences of execution.

(1) Planning should address the capability for CBRN hazard identification and assessment, protection, avoidance, and decontamination considerations, if necessary for CBRN hazards across the range of military operations.

(2) JIPOE and other threat analysis activities should include known or suspected CBRN hazards that may impact military operations.

(3) WMD CM activities in the homeland, conducted through CS operations, will require coordination at the interagency federal, state, and local levels.

(4) FCM activities not associated with combat operations may be required due to a specific HN request in response to an accidental or intentional release of CBRN hazards, generally in support of foreign disaster relief operations. Coordination will be required with the DOS, the American embassy or US consulate, and the affected or requesting nation.

(5) WMD CM during combat operations should consider the capabilities and limitations of US forces, multinational forces, and host or staging nation consistent with the assessed CBRN threat.

For further guidance on CBRNE CM planning considerations, refer to JP 3-41, Chemical, Biological, Radiological, Nuclear, and High-Yield Explosives Consequence Management, *JP 3-11,* Operations in Chemical, Biological, Radiological, and Nuclear (CBRN) Environments, *and FM 3-11.21/Marine Corps Reference Publication (MCRP) 3-37.2C/Navy Tactics, Techniques, and Procedures (NTTP) 3-11.24/Air Force Tactics, Techniques, and Procedures (Instruction) (AFTTP(I)) 3-2.37,* Multi-Service Tactics, Techniques, and Procedures for Chemical, Biological, Radiological, and Nuclear Consequence Management Operations.

k. **Interagency Coordination.** The involvement of a large collection of agencies and organizations is a common thread throughout CWMD operations. These interagency participants, many with indispensable practical competencies and significant legal responsibilities, often provide enabling functions critical to the success of CWMD operations. Close, continuous, interagency and interdepartmental coordination and cooperation are necessary to effectively accomplish CWMD missions.

(1) The JIACG and joint interagency task force (if authorized) can assist with coordination. JIACG activities include:

(a) Planning conferences with interagency partners as well as assessments that include realistic exercises to test plans.

(b) Advice on interagency plans and activities.

(c) Assistance resolving conflicts in interagency plans and operational issues.

(d) Providing civilian agency perspectives.

(e) Presenting unique interagency approaches, capabilities, and limitations.

(f) Providing linkage and reachback to parent organizations.

(2) Other considerations for interagency coordination include:

(a) Cooperate with each agency, department, or organization to obtain a clear definition of the role each plays. This is particularly important with organizations that provide enabling function for CWMD operations.

(b) Identify potential obstacles arising from conflicting departmental or agency priorities. Obstacles must be resolved early or forwarded up the chain of command for resolution.

(c) Establish responsibility. A common sense of ownership and commitment toward resolution is achievable when all participants understand what needs to be done and agree upon the means to do it. The resources required for a mission must be identified, with specific and agreed upon responsibility assigned to the agencies that will provide them.

(d) Plan for the transition of key responsibilities, capabilities, and functions. In most multiagency operations, civilian organizations will remain engaged long after the military has accomplished its assigned tasks and departed the operational area. Therefore, prior to employing military forces, it is imperative to plan for the transition of responsibility for specific actions or tasks from military to non-military entities. As plans and orders are developed, effective transition planning should be a primary consideration. An example of this is the transitioning from WMD elimination operations to the continued demilitarization of a WMD program and associated weapons and materiel as part of threat reduction cooperation.

(e) Because DOD will often be in a supporting role during CWMD operations, it may not be responsible for determining the mission or specifying the participating agencies. Appropriate organization, C2, and an understanding of the objectives of the organizations involved are all means to build consensus and achieve unity of effort, regardless of role. The reciprocal exchange of information is also a critical enabler.

(3) It is important to note that most interagency participants in CWMD missions have a different lexicon for CWMD matters. With the publication of the NS-CWMD, most interagency participants organize their CWMD tasks from the three pillar perspective: NP, CP, and CM. This is in contrast to the DOD that further describes those tasks using the eight MMAs.

(4) When conducting CWMD activities in concert with participants external to the USG, it is important to understand the differences between US national objectives, end state, and transition criteria and those of IGOs and NGOs. Although appropriate IGOs and NGOs may participate in defining the problem and working collaboratively with the United States, ultimately their goals and objectives are independent of our own.

For further guidance on interagency coordination, refer to JP 3-08, Interorganizational Coordination During Joint Operations.

Intentionally Blank

APPENDIX A
WEAPONS OF MASS DESTRUCTION ELIMINATION OPERATIONS

1. **Operational Construct**

    a. WMD elimination operations are actions to systematically locate, characterize, secure, disable, or destroy WMD programs and related capabilities. The objective of WMD elimination operations is to prevent the looting or capture of WMD and related materials; render harmless or destroy weapons, materials, agents, and delivery systems that pose an immediate or direct threat to the Armed Forces of the United States and civilian population; and exploit, for intelligence purposes, program experts, documents, and other media, as well as previously secured weapons and material to combat further WMD proliferation and prevent regeneration of a WMD capacity. Once these activities have been accomplished, WMD elimination operations may be transferred, if directed, to OGAs, IGOs, or HNs to continue destruction, redirection, and monitoring activities. If transfer is not directed, commanders should be prepared to accomplish the remaining activities, and should request coordination and technical assistance from applicable agencies, as necessary.

    b. WMD elimination operations consist of four principal operational level tasks: isolation; exploitation; destruction; and monitoring and redirection (see Figure A-1). WMD elimination operations may be conducted during any phase of a combatant command's campaign or as an independent operation. That is, the four steps of WMD elimination discussed below may be performed simultaneously at various geographically separate sites. JTF-E activities will require logistics and security to be drawn from resources possibly allocated to ongoing operations Most non-DOD agencies require a secure environment to support WMD elimination missions. Military planners should consider this when considering site security. In addition, requirements for WMD elimination should be considered when planning or conducting operations in all WMD MMAs. The following discussion assumes the formation of a functional JTF-E as described in Chapter III, paragraph 2, "Command Relationships." Figure A-2 illustrates the overall concept of operations.

    (1) Isolation is the overall encirclement of the WMD program.

        (a) The purpose of isolation is to physically secure suspected WMD sites, material, equipment, or personnel. The objective is to ensure suspected sites and materials are secure to prevent possible proliferation, pilfering, or destruction of potential forensic evidence; detain personnel; and prevent dispersion, contamination, or collateral effects of the release of dangerous WMD materials or agents. These actions ensure the safety of US and multinational forces and the surrounding civilian population. Forces must establish and maintain the conditions for elimination operations by securing sensitive sites. To accomplish this step, the Services must train and equip forces with the capacity to identify WMD and associated delivery systems and isolate them for further exploitation.

        (b) Isolation consists of four principal tasks: locate, isolate, seize or secure, and confirm or deny.

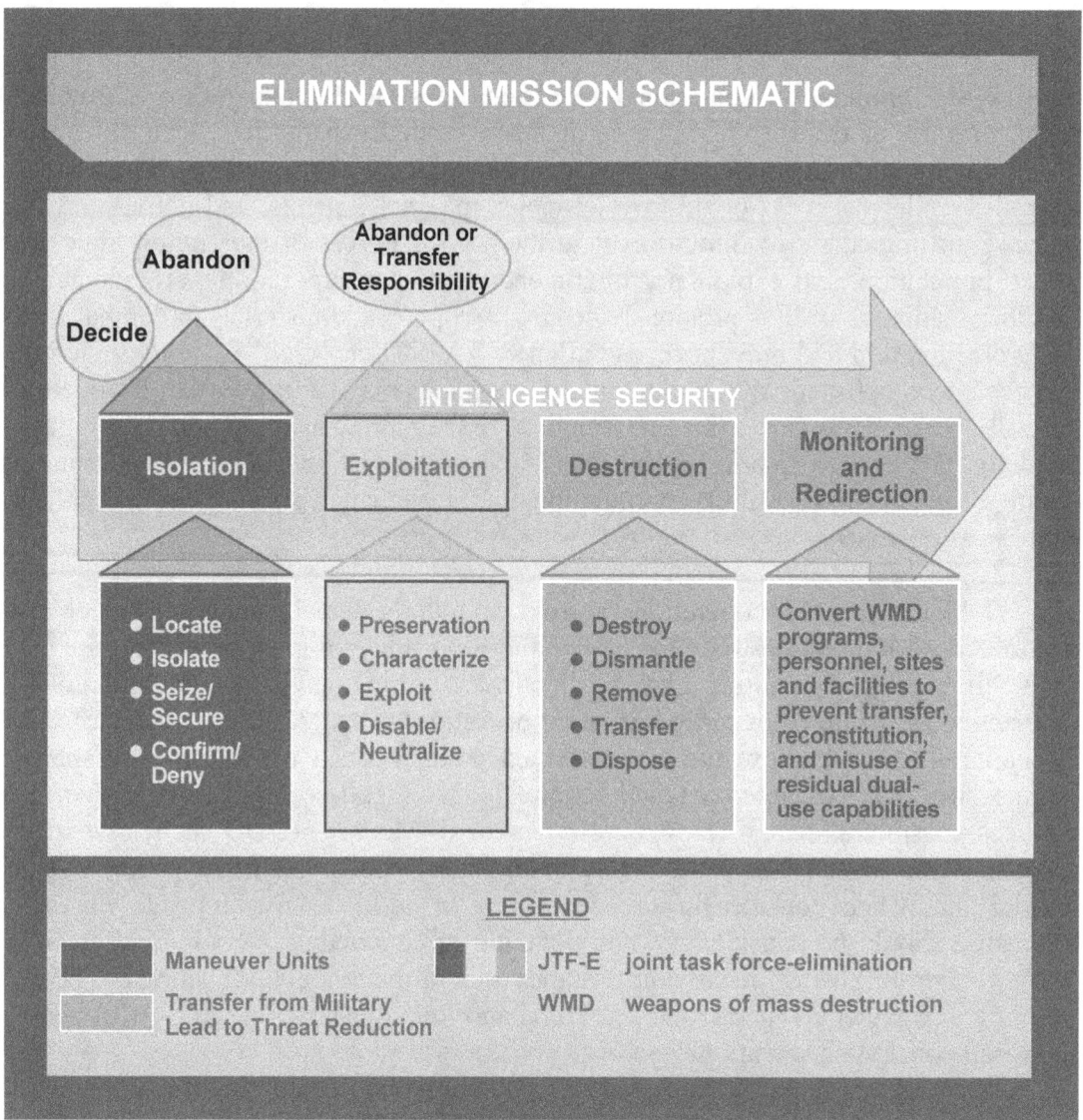

Figure A-1. Elimination Mission Schematic

1. **Locate.** This task includes continuously collecting actionable intelligence about adversary programs from the strategic to the tactical level. The new intelligence collected expands, redirects, and reprioritizes intelligence collection activities. During the prosecution of military operations, maneuver and support units act upon that intelligence to physically locate adversary WMD programs and associated networks or they may inadvertently encounter WMD sites. Planning should provide a target or site list prioritization method for determining sites that should be exploited. An all-source balance of ISR, to include technical intelligence and human intelligence, is essential to this task and to counter an adversary's CCD and hardening of WMD programs and facilities.

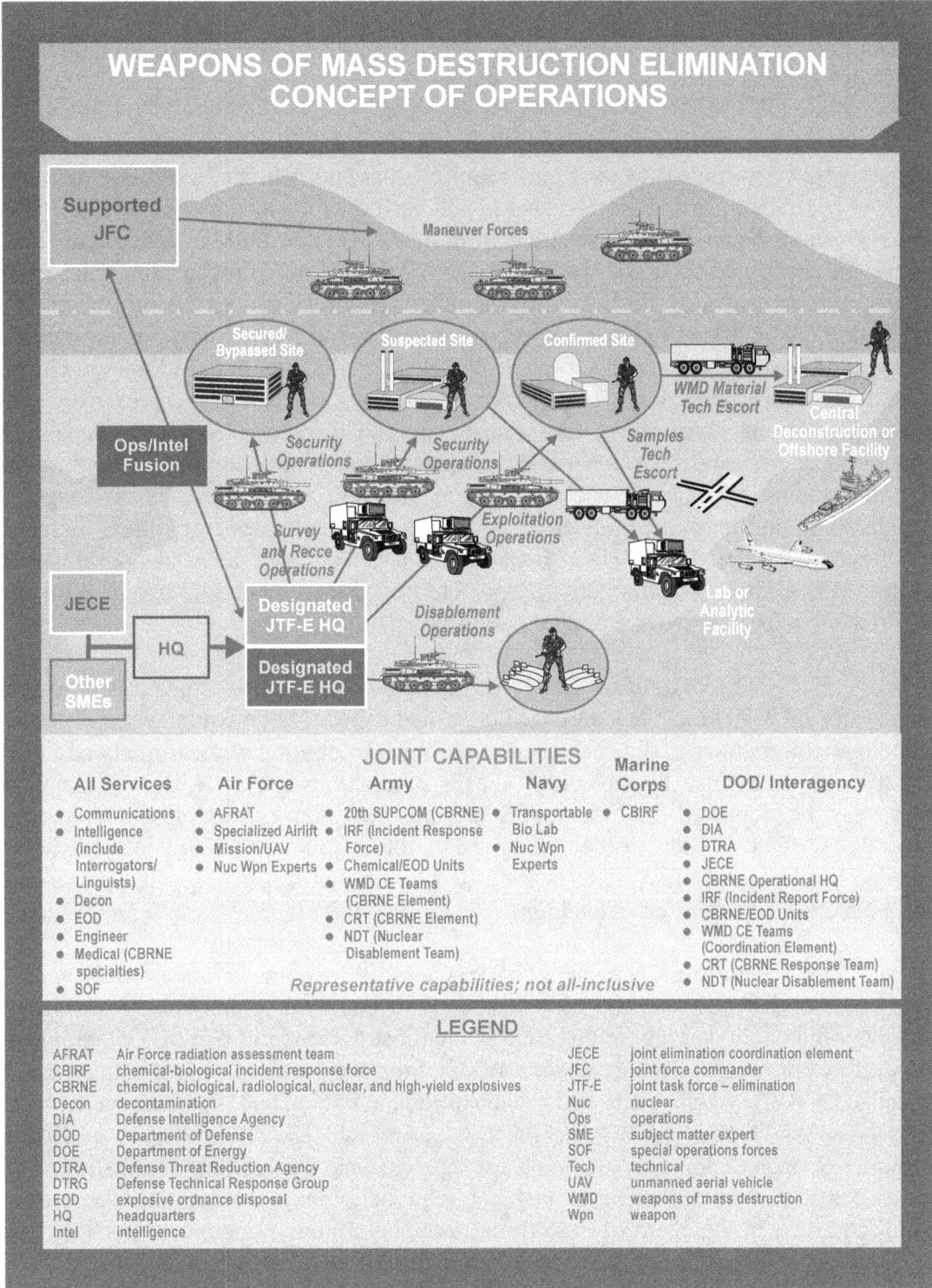

Figure A-2. Weapons of Mass Destruction Elimination Concept of Operations

2. **Isolate.** Once a known or suspected WMD site is located, actions are taken to physically isolate it. This task should be accomplished by forces and deconflicted with OGAs. During isolation, units must consider CBRN passive defense

and WMD CM measures due to the potential for material release. Consideration should be given to the need for additional security forces required in the event that unanticipated WMD sites are encountered by maneuver units.

3. **Seize or Secure.** WMD sites are likely to be protected by active and passive security measures, and may require lethal and nonlethal offensive actions to reduce or neutralize them. Planning should address how to detect, assess, and defeat site defenses; establish and maintain secure control of WMD sites until the absence of CBRN material is confirmed, or until the hazard is eliminated or removed; and transfer the mission and responsibility for security to another agency as part of the threat reduction cooperation CWMD MMA. This may require coordination for additional assets based on the extent of site defenses and size/type of WMD sites. Planning must address the impact of security requirements for a large number of sites (which may progressively drain organic assets) and transition of the security mission to other forces or organizations. Planning must also consider the need for robust/high bandwidth communications at each site. The responsibility for a site's long-term security, where there is no longer an immediate threat, may be transferred to the lead agency for the threat reduction cooperation CWMD MMA, when directed. JTF-E will plan for and coordinate the transfer of security to authorities responsible for threat reduction cooperation if a cooperative and permissive operational environment exists.

4. **Confirm or Deny.** Once a suspected site is isolated and secured, the presence of WMD must be confirmed or denied using organic equipment and specific predeployment training. If the presence of WMD cannot be confirmed, additional specialized low-density, high-demand WMD elimination survey and reconnaissance assets may be deployed. These assets are the next tier of response and augment conventional forces, when needed, must have the required training, equipment, and expertise needed to conduct initial survey of sites to confirm or deny the presence of WMD material, expertise, or technology.

(2) **Exploitation.** The intent of this task is to gain an understanding of an adversary's WMD programs and capabilities to attribute and connect to the adversary's network, which may determine future targets; collect evidence of a WMD program; and provide force protection from immediate WMD threats, if required. Exploitation requires specialized CBRN, intelligence, and technical augmentation forces within the Services, CSAs (such as DTRA), and OGAs (such as DOE and DOS) capable of conducting sensitive site exploitation operations. These agencies may require the establishment of a locally permissive environment to conduct their activities. Throughout the process, careful attention to the chain of custody is necessary. Four principal actions comprise exploitation: preserve, characterize, exploit, and disable or neutralize.

(a) **Preserve.** If the weapon's contents are unconfirmed or uncertain, further examination by specialized forces may be required. For suspected or known WMD sites, in addition to tactical security, a primary challenge is safeguarding suspected materials until specialized forces can characterize the material and exploit the site. Long-term security requirements for WMD elimination operations are potentially overwhelming. Additional security forces should be planned for, and assigned to, the elimination mission. The actual number required depends on the number and size of sites the unit is expected to locate and exploit. In the case of WMD materials located aboard vessels, identification of suitable airfields, ports, and capable facilities may be required to accomplish follow-on characterization and exploitation operations.

(b) **Characterize.** Once a site is isolated, dedicated exploitation assets or specialized technical forces exploit the site in accordance with the JFC commander's critical information requirement (i.e., initial characterization may occur during isolation). These assets have the necessary expertise and specialized equipment to characterize WMD weapons, materials, agents, equipment, infrastructure, and delivery means; provide a presumptive analysis; and package and transport WMD material for shipment to a pre-identified facility for confirmation. "Characterization" includes detailed assessments that may take hours to days to complete. USG or internationally designated laboratories with accepted confirmatory capabilities, as well as assets with other required capabilities, are not generally organic to a theater.

(c) **Exploit.** Exploitation assets conduct initial intelligence exploitation of program experts, documents, and other media as well as secure weapons, material, agents, delivery means, and related processes and facilities (e.g., R&D, production, test, and evaluation) found in and around the site. These assets also conduct necessary evidence packaging and handling. Detailed reports and imagery are sent to the appropriate headquarters/agencies for further analysis. This analysis can lead to a re-prioritization of WMD sites or identify additional sites or experts for investigation. Exploitation activities are essential for arresting further WMD proliferation and preventing WMD program regeneration. They also include taking full advantage of any information obtained for tactical, operational, or strategic purposes. Clear policy guidance with regard to incentives, amnesty, debriefing, and interrogation is essential to effectively manage these actions. Exploitation will require the fusion of multiple DOD and OGA organizations, as well as the integration of additional skill sets such as technical WMD and specialized intelligence analysts.

(d) **Disable/Neutralize.** Exploitation assets will render harmless or destroy weapons, materials, agents, and delivery systems that pose an immediate threat to the Armed Forces of the United States and civilian populations. The intent of "disable/neutralize" is to provide force protection from WMD rather than to conduct the destruction of the WMD program.

(3) **Destruction.** Once a site has been exploited and it has been determined that it is not a component of a dual-use industry that will be designated for redirection, destruction may begin. The purpose of this task is to destroy, dismantle, remove, transfer, or otherwise verifiably dispose of an adversary's WMD material, weapons equipment, and infrastructure. While the ideal case is to conduct destruction operations in a permissive environment, the military must plan for and, if necessary, conduct this step in a hostile or uncertain environment until conditions permit the transfer to another agency. Since these operations are subject to monitoring by various government agencies

or IGOs, planners should anticipate specific national level guidance. While destruction may be conducted at any time during the exploitation task to ensure safety, it is always coordinated and authorized at the appropriate level in accordance with approved supplemental WMD elimination-specific ROE or RUF.

(a) Planners must closely coordinate with higher HQ to plan destruction activities with OGAs and international agencies, or plan handover of these activities to nonmilitary entities. As soon as practical during an operation, the JTF-E, if established, should initiate planning activities to support transfer of associated long-term destruction activities to threat reduction cooperation activities. This is essential to ensure that the limited organizations with technical capabilities to conduct WMD exploitation and destruction are available to support combat operations.

(b) In the case where the military continues with destruction activities, the JTF-E will assess and make recommendations for what needs to be done and what resources are required. The JTF-E will adapt destruction procedures to cope with a program's scope, size, and expected duration. The personnel, equipment, and facilities required for destruction depend on the quantity and type of WMD material at the sites; the number of sites; the extent of the program's infrastructure; logistics; and the urgency in which to complete the operation. WMD destruction may be accomplished by military personnel, specialized technical experts, civilian organizations, or commercial companies from the United States or multinational partners.

(c) Depending on the situation, destruction may occur at the site or at a central processing site. DOD safeguards and maintains proper chain of custody from time of possession through destruction for all WMD and materials. All documentation will be maintained in accordance with existing treaties and conventions. For example, all chemical weapons and material must have chain of custody and destruction documentation in accordance with the Chemical Weapons Convention (CWC).

For detailed guidance, refer to CJCSI 2030.01B, Chemical Weapons Convention Compliance Policy Guidance, and CJCSI 3110.07C, Guidance Concerning Chemical, Biological, Radiological, and Nuclear Defense and Employment of Riot Control Agents and Herbicides.

(4) **Monitoring and Redirection.** As with the destruction task, this task is highly dependent on the interagency and IGOs. Planning cells should be formed early in the process to ensure the necessary coordination occurs.

(a) Monitoring requires continuous observation and examination of former WMD programs and sites to ensure eliminated programs are not reconstituted.

(b) Redirection involves the conversion of material, equipment, and personnel to peaceful purposes. This mission is normally performed by personnel from DOE, DOS, Central Intelligence Agency, and other interagency or international partners until such time as the complete CWMD program transition from WMD elimination to threat reduction cooperation is achieved, as allowed by the conditions of the operational environment. To successfully redirect an adversary's WMD program, an initial survey must be conducted. First, an overall assessment of the remaining dual-use facilities, technologies, and technical expertise is conducted to determine the expected level and type of legitimate output. Second, an assessment of the adversary's peaceful CBRN requirements is performed. These requirements may include, but are not limited to, vaccination and pharmaceutical programs, nuclear power, medical radiological requirements, and industrial chemical requirements. Once the level and type of capacity is established, all aspects of the program are monitored to ensure continued compliance.

(c) The final task associated with monitoring and redirection is the transition to threat reduction cooperation or similar mission. Threat reduction cooperation activities include long-term destruction, redirection, and monitoring, and are ideally conducted in a permissive environment, even if that environment is only local. However, these activities may commence in an uncertain environment. For example, as a result of hostilities, the appropriate authorities may no longer be effective or even exist.

(d) A JTF-E planning cell(s) should be formed as soon as the exploitation task/action identifies the locations and extent of a dual-use industry or expertise for redirection and monitoring. The planning cell(s) must develop a transition plan to threat reduction cooperation to support phase IV (Stabilize) and phase V (Enable Civil Authority) operations. At a minimum, planning considerations should include:

1. Determination of legal and policy authorities.

2. Identification of all agencies and organizations that should be involved.

3. Coordination of the changeover for providing security.

4. Coordination of leave behinds (e.g., specialized assets, chemical-biological defense equipment, nonlethal weapons, power generators, provisions).

5. Coordination of logistic support transition.

6. Coordination with HN for transition of the mission to threat reduction cooperation.

2. Operational Planning

a. Adversaries include state and non-state actors and the networks that support them. Planners must consider how to conduct elimination operations against both. Commanders should be prepared to conduct WMD elimination activities from the initiation of an operation until it is determined that a transfer of authority to another agency is warranted. The objective of elimination operations is to reduce or eliminate the threat to the United States and to support military and national objectives. Planners must determine how to conduct elimination operations that ensure the safety of the Armed Forces of the United States and multinational partners through the following:

(1) Security operations to prevent looting, use, or capture of WMD and related materials.

(2) CBRN passive defense or WMD CM operations in the event WMD is employed by an adversary (e.g., improvised WMD device, booby trapped WMD site).

(3) Rendering chemical, biological, and radiological WMD harmless or destroying weapons, materials, agents, and delivery systems that pose an immediate threat to the Armed Forces of the United States and civilian populations.

(4) Render safe operations of nuclear weapons are not covered in this document. These operations are specifically addressed in other plans or integrated into regional WMD elimination operations.

(5) Intelligence exploitation of program experts, documents, and other media, as well as, previously secured weapons and material. Specialized low-density/high-demand assets and linguists may be required to support the WMD elimination mission.

(6) In any phase of elimination operations, there is a potential to discover previously undetected threats. Credible information on imminent threats must be reported in accordance with JOPES and supported CCDR reporting procedures.

b. Once elimination operations have been planned, planners should turn their attention to the transition phase of WMD elimination. During this phase, operations may be transferred to the lead agency for threat reduction cooperation or some other entity, as directed by the SecDef, to continue destruction of WMD programs and to redirect and monitor dual-use industry and expertise capable of regenerating WMD capability.

c. Adversary WMD programs include, but are not limited to:

(1) Weapon systems and associated stockpiles.

(2) Raw sources/agents or precursor stockpiles.

(3) Delivery Systems. Adversary WMD delivery systems can include artillery or rocket systems (e.g., mortars, howitzers, and multiple rocket launchers); motor vessels; missiles and missile systems; aircraft; UASs; and other unconventional delivery means.

(4) Dual-use Facilities and Associated Expertise. Infrastructure, materials, and expertise that have legitimate civilian research and industry utility, but could be converted or employed to support WMD programs, are of particular concern in WMD elimination operations.

(a) Dual-use facilities include, but are not limited to: commercial nuclear power facilities; nuclear research reactors; civilian or academic R&D facilities, laboratories, or production facilities; facilities with capacities exceeding amounts deemed necessary for civilian or peaceful purposes; pharmaceutical research and production facilities; medical vaccination production/formulation programs; radioisotope thermoelectric generators; and food irradiation facilities.

(b) Dual-use expertise includes personnel and documents associated with WMD research, production, testing, storage, proliferation networks, or operations.

d. WMD elimination operations may be required for WMD programs characterized as small-scale, narrow scope through large-scale, broad scope. WMD elimination operations could be required for some or all of the four types of WMD (chemical, biological, radiological, and nuclear) and their delivery systems during the same operation. Based on threat estimates, CCDRs should ensure capabilities to conduct operations against each of these scenarios.

e. To increase the effectiveness of WMD elimination operations, CCDRs should integrate them into campaign plans from phase 0 (Shape) through phase V (Enable Civil Authority). The process for transferring this mission to OGAs or IGOs, at the appropriate time, must also be considered. If forces are permanently assigned, this planning should incorporate force training and exercising.

f. Since contamination may exist at any WMD site, WMD elimination operations require the ability to operate in a CBRN environment. WMD elimination operations may require WMD CM or CBRN passive defense activities.

3. **Command and Control of Weapons of Mass Destruction Elimination Operations**

a. Small-scale WMD elimination operations may be handled within a CCDR's pre-existing command structure by relying on limited technical augmentation capabilities. For medium to large scale WMD elimination operations, a JTF-E or combined joint task force-WMD elimination may be required. Medium to large-scale WMD elimination operations require specialized technical capabilities. The following describes organizational constructs to achieve this larger capability.

b. **Joint Task Force-WMD Elimination.** A JTF-E may be established, by an establishing authority, for the WMD elimination mission and be dissolved when the mission is complete or transitioned to an OGA or another organization assigned as lead for threat reduction cooperation or similar MMA. The JTF-E's activities must be coordinated and integrated by the supported combatant command. The JTF-E should possess capabilities to:

(1) Coordinate, through the supported CCDR, to ensure an interagency approach to isolate the adversary's WMD program. This includes capabilities used to isolate personnel, equipment, material, agents, weapons, and delivery systems that may

not be controlled at the tactical level. These include capabilities to monitor and coordinate denial measures to close down cross border proliferation and ex-filtration of WMD, related material, means of delivery, and program personnel.

(2) In coordination with, and with assistance from, maneuver forces, locate, seize and secure WMD, WMD sites, means of delivery, related-material, and expertise across a broad scope of programs.

(3) Coordinate exploitation of WMD sites and individuals associated with WMD programs.

(4) Conduct rapid destruction/render harmless nonnuclear WMD or WMD agents (e.g., mixed chemical and biological agents) in various dispositions (bulk, rounds, submunitions) for force protection purposes.

(5) Integrate the exploitation of WMD infrastructure (e.g., plutonium re-processing and high-enrichment uranium facilities); WMD R&D (e.g., nuclear research reactors); and WMD weapons, components, and materials.

(6) Redirect expertise. When directed, transfer former adversary's personnel with WMD-related expertise or their personnel files to the lead USG agency for threat reduction cooperation.

(7) When directed, initiate redirection of WMD programs and catalogue dual-use facilities in preparation for transfer to the lead OGA for threat reduction cooperation or similar mission.

(8) Locate, seize, and control illicit or excess radiological materials.

(9) Exploit and, if necessary, destroy WMD-capable missile systems and other delivery systems.

(10) Report potential imminent threats discovered in accordance with JOPES and supported CCDR procedures.

(11) Recommend reprioritization of WMD program components based on exploited sites.

(12) Remain in compliance with related treaties; and establish and maintain chain of custody of seized materials, records, and personnel for further exploitation or transfer to legal authorities.

(13) Coordinate and deconflict existing nuclear render safe capabilities with JTF-E operations.

For detailed guidance on JTFs, refer to JP 3-33, Joint Task Force Headquarters.

c. **JTF-E Headquarters** (see Figure A-3). When formed, a JTF-E HQ would be drawn from three sources:

(1) Portions of an existing standing joint force or subordinate component as directed by the supported CCDR; and

(2) The Joint Elimination Coordination Element (JECE); and

(3) Other capabilities from the Services and specialized joint activities including CSAs.

(4) Elements of the JTF-E HQ will be a combination of DOD functional and technical experts; be augmented by non-DOD personnel, as appropriate; and have real time reachback capability to national level technical experts. At a minimum, and as required by the supported CCDR to conduct specific WMD elimination operations, the JTF-E HQ should possess the capabilities to:

(a) Load for movement to a port of embarkation.

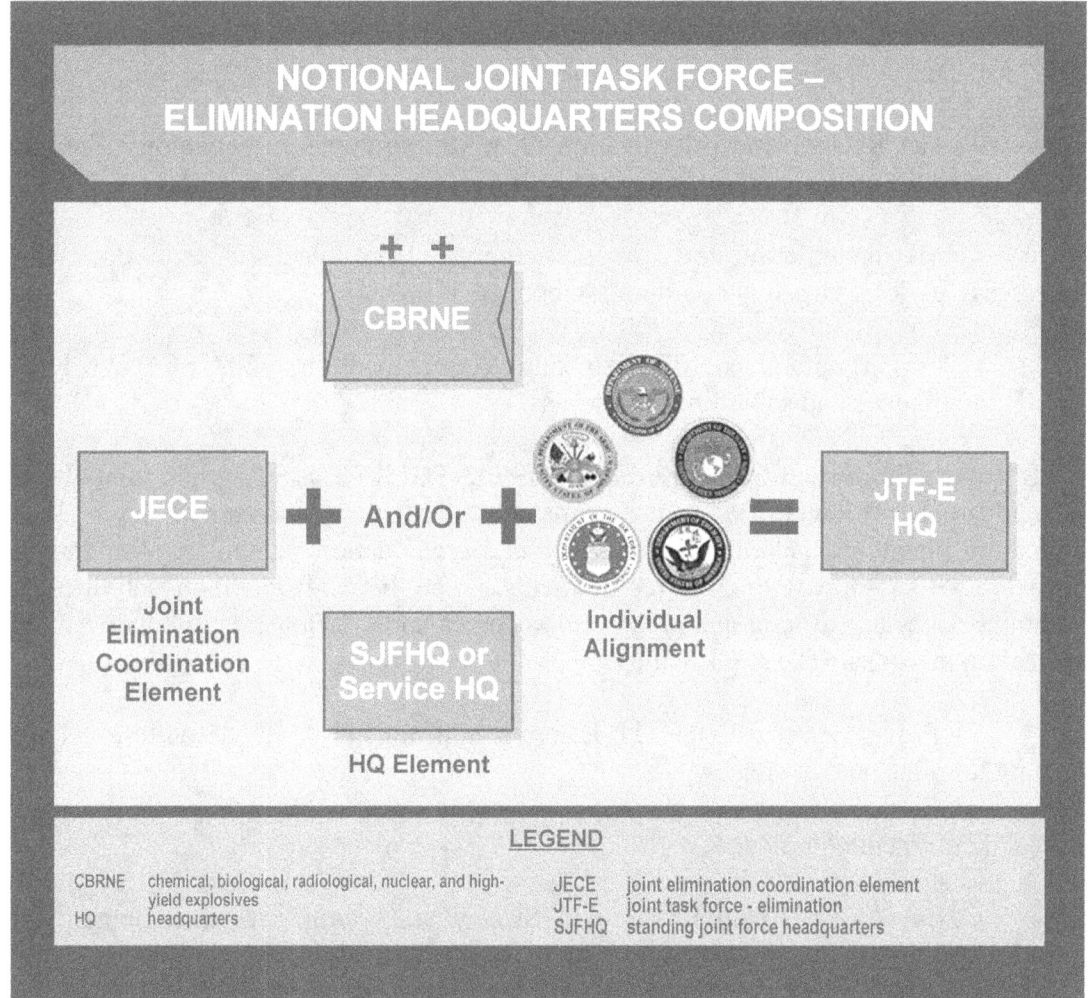

Figure A-3. Notional Joint Task Force-Elimination Headquarters Composition

(b) Deploy into an operational area to C2 WMD elimination operations.

(c) Coordinate operations with friendly forces, OGAs, foreign governments, IGOs, and HNs.

(d) Provide overall assessment, analysis, and planning for elimination operations.

(e) Coordinate planning activities with other commands.

(f) Plan for JTF-E deployment, employment, and redeployment.

(g) Plan for transfer of responsibility of elimination operations to or from CCDR from or to other agencies.

(h) Plan for mitigation of potential WMD elimination collateral effects.

(i) Conduct WMD elimination operations training and rehearsals.

(j) Maintain situational awareness of all elimination activities within the AOR.

(k) Recommend prioritization of WMD equipment, technology, facilities, and personnel for elimination activities.

(l) Integrate into the supported combatant command's C2 and coordination processes (e.g., joint targeting coordination board).

(m) Maintain coordination and communication with SCC-WMD for CWMD intelligence and situational awareness.

d. **Joint Elimination Coordination Element.** The JECE is a standing joint element assigned to USSTRATCOM and designated to conduct operational level WMD elimination planning (including contingency and crisis action planning), joint training, and exercises in support of JFC requirements. The JECE focuses on activities and operations necessary to train and prepare joint forces and C2 elements to conduct WMD elimination missions. The JECE will:

(1) Provide support to the JTF-E commander for JTF-E HQ activities, including planning, training, and exercises.

(2) When requested,

(a) Assist CCDRs, through SCC-WMD, with the development and execution of joint training exercises involving WMD elimination.

(b) Assist CCDR's subordinate commands in the development of their operational and tactical level planning for WMD elimination missions (contingency and crisis action planning).

(3) Coordinate with SCC-WMD for planning support to CCDRs and assist with development of joint and Service WMD elimination operations doctrine and tactics, techniques, and procedures.

(4) Plan, participate in, and conduct joint elimination training and exercises in support of CCDR requirements and ensure the readiness of JECE personnel.

(5) Maintain world-wide situational awareness of WMD elimination operations to focus activities in support of CCDR requirements.

(6) Assist USSTRATCOM in prioritizing DOD WMD elimination planning and support activities.

(7) In a contingency and upon request, deploy to either augment an established JFC's HQ as a specialized WMD elimination element, or provide the core joint element to enable a Service or existing JTF HQ to function as a JTF-E HQ. The JECE is normally transferred to the JTF-E commander when a JTF-E is established or to a supported JFC if a JTF-E is not established. The gaining commander is assumed the operational control of the JECE. The supported JFC will define specific C2 relationships.

e. Figure A-4 provides a notional JTF-E construct and task organization. This is a notional organization to assist planners in JTF-E development. The supported GCC will task organize a JTF-E to meet mission specific requirements.

4. **Weapons of Mass Destruction Elimination Organizations and Functions**

The following roles and responsibilities are specific to the WMD elimination mission and are in addition to those listed in Chapter III, "Organizational and Command Relationships."

a. **Geographic Combatant Commanders**

(1) Plan and, as required, execute WMD elimination operations.

(2) In coordination with the intelligence community, assess the importance of a current or pending movement/transfer of WMD-related materials, technology, precursors, funding, information, or personnel.

(3) In coordination with the intelligence community, develop a WMD elimination target list.

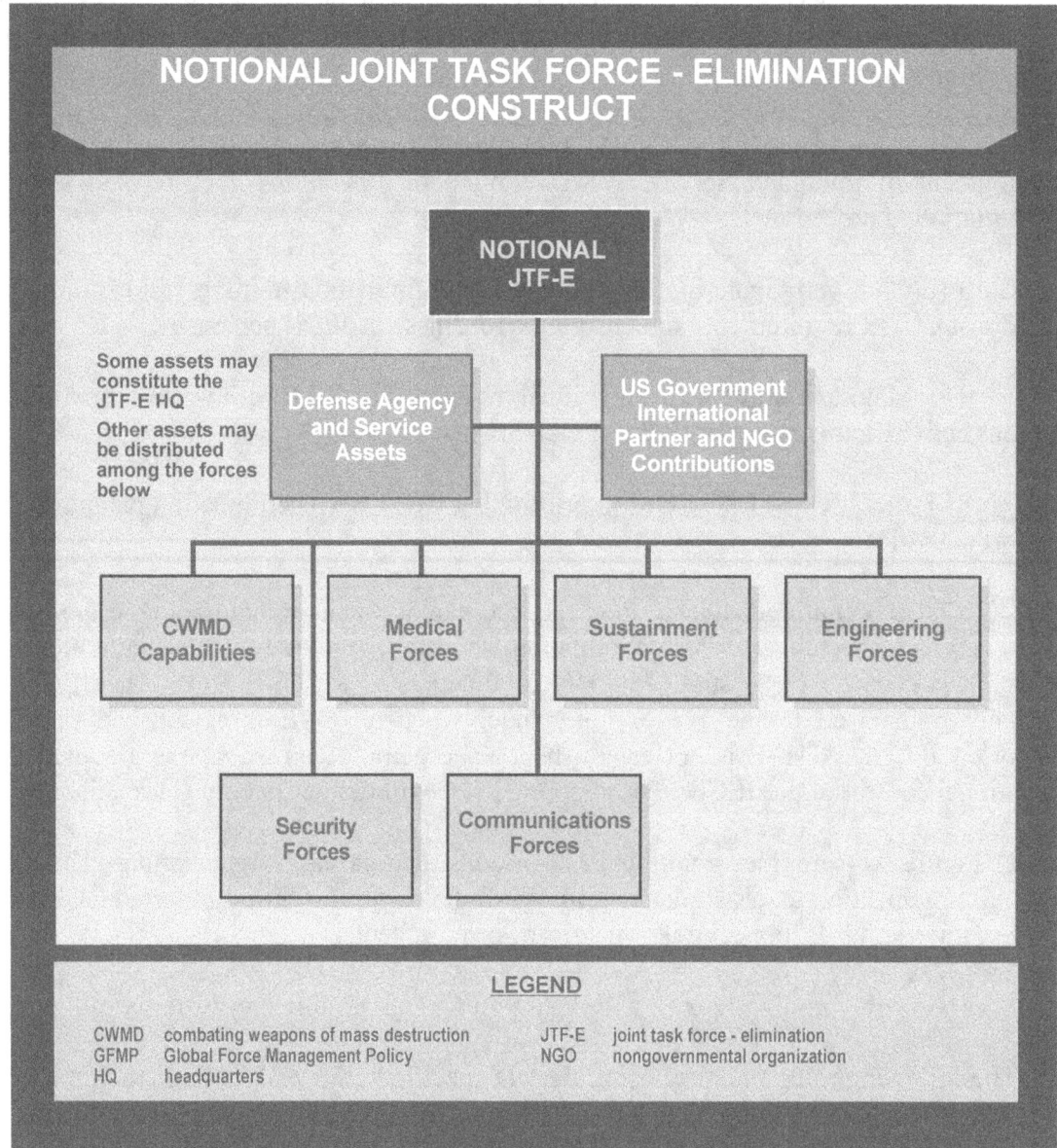

Figure A-4. Notional Joint Task Force- Elimination Construct

(4) Assess WMD elimination implications of the theater proliferation situation.

(5) Establish WMD material temporary safe storage for WMD elimination missions.

(6) Provide security and logistic support to WMD elimination elements.

(7) Provide for intratheater movement of WMD elimination personnel and specialized WMD equipment.

(a) Where applicable, develop threat reduction cooperation plans to allow for transfer and termination of WMD elimination missions.

(b) Coordinate with the Office of the Under Secretary of Defense for Policy and JS to ensure WMD elimination operations are in compliance with US international treaty and agreement obligations.

(8) In coordination with the intelligence community and exploitation efforts, exploit data, personnel, information, and materials obtained during WMD elimination operations, and report any potential or likely threats to the United States, the Armed Forces of the United States, multinational partners, or interests in accordance with JOPES and supported CCDR reporting procedures.

(9) Provide after action reviews and lessons learned to facilitate future WMD elimination mission planning.

b. **Commander, United States Joint Forces Command**

(1) As the joint force provider and trainer, provides forces and training when directed, using established policies and procedures.

(2) As the designated establishing authority for the JTF-E, comply with guidance in JP 3-33, *Joint Task Force Headquarters*, applicable to a functional CCDR.

(3) Supports the development of joint concepts and joint doctrine for WMD elimination.

(4) When directed, assesses and recommends modifications to joint force HQ and structures as they relate to WMD elimination missions.

(5) When directed, collects, compiles, and catalogs lessons learned for WMD elimination missions.

(6) As DOD lead for joint force integration, coordinates WMD elimination integration efforts with USSTRATCOM.

c. **Commander, United States Special Operations Command**

(1) Provides technical means to disable WMD, as required.

(2) Provides special reconnaissance teams to monitor WMD sites, border crossings, and likely exfiltration locations as part of the isolation step.

(3) Provides teams to conduct direct action operations in limited access areas, as required.

(4) Provides expertise, material, and teams to locate, tag, and track WMD, as required.

d. **Commander, United States Strategic Command**

(1) Assesses WMD elimination implications of the global proliferation situation.

(2) Provides recommendations for global force management of WMD elimination related assets.

(3) Provides ISR planning, integration, and coordination support to a CCDR's WMD elimination plans and operations.

(4) Exercises combatant command (command authority) over the JECE.

(a) Maintains the JECE, as a deployable capability, to support a request for forces.

(b) The JECE will operate in direct support of the 20th Support Command for JTF-E planning, operations, training, and exercises. During day to day operations, SCC-WMD assigns JECE tasks and designates its objectives; directs JECE administration, organization, and training; and provides other directions necessary to accomplish its mission (see Deputy Secretary of Defense Memorandum, dated 3 December 2007).

SECTION A. OVERVIEW

INTERDICTION

"Effective interdiction is a critical part of the US strategy to combat weapons of mass destruction (WMD) and their delivery means. We must enhance the capabilities of our military, intelligence, technical, and law enforcement communities to prevent the movement of WMD materials, technology, and expertise to hostile states and terrorist organizations."

National Strategy to Combat Weapons of Mass Destruction

1. General

a. **Purpose.** This appendix provides a reference for staff officers assigned to a geographic or functional combatant command, JTF, or other major staff and operational elements responsible for planning and executing WMD interdiction operations. It addresses:

(1) Interagency roles and responsibilities for WMD interdiction;

(2) CCDR roles, responsibilities, and employment of WMD interdiction capabilities as part of a theater campaign to combat WMD in support of national strategic goals; and

(3) Linkages between WMD interdiction, WMD security cooperation and partner activities, WMD elimination, and threat reduction cooperation MMAs necessary to prevent, dissuade, and deny adversary attempts to proliferate WMD.

WEAPONS OF MASS DESTRUCTION (WMD) INTERDICTION

WMD interdiction encompasses operations directed towards weaponized chemical, biological, radiological, and nuclear devices/warheads and delivery vehicles; dual-use items required to produce devices/warheads, their precursors, or related items; related technology; financial and transportation intermediaries which facilitate trade in WMD; and individuals associated with all the above.

VARIOUS SOURCES

b. **Background.** WMD interdiction operations are those operations conducted in support of national efforts to prevent, dissuade, and deny adversary attempts to proliferate or acquire WMD. It is important to note that since the majority of WMD interdiction operations involve dual-use items, precursors, and associated technology and personnel, and not finished weapons, most other USG agencies refer to the mission as CP interdiction. DOD's use of the term WMD interdiction is intended to capture the same mission.

(1) The overall national objective is to deny rogue states and violent extremist organizations (VEOs) access to WMD by disrupting procurement networks that seek access to finished WMD, dual-use materials and technology required to produce WMD, and expertise necessary to develop and employ WMD. Ultimately, reducing the proliferation of WMD is likely to depend on neutralizing WMD network functions (e.g., financial, production, logistic, C2, scientific) that support WMD proliferation. The United States pursues this objective through a national-level campaign targeted at state and non-state actors of proliferation concern orchestrated through the National Security Council (NSC). This campaign links the NP activities of active diplomacy, threat reduction cooperation, controls on nuclear materials, US export controls, and NP sanctions, with the CP activity of interdiction. These activities are dependent upon, and mutually supported by, targeted SC and focused intelligence gathering and analysis. WMD interdiction operations support the following national-level tasks derived from national guidance:

(a) Establish or reinforce global norms against unsanctioned possession or proliferation of WMD, especially to VEOs, through diplomatic means;

(b) Globally monitor through an intelligence effort, to detect attempts to proliferate WMD;

(c) Dissuade WMD suppliers from participating in proliferation activity through coordinated diplomatic, economic, and information campaigns;

(d) Enable allies and partner nations to develop and enforce appropriate export control regimes within their own sovereign territory through security assistance for law enforcement and military activities; and

(e) Enforce the norms against unsanctioned proliferation through military WMD interdiction operations in the global commons as necessary.

(2) The DOD plays a critical role in executing these tasks. Of most relevance to WMD interdiction are the following DOD activities, derived from national guidance:

(a) Build the capacity and will of allies and partner nations to enforce export controls within their sovereign territory;

(b) Establish and maintain global situational awareness of WMD proliferation activities and attempts;

(c) Support SC themes and messages;

(d) Support intelligence collection and exploitation, as well as law enforcement activities of OGAs;

(e) Integrate WMD interdiction into command's regional plans;

(f) Support coordinated interagency actions to delay and disrupt identified proliferation shipments; and

(g) Establish supremacy over selected areas of geography, as required, enabling physical interdiction of WMD by forces appropriate in each circumstance.

(3) Geographic and functional combatant commands conduct WMD interdiction shaping activities as part of their regional CWMD efforts and broader trans-regional efforts. Security cooperation, military-to-military engagement, and intelligence/information sharing with allies and partner nations are the primary tools CCDRs employ to shape the regional environment. In response to appropriate cueing from intelligence, and upon receiving direction from the President or SecDef, or within existing authorities, commanders prepare the operational environment and interdict specific WMD-related shipments.

(4) Commanders cannot plan or conduct WMD interdiction activities irrespective of interagency and international considerations. In most cases, DOD will not have the lead for WMD interdiction actions. However, DOD must remain prepared to serve as the lead federal agency (LFA) or lead coordinating agency in WMD interdiction scenarios. To this end, geographic combatant commands must not only support overall USG WMD interdiction efforts but also prepare to conduct follow-on actions which may involve more aggressive postures. These postures include preparing for follow-on missions such as, but not limited to, WMD elimination or offensive operations to destroy WMD or WMD-related material in development, storage, or transit.

> *"Interdiction operations are designed to stop the proliferation of WMD, delivery systems, associated and dual-use technologies, materials, and expertise from transiting between states of concern and between state and non-state actors, whether undertaken by the military or by other agencies of government (e.g., law enforcement)."*
>
> **National Military Strategy to Combat Weapons of Mass Destruction**

2. Guidance

This appendix derives its foundation from, and is supplemental to, existing WMD interdiction policy and guidance.

a. **International Treaties and Agreements and United Nations Security Council Resolutions.** Various international treaties, agreements, and United Nations Security Council resolutions obligate member states to prevent WMD proliferation. US support for United Nations Security Council resolutions provides a basis for action under existing legislative and executive authorities. In some cases, additional legislation and executive orders are necessary. Where combatant commands believe they require additional legal authority to conduct WMD interdiction activities, they should seek guidance from OSD and JS. United Nations Security Council resolutions form the international legal basis for conducting WMD interdiction operations against the unsanctioned WMD transfer, possession, or use. The following lists of treaties and agreements are not all inclusive.

(1) **International Treaties.** Signatories of *The Treaty on Nonproliferation of Nuclear Weapons* prohibit the proliferation, development, and transfer of nuclear weapons, related materials, and technology to any recipient. The CWC prohibits possession, development, or transfer of chemical weapons and limits transfer of dual-use technology used to make chemical weapons to states that are not signatories to the CWC. The Convention on the Prohibition of the Development, Production, and Stockpiling of Bacteriological (Biological) and Toxin Weapons and on their Destruction (The Biological Weapons and Toxins Convention) prohibits development or possession of biological weapons. The Missile Technology Control Regime limits the transfer of long-range (i.e., greater than 300 kilometers in range or 500 kilograms in payload) missiles and associated technology to any state.

(2) **United Nations Security Council Resolutions.** United Nations Security Council resolutions *1540 and 1673* require member states to "detect, deter, prevent, and combat, including through international cooperation when necessary, the illicit trafficking and brokering" of WMD and delivery systems to non-state actors. United Nations Security Council resolutions *1695 and 1718* require member states to prevent proliferation of WMD and missile technology to and from North Korea. Similarly, United Nations Security Council resolutions *1696, 1737, and 1747* require member states to prevent proliferation of nuclear and missile technology to and from Iran. It is important to understand that United Nations Security Council resolutions do not automatically become US law. The United States will put in place either legislation, executive orders, or regulations which support United Nations Security Council resolution goals, or use existing authorities which can support United Nations Security Council resolution enforcement in their current form to create a basis for US WMD interdiction actions.

b. **US Domestic Law and Orders.** The Arms Export Control Act and the Export Administration Act establish the framework for US export controls. Various executive orders under the International Emergency Economic Powers Act implement sanctions on specific entities for WMD-related activities.

c. **Strategic Guidance.** There are various USG interagency coordination groups that focus national efforts on countering WMD threats and proliferation. National security Presidential directives (NSPDs) and legislation codify these bodies and create new agencies such as the National Counterproliferation Center and the Domestic Nuclear Detection Office (DNDO). The *National Military Strategy of the United States* and the

National Military Strategy to Combat Weapons of Mass Destruction provide additional strategic guidance.

3. Legal Considerations for Weapons of Mass Destruction Interdiction

The JFC must consider the legal issues inherent in WMD interdiction operations to attain US national objectives. WMD interdiction operations must comply with US law, treaties, and bilateral agreements. Planners should involve their respective general counsel or SJA representative early in the campaign design or mission analysis phase and throughout execution to identify key issues and work to resolve them (see JP 1-04, *Legal Support to Military Operations*). Additionally, international allies and partner nations may have differing interpretations of rights and obligations under international law than the United States. This will require sensitivity, cooperation, and negotiation when operating in a multinational environment.

a. Treaties, US laws, US regulations, and bilateral agreements identify certain rights and obligations of states, ships, and aircraft related to search and seizure in territorial and international seas and airspace. These issues include state of belligerency, territorial rights, legal status of the target vessel, aircraft, or vehicle, use of military forces, seizure of material and detention of persons, preservation of evidence, and ROE/RUF during interdiction. WMD interdiction in cyberspace poses additional legal concerns.

b. **State of Belligerency.** International law recognizes a difference in the rights of states during conflict (state of belligerency). Belligerent states may seize and condemn enemy vessels or vehicles, stop and search neutral vessels or vehicles for contraband, and blockade enemy port(s) and airspace on both the high seas and within the enemy's territorial seas. This right does not extend to the territorial seas of neutral states or to international straits.

c. Less clear are circumstances where no declared state of belligerency exists. This is the circumstance under which most WMD interdiction activities will occur. There is no definitive customary international law in this case. Article 51 of the United Nations Charter (right to self-defense) may provide some basis for action in this circumstance. United Nations Security Council resolutions may also provide basis for action under certain circumstances.

d. **Territorial Rights.** The authority to stop and inspect a ship, aircraft, or ground vehicle resides with the nation in whose territory the vessel, aircraft, or vehicle is transiting. Key, but not all-encompassing, international agreements are the United Nations Convention on the Law of the Sea (UNCLOS) and Chicago Convention on International Civil Aviation. Although the US may not be a party to the UNCLOS or to all provisions of the Chicago Convention, many provisions of these treaties reflect customary norms, which give rise to rights and obligations under international law.

(1) **High Seas or International Airspace.** UNCLOS identifies five circumstances in which a warship or military aircraft may exercise a right of visitation and board a ship otherwise engaged in legitimate commerce on the high seas. These are:

(a) Vessel is engaged in piracy,

(b) Vessel is engaged in slave trade,

(c) Vessel is engaged in unauthorized broadcasting and the warship's flag state has jurisdiction,

(d) Vessel is without nationality, or

(e) Vessel is same nationality as warship.

(2) It is important to note that some military actions, such as hailing and querying vessels on the high seas, can be supportive of USG CP goals without being classified as interference with ships otherwise engaged in legitimate commerce.

(3) **National Airspace.** Under the Chicago Convention, a state has the right to enforce its domestic laws and regulations on aircraft transiting its national airspace to include the airspace above its territorial borders and waters and to ensure the observance of any obligation of such state under a multilateral international agreement. A state may compel an aircraft entering its national airspace to land.

(4) **Territorial Waters and the Right of Innocent Passage.** Under international law, states generally have the authority to enforce their domestic law within their territorial waters. However, the right of innocent passage constrains this right. Innocent passage is the right of a ship to transit territorial waters without undue impediment as long as it does not interact with any agency, business, or person of the state.

(5) **International Strait and Archipelagic Waters.** Within international straits and archipelagic waters, ships and aircraft enjoy transit rights to proceed without impediment, other than that required to ensure safe navigation.

e. **Legal Status.** The commercial maritime shipping and aviation industries often involve multiple layers of nationality in ownership, operating company, voyage contracting, leasing, flagging, vessel's master/captain, etc. Each country associated with a specific transaction can be approached in some fashion to cooperate with WMD interdiction efforts.

(1) **Flag State Consent.** Unless a UN Security Council resolution expressly states otherwise, the authority to stop and inspect a ship, civil aircraft, or ground vehicle (hereafter referred to collectively as a transport), or authority to authorize a third-party nation to stop and inspect, depends upon the "flag" registry of the transport. The flag

state of a transport can be different from the owner or operator nationality, and a transport is considered under the jurisdiction of the laws and directives of competent authority of the flag state. Generally, states have the right to stop and search any transport flagged (registered) by the state or authorize a third party to do the same. Under the PSI, the United States has negotiated a series of "boarding agreements" with certain other participants. These agreements provide for US boarding of these states' flag shipping transport under specific circumstances and conditions. Planners should consult their command's political advisor and SJA on these specific agreements.

(2) **Master's or Command Pilot's Consent.** The United States holds that it may board and carry out certain activities on ships otherwise immune if the master (captain) of the ship provides consent. Although such boarding, while in international waters, is technically limited to a visit only, the master may authorize a boarding party to examine any portion of the ship. The master is, however, not obligated to provide extended authorization unless directed by competent authority of the flag state. With respect to aircraft in international airspace, the command pilot of a civil aircraft may consent to have the aircraft diverted from its original destination to a designated airport so it can land and be boarded for inspection. Some states do not necessarily concur with the US position.

(3) **Sovereign Immunity.** Warships and military aircraft of a state enjoy sovereign immunity. Coastal states may not stop and search warships and military aircraft, but may direct them to depart the coastal state's territorial waters.

f. **Posse Comitatus and Use of US Military Forces in Law Enforcement**

(1) **Posse Comitatus.** The "Posse Comitatus Act" (Title 18, USC, Section 1385) prohibits use of the federalized US Army (USA), US Air Force (USAF), US Navy (USN), and US Marine Corps (USMC) to enforce domestic law unless authorized by the President, the Constitution, or Congress by Title 10, USC, Section 375, and DOD regulations. This includes active duty Soldiers in a Title 10, USC, status; reservists placed on active duty (Title 10, USC), active duty for training, or inactive duty for training status; National Guard Soldiers in federal service; and DOD civilian and contract personnel under the command of an officer in active duty status under Title 10, USC. There are a number of exceptions to the statute that allow military support for civilian law enforcement (see Title 10, US Code, Section 371). Posse Comitatus does not apply to National Guard personnel serving in a state on state active duty or Title 32, US Code status. In addition, Posse Comitatus does not apply to US Coast Guard (USCG) per Title 14, US Code authority. However, the USCG is subject to Posse Comitatus Act when it is brought under the Navy by Presidential order during wartime. The servicing SJA must review all operations to ensure that they comply with the Act, other domestic laws, and DOD policy.

(2) **Title 10, US Code.** Title 10 is the "Armed Forces" portion of the US Code. Chapter 18, "Military Support for Civilian Law Enforcement Agencies," gives basic guidance for the interaction of military and civilian law enforcement agencies. Title 10,

USC, Section 375 directs SecDef to prescribe such regulations to prohibit a member of the USA, USN, USAF, and USMC from directly participating in arrests, searches, seizures, or other similar activity unless authorized by law (e.g., arrests on military property).

(3) **Title 14, US Code.** Title 14, US Code applies to USCG personnel when they are performing their normal duties, which include enforcing US laws. USCG personnel can be used to enforce US laws anywhere in the world, with certain restrictions, and can participate in regular DOD-led interdiction operations retaining their Title 14, US Code authorities, even if assigned as additional Title 10, US Code forces. Roles and responsibilities for USCG personnel must be clearly laid out by area commanders prior to interdiction operations.

g. **Seizure of Material and Detention of Persons.** Seizures and detentions must have basis in international law, US law, or HN law. Specific cases and circumstances are too numerous to be recounted here. It is critical to involve the SJA as early as possible in the planning process to aid in determining requirements to support seizures, detentions, and expedite disposition.

h. **Disposition - Availability of Evidence and Chain of Custody.** In cases involving probable prosecution by the United States or prosecuting state, agencies should take measures and provide guidance to field units regarding preservation of relevant evidence and establishing chain of custody. Preservation of the chain of custody is also essential to support attribution.

(1) In cases involving possible foreign prosecutions arising from US interdictions and investigations, the interagency team should ascertain whether US investigators intend to make available all unclassified and relevant evidence to their counterparts in the prosecuting state for use by the prosecuting state in any hearings, trials, etc. This may include testimony, weapons, ammunition, imagery, small vessels, and other physical evidence requiring special handling or storage.

(2) The prosecuting state should consider its transport and storage options (items are often located in third-party states or at-sea), as well as chain of custody procedures it may wish to communicate to the United States and other investigators. The prosecuting state may wish to engage in immediate coordination with officials and investigators of other concerned states to establish early chain of custody and collection and preservation of evidence in ways that ensure admissibility in prosecuting state courts.

(3) The United States will, in appropriate circumstances, facilitate delivery of statements from US military witnesses to the prosecuting state. All requests for such personnel or their statements will normally be made to the cognizant US embassy for forwarding to DOD, the DHS (for the USCG), and DOJ. Consideration should be given to the availability of witnesses and facilitating contact with (including travel of) potential prosecuting state investigators while the witnesses remain available.

4. Relationship of Joint Interdiction to Weapons of Mass Destruction Interdiction

a. **JP 3-03, *Joint Interdiction,* and WMD Interdiction.** The NMS-CWMD defines WMD interdiction as operations "designed to stop the proliferation of WMD, delivery systems, associated and dual-use technologies, materials, and expertise from transiting between States of concern and between state and non-state actors, whether undertaken by the military or by other agencies of government (e.g., law enforcement)." JP 3-03, *Joint Interdiction,* defines interdiction for use across the range of military operations as "1. An action to divert, disrupt, delay, or destroy the enemy's military surface capability before it can be used effectively against friendly forces, or to otherwise achieve objectives. 2. In support of law enforcement, activities conducted to divert, disrupt, delay, intercept, board, detain, or destroy, as appropriate, vessels, vehicles, aircraft, people, and cargo."

b. **The NMS-CWMD** addresses WMD interdiction more broadly than JP 3-03 by placing WMD interdiction within the context of the *National Strategy to Combat WMD* and addressing not only the actual interdiction, but a broader national effort. Within the context of JP 3-03, the purpose of WMD interdiction can be interpreted as to **divert** adversary proliferation assets by forcing urgent movement, thereby revealing the networks supporting WMD proliferation or channeling movement into less desirable, more costly, and more vulnerable avenues. Ultimately, WMD interdiction operations seek to **disrupt** the adversary's ability to produce, transport, or acquire WMD, associated materials, technology and expertise, and modes of delivery by constricting the adversary's logistic system supporting WMD development, imposing excessive costs, publicly revealing illicit behavior, and enforcing of sanctions.

c. WMD interdiction operations may occur throughout the operational environment. WMD interdiction operations may occur in all conditions – permissive, uncertain, and hostile, and the specific condition can be subject to rapid change during conduct of operations. Specific activities may occur as stand-alone activities or as part of a larger theater campaign. Regardless, JFCs must ensure integration of their operations with the global USG campaign to combat WMD.

SECTION B. INTERAGENCY ROLES AND RESPONSIBILITIES

5. Overview

a. Successful WMD interdiction requires careful coordination and integration across all government agencies to appropriately engage all instruments of national power. Interagency coordination is the vital link between the military and the diplomatic, informational, and economic instruments of national power. Successful interagency coordination enables the USG to conduct coherent operations to achieve shared goals with maximum efficiency and effectiveness, build international support, and conserve resources. Understanding roles and relationships among agencies and organizations, geographic and functional combatant commands, US state and local governments, and the US chief of mission (COM) and country teams in US embassies or consulates, is essential to successful planning and execution of WMD interdiction throughout several phases.

b. Illicit WMD-related trade and transfer is a dynamic process, featuring constant evolution of the relationships among suppliers, recipients, and intermediaries responsible for the sale, manufacture, and methods of obtaining or transporting WMD materials. A versatile and well-coordinated USG response is necessary. Specific roles, responsibilities, and relationships vary depending upon the circumstances surrounding each case and the phase of a WMD interdiction operation. Oversight of the WMD interdiction process is critical to ensure timely, appropriate tasking and coordination for interdiction activity outside of the United States. Interagency coordination across the USG is essential to developing the USG's desired outcome for a situation, the successful execution of targeted strategies against state and non-state actors, and the disruption of proliferation programs and transactions.

6. National Security Council and Homeland Security Council Role

The NSC and Homeland Security Council (HSC) have similar structures, depicted in Figure B-1. Decisions are made at the lowest possible level or forwarded to the next senior committee or council for action. Each represented agency or department participates in NSC or HSC deliberations to address specific security policy issues and to identify specific agency contributions to selected actions. Both NSC and HSC coordinate the actions of individual groups called policy coordination committees (PCCs); some PCCs are coordinated jointly by NSC or HSC leadership. These joint and sometimes overlapping AORs can create potential for duplication of efforts or uncertainty as to which element carries higher authority. Interagency integration seeks to mitigate these problems through close coordination between NSC, HSC, and other interagency groups.

7. Supporting Weapons of Mass Destruction Interdiction Organizations and Agencies

The following department or agency descriptions of roles, responsibilities, and actions are representative in nature and not to be construed as all-inclusive or static. USG CP capabilities, much like the mission space they address, are constantly evolving.

a. **Department of Defense**

(1) **Office of the Secretary of Defense and the Joint Staff.** SecDef has overall responsibility to the President for DOD CWMD responsibilities. The Assistant Secretary of Defense for Global Security Affairs is responsible for CP policy development and coordination within DOD. CJCS provides military advice to the President regarding CWMD. JS Strategic Plans and Policy Directorate provides military advice on WMD interdiction policy issues. JS Operations Directorate provides military advice on WMD interdiction operations.

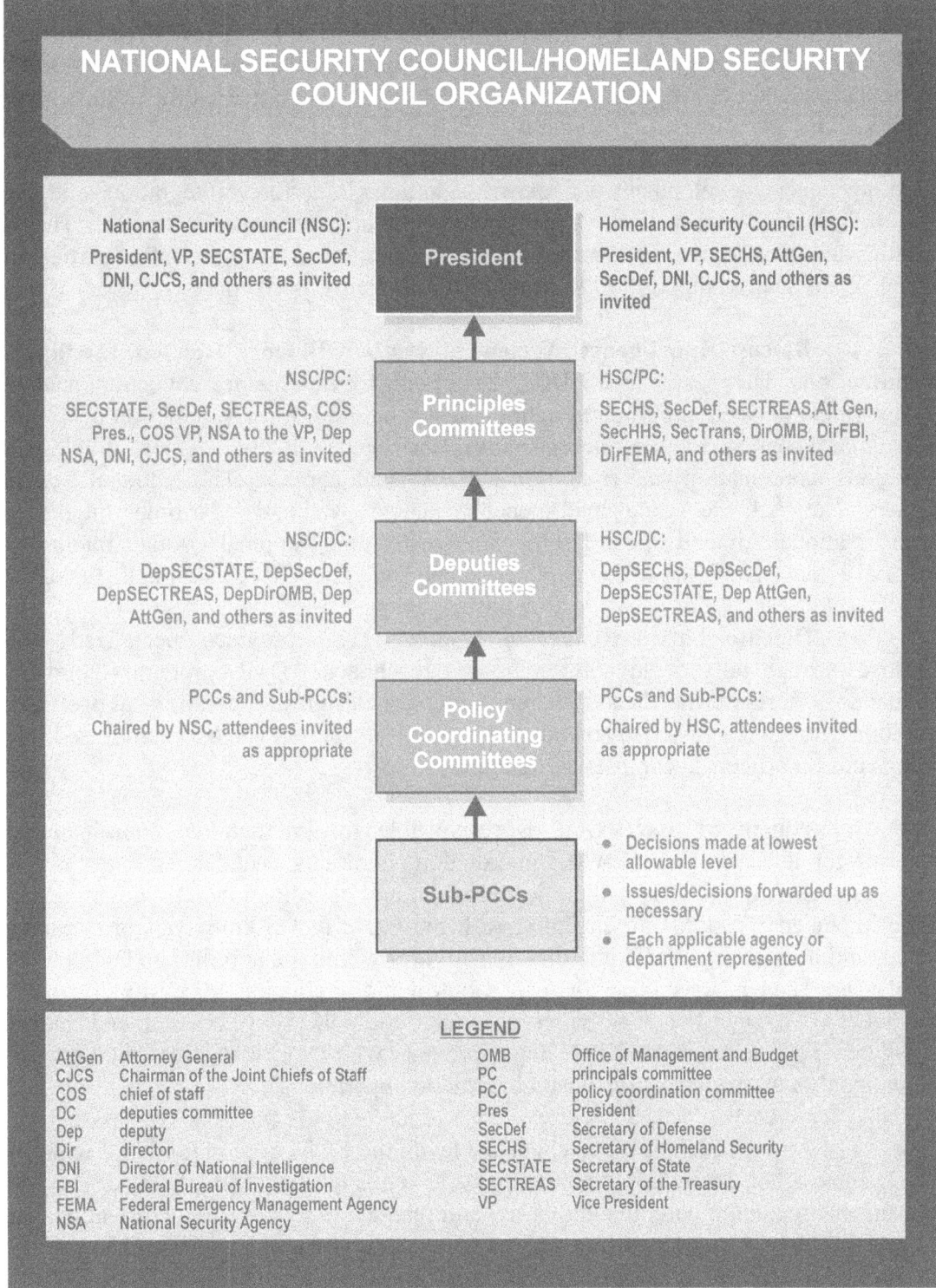

Figure B-1. National Security Council/Homeland Security Council Organization

(2) **Combatant Commands.** USSTRATCOM develops the global campaign plan that provides a planning construct designed to synchronize military activities in support of national CWMD efforts, including WMD interdiction. CDRUSSTRATCOM delegates authority for the interdiction mission to the SCC-WMD. USSTRATCOM is

responsible for advocacy of CWMD capabilities and synchronizing CWMD planning for DOD CWMD. USSTRATCOM provides the primary military representation to other USG departments, US commercial entities, and international agencies for matters related to CWMD, as directed. Finally, CDRSTRATCOM provides prioritization recommendations to the SecDef regarding CWMD efforts. USJFCOM provides support for joint concept development and experimentation, joint force integration, and joint force training for interdiction. Geographic combatant commands conduct shaping activities and execute specific WMD interdiction operations. They are active participants in the PSI and feature support to PSI prominently in their CWMD plans.

(3) **Defense Intelligence Agency and other Defense Related Intelligence Organizations.** DIA serves as the DOD focal point for intelligence collection, analysis, and dissemination as appropriate to help plan, shape, and inform interdiction operations. DIA's main conduit for interdiction-related intelligence is the Defense Intelligence Operations Coordination Center housed at DIA headquarters. The National Security Agency, National Geospatial-Intelligence Agency, National Maritime Intelligence Center, National Air and Space Intelligence Center, and National Ground Intelligence Center also play significant roles in collecting and analyzing CP-related intelligence.

(4) **Defense Threat Reduction Agency.** DTRA provides specialized WMD expertise through fully deployable teams and reachback. DTRA supports combatant commands' efforts during theater shaping, exercise design and creation, as well as at execution through reachback to technical expertise. To support CWMD activities, DTRA stations liaison officers at combatant commands.

b. **Department of State.** DOS is responsible for international coordination in preparing for, and engaging in, WMD interdiction operations. The Secretary of State has direct responsibility for DOS policy development and coordination activities in support of the interagency process, in engaging with the COM at US embassies or consulates abroad, and in directing WMD interdiction activities within the appropriate DOS bureaus and offices. The Undersecretary for Arms Control and International Security (Terrorism) leads DOS WMD interdiction activities, programs, and policy development, and leads the interagency policy process on NP. They coordinate with DOD to facilitate and integrate international military support for WMD interdiction operations.

(1) At the US embassy or consulate level, the COM acts on guidance regarding WMD interdiction activities, instructions on engagement with host or regional governments regarding coordination of law enforcement, intelligence, investigations, and PA, and multilateral organization or international legal implications of WMD interdiction activities.

(2) Official USG communication with foreign governments is conducted via demarche. All USG demarches are delivered by DOS via cable to the embassy or consulate with specific delivery instructions. The demarche is prepared and delivered to the recipient government by the COM or assigned representative to reinforce that the demarche represents the official USG position. Typical WMD interdiction-related

demarches request information on items, people, or transactions of proliferation concern identified through intelligence community collection and analysis or recommended actions to address the proliferation concern.

(3) Other DOS interdiction-related activities include:

(a) Confirmation of transport registry information.

(b) Waivers of objection or consent to US law enforcement.

(c) Coordination of flag state consent to stop, board, and search suspect transports.

(d) Coordination of operations in foreign territorial waters and airspace.

(e) Coordination of diverting a transport to an unscheduled location (e.g., port-of-entry).

(f) Coordination of disposition of suspect transports, cargo, and personnel.

(g) Coordination of technical law enforcement assistance and handoff.

c. **Department of Homeland Security.** DHS is responsible for preventing and deterring terrorist attacks against the United States and its interests, and protecting the United States and its interests from and responding to these threats, as well as natural hazards. Four elements of DHS play a role in WMD interdiction.

(1) **US Coast Guard.** The USCG protects US economic and security interests in maritime regions at risk. USCG has broad maritime jurisdiction authority in US coastal areas, is the LFA for maritime security, provides expertise in maritime security C2 and transportation, and provides support for USG agencies operating in the maritime domain. USCG boarding teams will board vessels suspected of carrying WMD as far offshore as possible. These teams can be inserted by small boats or helicopter. USCG may provide law enforcement detachments to DOD during execution of WMD interdiction to arrest individuals suspected of violating US law. USCG supports foreign government outreach through maritime law enforcement training and exercises and supports DOS development of foreign ship boarding agreements in support of the PSI. The JFC should consider the suitability of using USCG and its personnel in theater security cooperation plans and WMD interdiction operations.

(2) **Immigration and Customs Enforcement (ICE).** ICE is responsible for enforcing US immigration and customs laws outside of the border areas. ICE identifies and works to eliminate vulnerabilities in US border, economic, transportation, and infrastructure security. ICE is the lead DHS agency for investigation of violations of US technology control, customs, and immigration laws. ICE maintains representation at US

embassies or consulates worldwide and provides intelligence and investigative support for countering terrorist threats against the United States.

(3) **Customs and Border Protection (CBP).** CBP protects US borders and ports of entry. It provides technical support to international partners through training, expertise, and border security equipment or technology maintenance and grants, and expertise regarding entry, inspection, and admissibility of persons, items, and vessels arriving from foreign locations. CBP maintains a National Targeting Center, providing WMD interdiction and WMD-terrorism analytical and targeting capabilities. CBP operates the Container Security Initiative as part of a partnership with DOE in the Megaports initiative, deploying agents to major foreign seaports to work with HN counterparts to target all containers that pose a potential threat, and to prevent the transport of WMD on container vessels destined for the United States. CBP Laboratories and Scientific Services staff WMD response teams in strategic domestic locations.

(4) **Coordination of US Coast Guard, Immigration and Customs Enforcement, and Customs and Border Protection.** Pre-interdiction, DHS components support efforts to build an environment hostile to WMD proliferation. CBP is responsible for customs mutual assistance agreements, international outreach for customs information sharing between national customs authorities, and all-source customs analysis outputs into the intelligence process. ICE is responsible for supporting and coordinating with DOS on WMD interdiction activities. During interdiction, USCG participates directly in interdiction activities, or provides assistance to USG interagency and foreign partners, including technical assistance to maritime law enforcement efforts, as described above. Post-interdiction, ICE conducts investigations as necessary to develop additional intelligence and law enforcement information.

(5) **Domestic Nuclear Detection Office.** DNDO is responsible for the development of an enhanced global nuclear detection architecture and is responsible for the implementation of the domestic portion of that architecture. DOD is responsible for implementation of defense radiological/nuclear detection requirements both within and outside the United States. DOS, DOD, and DOE maintain their responsibilities for policy guidance and implementation of the portion of the global architecture outside the United States.

d. **Department of Energy and National Nuclear Security Administration (NNSA).** Pre-interdiction, DOE supports all-source analysis and intelligence activities. During interdiction, DOE supports cargo search and analysis. Post-interdiction, DOE supports the disposition of seized transports and cargo, and exploitation. DOE/NNSA also supports WMD interdiction through:

(1) Intelligence gathering and analysis;

(2) Reachback to national laboratories on nuclear or radiological, dual-use, precursor, and associated technology issues;

(3) Specialized radiation search capabilities which can be forward deployed; and

(4) Outreach to foreign governments for radiation detection and monitoring.

e. **DOJ and Federal Bureau of Investigation.** DOJ coordinates the USG legal position and law enforcement aspects of the USG related to WMD interdiction. The US district attorneys are responsible for conducting criminal prosecutions resulting from WMD interdiction operations. The FBI gathers evidence to support prosecutions, serves warrants for search and arrest, and conducts related law enforcement activities. It is important to involve appropriate DOJ and FBI elements early in the planning and execution of WMD interdiction to leverage their unique authorities while avoiding compromise of criminal cases. The FBI also maintains response capabilities for domestic WMD incidents in permissive, uncertain, and hostile environments.

(1) Pre-interdiction, DOJ conducts law enforcement outreach with partner nations, gathers evidence for use in future prosecutions, and, through the FBI, contributes law enforcement information to all-source intelligence collection and analysis. Of note is the need to balance DOJ requirements to protect evidence for future prosecutions with the need for timely, detailed intelligence.

(2) During interdiction, DOJ provides legal opinions on potential WMD interdiction operations and supports law enforcement activities. Post-interdiction, DOJ, through the FBI, is responsible for conducting evidence collection and exploitation, as well as investigating and detaining seized items and persons for follow-on prosecution by the United States or transfer to another prosecuting state.

f. **Department of Commerce and Bureau of Industry and Security (BIS).** BIS is responsible for international outreach to foreign governments and the international private sector for a number of USG programs. BIS maintains and strengthens the dual-use export control system and is responsible for strengthening multilateral coordination and compliance with multilateral export control regimes and relevant treaties. Pre-interdiction, Department of Commerce is responsible for export control outreach and all-source intelligence analysis. Post-interdiction, Department of Commerce reinforces and communicates dissuasion messages, consistent with USG national NP policy, through business outreach.

g. **Department of Treasury and Financial Crimes Enforcement Network (FinCEN).** The Department of Treasury's Office of Foreign Assets Control (OFAC) maintains awareness on export/import activities to countries of proliferation concern. FinCEN maintains intelligence on financial activities of suspect front companies/countries/other entities of proliferation concern. FinCEN conducts all-source financial intelligence collection and analysis. FinCEN conducts financial freezes and seizures which support interdictions, and WMD interdiction intelligence activities by tracking and reporting financial activities of suspect entities including terrorist financing, money laundering, and other illicit transactions.

(1) Pre-interdiction, the Department of Treasury notifies the intelligence community of suspect transactions and provides intelligence to partner states on suspect entities. During interdiction, OFAC imposes controls on transactions and freezes foreign assets under US jurisdiction.

(2) Post-interdiction, the Department of Treasury is responsible for financial forensic analysis and provides findings to the interagency. The Department of Treasury engages in international outreach activities pre- and post-interdiction.

SECTION C. WEAPONS OF MASS DESTRUCTION INTERDICTION OPERATIONAL PLANNING

8. General

This section details WMD interdiction operational concepts as they pertain to the JFC. It is intended to aid commanders and staffs by providing a basic overview of joint planning and operations concepts for the WMD interdiction mission, and a more detailed discussion designed to promote understanding of the requirements for planning military operations normally considered during the interagency decision-making process described in Section B, "Interagency Roles and Responsibilities." This section builds on JP 3-0, *Joint Operations,* and JP 5-0, *Joint Operation Planning.*

9. Campaign Plan Design and Terms Overview

a. **Design Element Overview.** USG interagency solutions to problems depend on how well the USG and partner nations integrate all instruments of national power—diplomatic, informational, military, and economic—as well as the elements of those instruments (financial, intelligence, and law enforcement) (the means). CWMD planners can use MSOs to describe the military contribution as an instrument of national power, as depicted in Figure B-2.

(1) **Interagency Efforts.** Due to strong interrelationships between actions of elements of the USG interagency, efforts in one portion often affect others. Commanders should consider these relationships when building plans targeting critical nodes and links of a proliferation transaction, pathway, or network as depicted in Figure B-3.

(2) **Adversary Vulnerabilities.** By identifying characteristics of actor and entity relationships, nodes, and links throughout an entire proliferation transaction, commanders may identify adversary vulnerabilities. Planning operations against these vulnerabilities, in turn, involves considering strategic guidance, strategic enablers, LOOs, phases, and termination criteria.

(3) **Ends.** End states, or ends, describe the desired outcome(s) of specific action. CWMD end states are usually achieved through DOD's collaborative work with other instruments of US national power. The most pertinent WMD interdiction end states defined in the NMS-CWMD are:

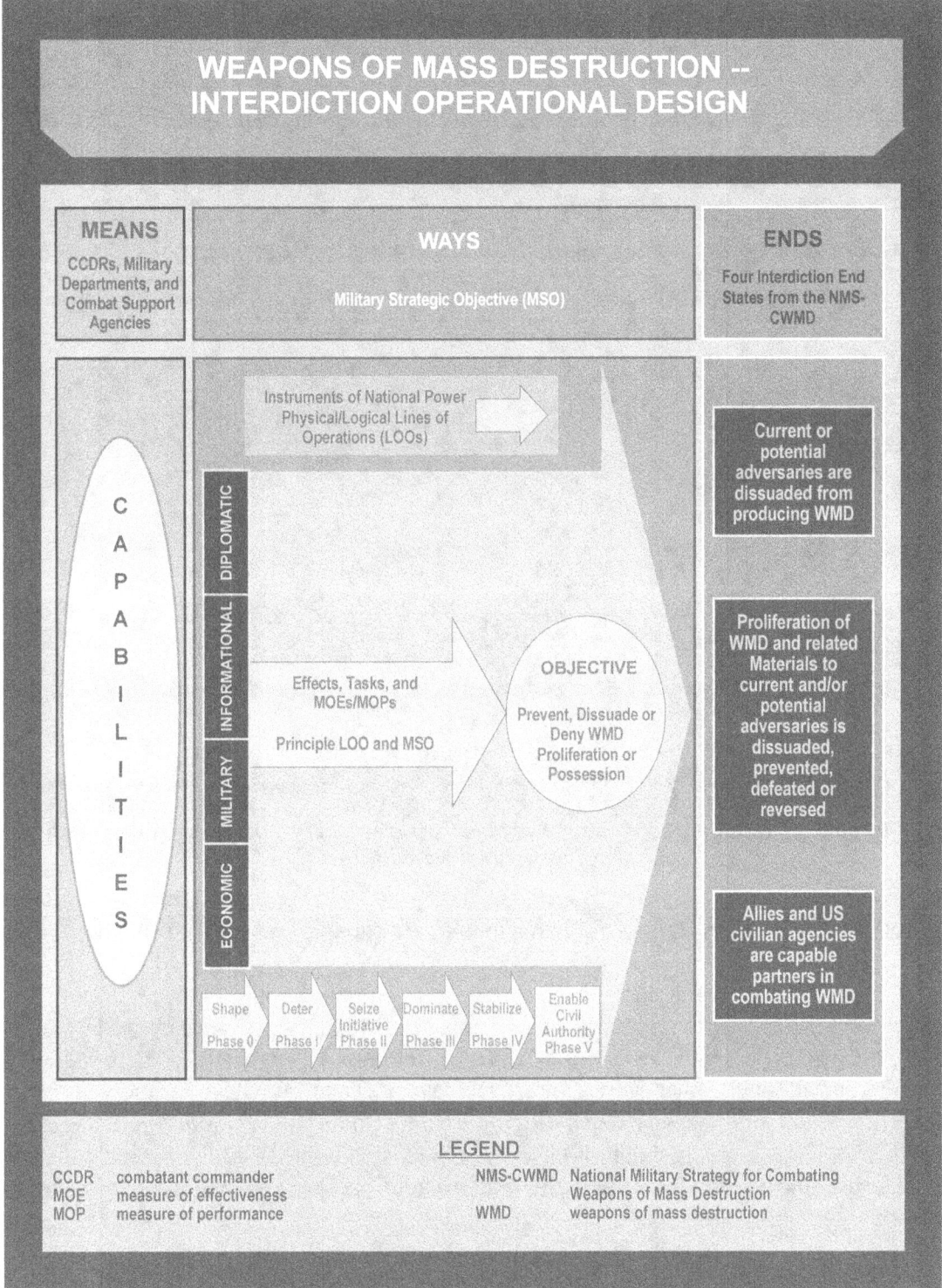

Figure B-2. Weapons of Mass Destruction-Interdiction Operational Design

(a) Current or potential adversaries are dissuaded from producing WMD;

(b) Proliferation of WMD and related materials to current or potential adversaries is dissuaded, prevented, defeated, or reversed; and

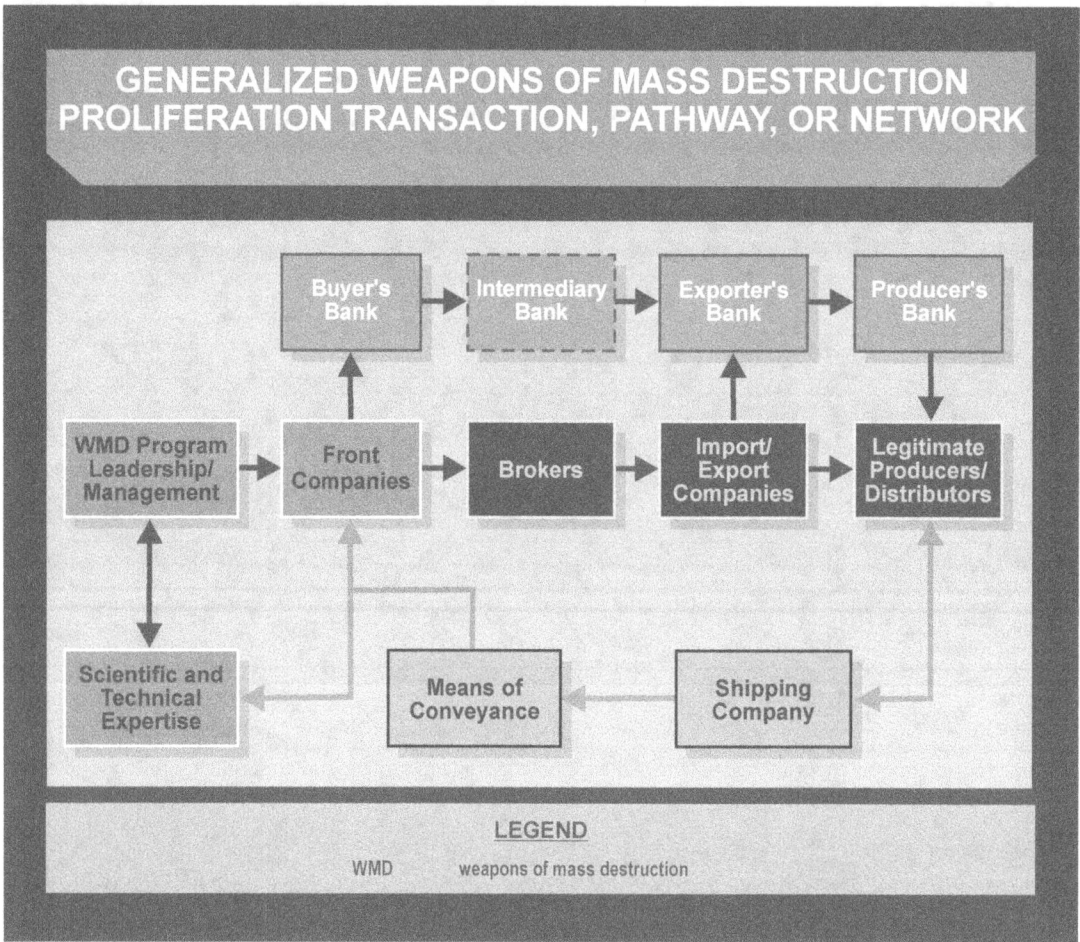

Figure B-3. Generalized Weapons of Mass Destruction Proliferation Transaction, Pathway, or Network

(c) Allies and US civilian agencies are capable partners in CWMD.

(4) **Ways.** Ways can be interpreted as general actions taken to help achieve desired end states. In that regard, we can consider MSOs as ways. The NMS-CWMD MSO, "Prevent, Dissuade, or Deny WMD Proliferation or Possession," best fits WMD interdiction, although other MSOs like, "Defeat and Deter WMD Use and Subsequent Use," may be complementary depending on phase or activity. Actions supporting these "ways" can include enforcement of USG CP objectives, United Nations Security Council resolutions, and standing multilateral and bilateral security cooperation and partner activities.

(5) **Means.** Means describes the tools, including forces, organizations, allies, partners, etc., used to employ the "ways" to achieve the "ends." The combatant commands, working either individually or in conjunction with interagency and international partners, military departments, and CSAs are the means.

b. **Strategic Enablers.** Strategic enablers are capabilities that facilitate execution of a military strategy. The most significant CWMD strategic enablers are intelligence, partnership capacity, and SC support. Section D, "Considerations," provides additional information on these areas.

c. **Line(s) of Operations.** Commanders use LOOs to focus military actions toward achieving a desired end, or end state. Generally speaking, WMD interdiction includes two elements that can be considered as LOOs: shaping the environment and conducting specific WMD interdiction operations. See Figure B-4.

(1) **Shaping the Environment.** Shaping the environment in support of WMD interdiction is a steady-state, continuous activity. Commanders, working in support of broader interagency efforts, continually shape the theater environment to dissuade trafficking in WMD, persuade allies and partners to interdict WMD, and disrupt use of proliferation pathways. Examples include:

(a) Building allied and partner military capabilities to conduct WMD interdiction in support of their own national authorities through security assistance activities. During execution of specific WMD interdiction operations, CCDRs may leverage these allied or partner relationships to gain assistance and reinforce their will to act.

(b) Helping establish global situational awareness through activities supporting intelligence collection, and helping facilitate unilateral, multinational, or partner nation WMD interdiction activities through timely information and intelligence sharing.

(c) Contributing to targeted SC campaigns by developing and communicating messages and taking concrete actions to reinforce these messages (e.g., force demonstrations, multilateral exercises, and overt surveillance activities such as approach and query).

(d) Performing other shaping activities, as appropriate, to support the ability to establish supremacy in time and space over selected geographic areas to deny maneuver space to WMD proliferators, channel and restrict their movement into less desirable or more susceptible routes, and help facilitate the intercept of specific shipments.

(2) **Specific Weapons of Mass Destruction-Interdiction Operations.** Specific WMD interdiction operations covered in this appendix include actions and activities to identify or track; intercept; search or inspect; dispose of intercepted WMD, related material, persons and vessels; and transition residual material and persons to appropriate authority. Although these actions can be depicted sequentially in the same LOO, it is not required they be performed as such. Commanders should plan for and understand their role and the role of the interagency in executing any of these actions or activities at any time.

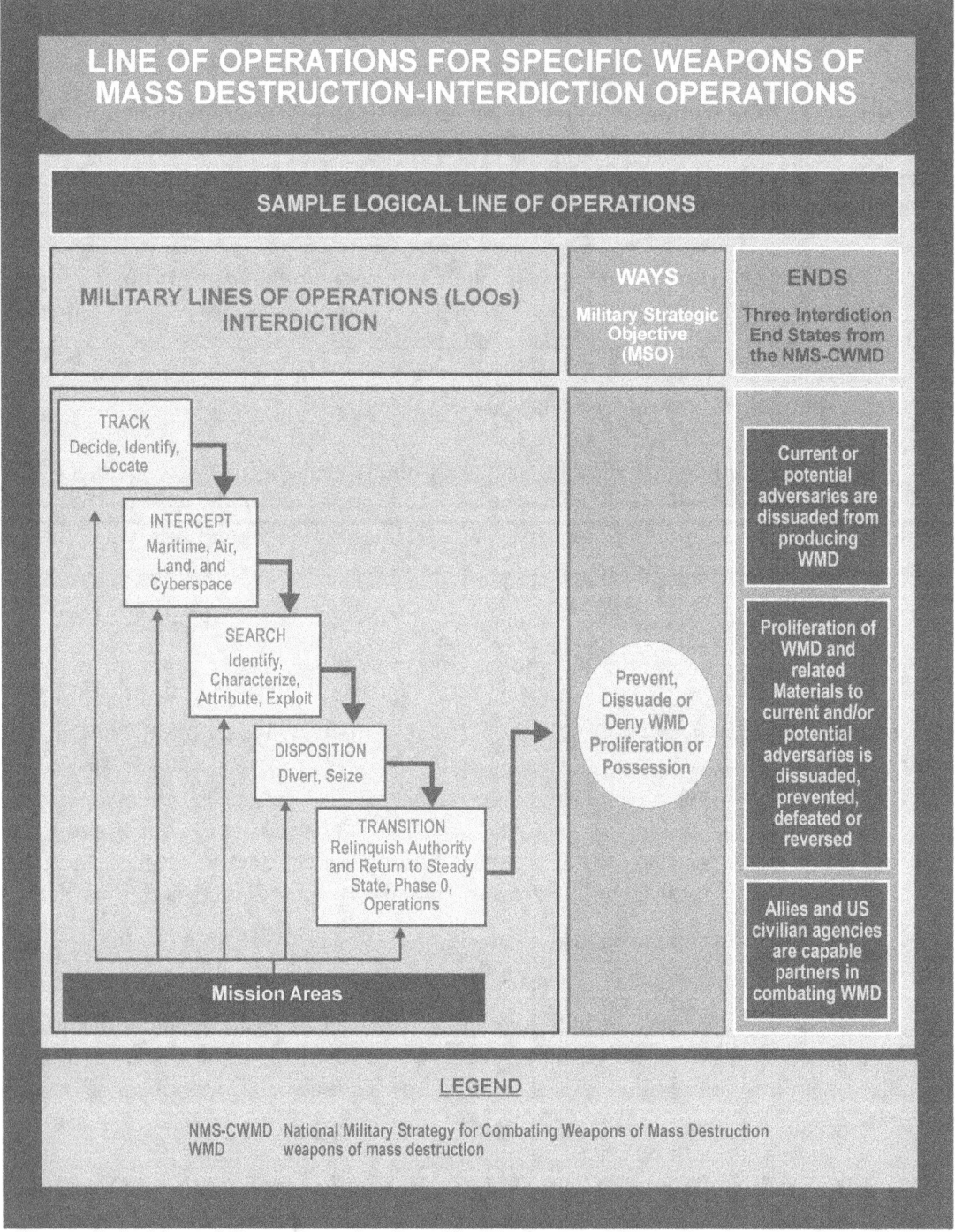

Figure B-4. Line of Operations for Specific Weapons of Mass Destruction-Interdiction Operations

(3) In coordination with interagency partners, collaborative planning considerations should include, at a minimum:

(a) Determining legal and policy authorities;

(b) Identifying all agencies and organizations that should be involved;

(c) Coordinating the change of responsibility for providing security;

(d) Identifying training requirements for boarding teams with respect to CWMD interdiction missions;

(e) Identifying expected law enforcement evidence collection procedures and requirements;

(f) Coordinating the leave-behinds (e.g., specialized personnel, equipment, provisions); and

(g) Coordinating the transition of logistic support.

(4) **Identify or Track.** This action is an ongoing, intelligence-intensive process that begins with the study of proliferators, transactions, pathways, and networks. An understanding of these networks and possible suppliers and recipients will help focus intelligence collection on possible transfer methods and activities to identify and track the potential transfer of WMD-related material, technology, or expertise. In some cases, merely the knowledge that WMD-related transactions are being monitored may deter some actors from entering into those transactions. In other cases, that knowledge may lead to changes in proliferation activity which help further characterize the full scope of that activity. One goal of intelligence collection and analysis is to discover and identify specific shipments or items intended to be transferred before the transfer is attempted.

(5) **Intercept.** This action begins with a decision to place military assets in the vicinity of a suspect transport shipment to perform some type of WMD interdiction activity. With respect to maritime CP interdiction, activities may range from surveillance (overt and covert), to hail and query, to boarding for visit or search. The intercept phase ends either with departure of the military asset upon completion of surveillance or hail or query operations or with the inspection of the shipment following a boarding. The decision to stop and inspect a shipment will most likely be made outside of military channels. Commanders must be prepared to intercept a shipment in accordance with standing orders or as directed by case-specific orders.

(a) **Air.** Interdiction of transfers by air are the most time-sensitive and require accurate and rapid ISR cueing to position assets to intercept the transfer. It is most likely that interception and inspection of air cargos will occur on the ground at the point of origin, transshipment point, or destination. Although possible, it is unlikely that intercepting air shipments would involve the actual aerial intercept of an aircraft and forcing it to land at an airport other than its intended destination. Although tracking and identifying the aircraft containing a suspect shipment will likely be accomplished through national or ground-based means, air assets may also be required. It is also possible that an aircraft containing a suspect shipment will land at a different destination or transshipment airport than planned or expected. This possibility requires the capability to track the aircraft from takeoff to landing and, if retaining the capability to stop and inspect the shipment is desired, the ability to rapidly relocate security and inspection assets to that location.

(b) **Land.** One challenge in land interdiction is the variety of transportation methods, from individuals carrying small items on foot to large containers on heavy rail transport. A significant complication is that while air and sea operations may occur in international airspace and waters, all land operations occur in sovereign territory. Regardless of whether the operation involves intercepting a shipment in transit or inspecting it at a point of departure or port of entry, land operations require close coordination with HN, federal, state, local law enforcement and customs officials. Military operations and personnel will nearly always be in a supporting role to another agency and will likely have significant constraints on actions during land operations. The DOS will assist coordinating with HN authorities.

(c) **Cyberspace.** A more accurate and complete understanding of the full range of WMD threats arrayed against the United States and its allies remains among the highest US intelligence priorities. Determining legitimate cyberspace activities from WMD-related cyberspace activities will become increasingly difficult as several nations of interest are becoming more adept at using it as a conduit for the transfer and procurement of foreign technology and equipment, and as a vehicle for collaboration with proliferation partners. Countries of interest and others are exploiting information technology to advance their strategic interests by developing a cyberspace warfare capability (albeit of uncertain effectiveness) and to expand their propaganda efforts. Improving our ability to obtain timely and accurate knowledge of adversaries' cyberspace capabilities, plans, and intentions is central to developing effective CP and NP policies and capabilities. Particular emphasis must be accorded to improving intelligence regarding WMD-related cyberspace nodes and activities, USG interagency interaction throughout instruments of national power, and cooperation with international friends and allies.

(6) **Search or Inspection.** This action commences once a boarding team or inspectors are established on-site in the vicinity of suspect cargo either afloat or on shore. It covers inspection of, or the general activity of attempting to locate or discover, WMD-related items as previously defined in this appendix. Physical interception and inspection of a shipment will likely be in support of initial or ongoing efforts by other USG agencies or their international counterparts. Search or inspections of air, land, and sea cargos and transactions in cyberspace each present a different challenge; however, the overall objective is the same: to allow subject matter experts to examine the shipment or transaction in a secure environment to determine if it contains WMD-related material or technology. If conventional forces confirm or suspect the presence of WMD, further examination by specialized forces may be required. A primary challenge is to safeguard suspected materials until specialized forces can characterize the material and further exploit it. There are three primary sub-activities or actions of search: identify and characterize; attribute; and exploit:

(a) **Identify and Characterize.** Specialized exploitation teams or capabilities may be required to assist conventional forces or boarding parties once a vessel, aircraft, or site is secure, and the decision has been made to remain on site to perform some type of identification and characterization. Conventional forces should have, at a minimum, the necessary expertise and equipment to either conduct a preliminary analysis themselves or to communicate discovery details in appropriate fashion through reliable means to subject matter experts for their preliminary analysis. Specialized exploitation teams should provide a more comprehensive analysis, packaging, transport, and escort capability for shipment of WMD material to pre-identified facilities for confirmation.

(b) **Attribute.** The intent of this step is to gain an understanding of an adversary's WMD program development, capabilities, and needs, and to discover additional details about proliferation transactions from supplier to end user. Understanding how the contents or details of a specific shipment contribute to the adversary's overall WMD program may determine future intelligence collection or interdiction requirements. Successful attribution may require specialized CBRN forces or capabilities from the Services, CSAs such as DTRA, or OGAs (e.g., DOE, DOS) that are capable of conducting sensitive site exploitation operations. Selected elements of the intelligence community who specialize in adversary CP and WMD-related programs can also provide valuable assistance. Most of these personnel will require a locally permissive environment to conduct their activities. Throughout the attribution process, careful attention to the chain of custody is necessary in order to preserve law enforcement options. Commanders should liaise as required with law enforcement personnel.

(c) **Exploit.** Exploitation activities are essential to counter further WMD proliferation and prevent WMD program regeneration or maturation. Exploitation can occur in limited fashion in the field or more extensively in highly supportive environments such as a laboratory. These activities include taking full advantage of any information obtained for tactical, operational, or strategic purposes. Exploitation personnel conduct detailed analysis of weapons, materials, agents, documents, technical experts, and other media found in and around the search site. Clear policy guidance on the depth of exploitation, including incentives, amnesty, and interrogation, is essential to effectively managing these actions.

> *"Characterization includes detailed assessments that may take hours to days to complete. USG [US Government] or internationally designated laboratories with accepted confirmatory capabilities as well as assets with other required capabilities are not generally organic to a theater."*
>
> **Handbook for Joint Weapons of Mass Destruction (WMD) Elimination Operations**

(7) **Disposition.** Disposition of the intercepted entity may involve return to originator, diversion, seizure, or destruction. Since the majority of these actions involve working with the interagency, other nations, commercial shipping entities, and businesses, planners must consider potential legal and financial implications. DOD's interagency partners can facilitate disposition efforts based on agency authorities (e.g., DOS can assist in negotiating financial arrangements with shippers and other commercial enterprises, as required).

(a) **Return to Originator.** If no WMD or related materials are found during the search or inspection phase, the suspect entity will be returned to the originator. Alternately, the purpose of interdicting a shipment may be to either facilitate its return to the originator, or provide time for diplomatic actions to result in the shipment's recall by the originator. Such actions are in keeping with the USG desire to assist other countries in enforcing their own laws or in enforcing compliance with applicable international laws, treaties, agreements, or United Nations Security Council resolutions.

(b) **Diversion.** If WMD materials are located aboard a transport during search operations, and the decision is made to characterize, delay, seize, return, or otherwise disrupt the shipment, identification of suitable locations may be required to accomplish follow-on disposition efforts. Planners must consider the need to preserve evidence for intelligence collection and exploitation, attribution, including possible law or treaty enforcement. Significant liaison with interagency partners remains critical prior to and during the disposition phase.

(c) **Seizure.** If WMD material is identified, seizure could include control and security of the site or vessel beginning with characterization of the material through transfer of control to appropriate authorities. Planning should address how to establish and maintain secure control of the site or vessel as well as opportunities for intelligence collection and exploitation. This may require coordination for additional personnel or material based on the extent of the site or vessel (e.g., quantity of WMD, risk). Specialized exploitation personnel, if required, should be capable of ensuring weapons, materials, CBRN agents, and delivery systems are not armed or can be handled safely.

(d) **Destruction.** It is possible, although highly unlikely, that the final disposition of an interdicted cargo will be its destruction. This action will involve a great deal of coordination between the existing security forces, required transportation elements, legal authorities, and WMD elimination experts. Nothing, however, shall impinge on a commander's right to act in self-defense.

(8) **Transition.** The final step in the interdiction process (although other activities such as exploitation, attribution, and legal prosecution may still be ongoing) is reconstitution of the forces. Reconstitution includes the relinquishing of authority from the interdiction team to HN or other authority, and return to other assigned missions.

ACTIONS ON DECISIVE POINTS OR NODES

The October 2003 diversion of the German-owned *BBC China* carrying centrifuge parts to Libya provides an excellent example of the strengths of international cooperation in weapons of mass destruction (WMD) interdiction and the potential strategic benefits from a seemingly simple action. The United States and the United Kingdom gleaned intelligence that the *BBC China* was potentially carrying an illegal shipment of WMD components to Libya (*Identify/Track*). In the case of the *BBC China*, Germany was involved as the vessel was German-owned. Italy was also involved, because it had ports close to the vessel's ultimate destination. US and British naval assets intercepted the ship once it passed through the Suez Canal on its way to Libya (*Intercept*). The German government contacted the German-based owner, BBC Chartering and Logistic GmbH, [Gesellschaft mit beschränkter Haftung], and asked it to divert the vessel to an Italian port for inspection (*Divert*). The inspection revealed thousands of parts for centrifuges in containers marked "used machine tool parts" (*Search*). This material was seized (*Disposition/Seize*), and shortly thereafter, Libya agreed to give up its WMD programs and to submit to international verification (*Transition*). Government officials in both the United States and the United Kingdom have argued that the interdiction and seizure helped turn the tide and led to Libya's much-sought-after nonproliferation posture and Libya relinquishing its WMD programs. The military strategic objective (MSO) of *prevent, dissuade, and deny* adversary attempts to proliferate WMD was complementary to the MSO of *reduce, destroy, or reverse WMD possession,* as Libya's WMD program was being cooperatively reduced *(reversed).*

VARIOUS SOURCES

d. **Weapons of Mass Destruction-Interdiction Phasing.** Arranging operations in phases is a key aspect of military planning. Phasing assists commanders and planners in visualizing and thinking through the entire operation or campaign and helps define requirements and guide planning in terms of forces, resources, time, space, purpose, and mitigating risk. Phasing can be applied to WMD interdiction operations (Figure B-5). Note that operations and activities in the shape and deter phases normally are outlined in theater security cooperation plans and those in the remaining phases are outlined in Joint Strategic Capabilities Plan-directed operation plans.

(1) **Phase 0 (Shape).** The intent of this phase is to create a theater environment hostile to proliferation activity in order to dissuade or deter state and non-state actors from proliferating WMD. This phase is continuous, with actions emphasizing international legitimacy and multinational cooperation in support of defined national strategic and MSOs. Phase 0 (Shape) activities should focus on shaping perceptions and influencing the behavior of both adversaries and allies; developing credible allied and friendly military capabilities for self-defense, coalition operations, and deterrence;

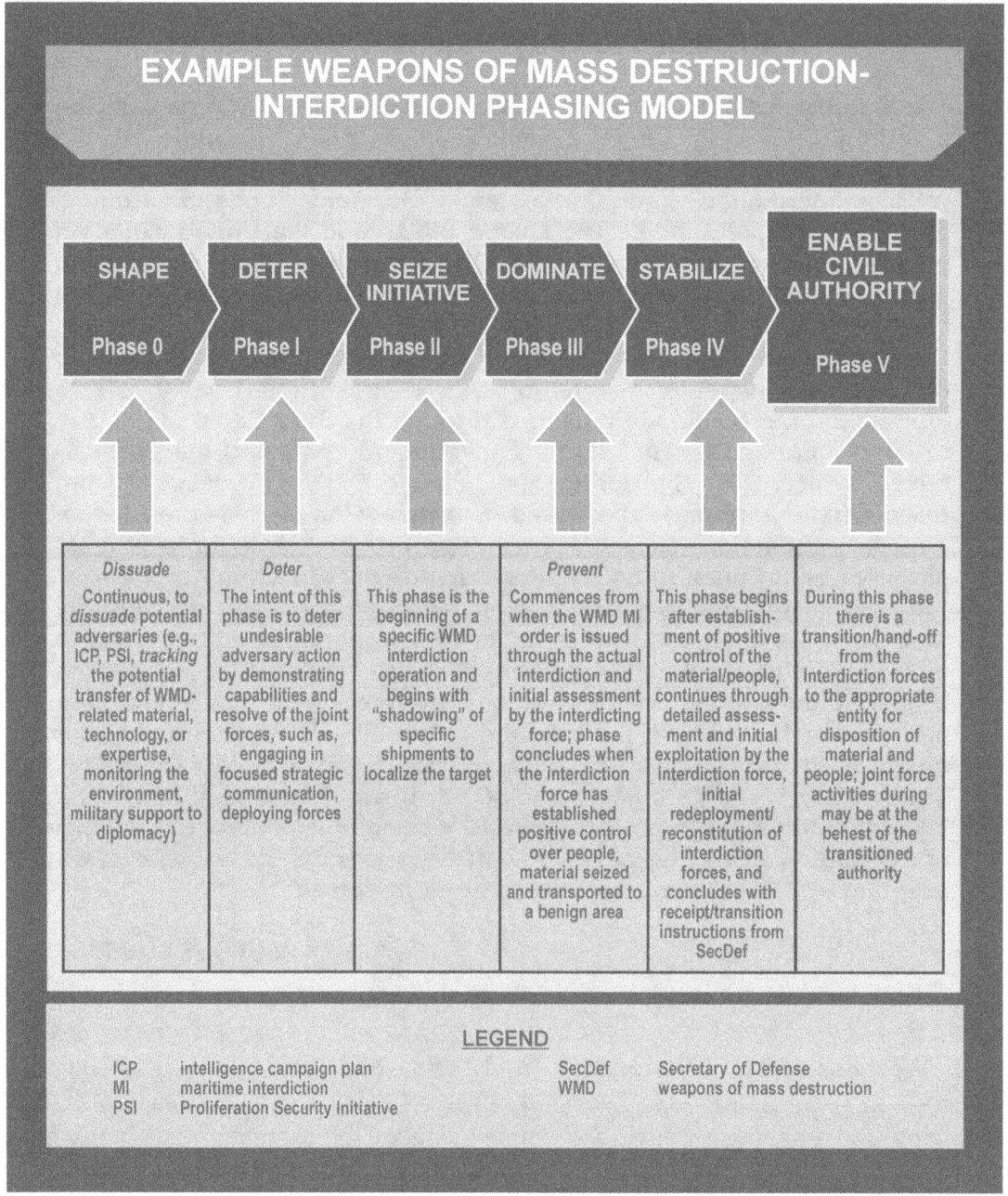

Figure B-5. Example Weapons of Mass Destruction-Interdiction Phasing Model

improving information exchange and intelligence sharing; and providing US forces with peacetime and contingency access to overseas operating environments through activities such as the PSI and pursuit of ship boarding agreements. Planning that supports most "shaping" requirements typically occurs in the context of day-to-day security cooperation, and combatant commands may incorporate phase 0 (Shape) WMD interdiction activities and tasks into their theater security cooperation plans.

(2) **Phase I (Deter).** The intent of this phase is to deter undesirable adversary action by demonstrating the capabilities and resolve of the joint force through actions such as deploying forces, engaging in focused SC, and conducting demonstrations. Phase

I (Deter) deterrence differs from phase 0 (Shape) deterrence in that it largely involves preparatory actions that specifically support or facilitate the execution of subsequent phases of the operation or campaign. These actions may include:

(a) Mobilization, tailoring of forces, and other predeployment activities;

(b) Deployment into a theater;

(c) Employment of ISR assets to provide situational awareness;

(d) Operations at en route locations to support shore-based disposition actions;

(e) Establishment of liaison with interagency and international WMD interdiction partners;

(f) Public exercise of coalition shipboarding capabilities to include inter-governmental coordination; and,

(g) Development of mission-tailored C2, intelligence, force protection, FHP, HSS, transportation, and logistic requirements to support the JFC's concepts of operations.

(3) **Phase II (Seize Initiative).** This phase is the beginning of a specific WMD interdiction operation and, as an example, may begin with "shadowing" a specific shipment to localize the target. It terminates with a decision by the commander, or order by SecDef, to conduct an interdiction or interdiction-related activity, such as an at-sea hail and query. During this phase, the JFC continues to coordinate actions designed to support follow-on operations should they be required.

(4) **Phase III (Dominate).** The intent of this phase is to gain and maintain control of the operational environment. Phase III (Dominate) commences when the WMD interdiction order is issued and continues through the actual interdiction or interdiction-related activity and initial assessment by the interdicting force. This phase concludes when the interdiction force has established positive control over suspect people or material, if such control was a desired goal of the interdiction activity, and the environment is deemed permissive (includes render safe/disablement operations if a device is discovered).

(5) **Phase IV (Stabilize).** Phase IV (Stabilize) begins after establishment of positive control of the material or people, continues through assessment and initial exploitation by the interdiction force, can include initial redeployment or reconstitution of interdiction forces, and concludes with receipt of transition instructions from competent authority. The joint force may be required to initially integrate the efforts of other supporting or contributing agencies, forces, and organizations until legitimate authorities or entities establish control. Throughout phase IV (Stabilize), the JFC must continue to

assess requirements to facilitate transfer of overall authority to a legitimate entity, leading to phase V (Enable Civil Authority).

(6) **Phase V (Enable Civil Authority).** During this phase, there is a transition or handoff from the interdiction forces to the appropriate entity for disposition of material and people. The goal is for the joint force to enable the viability of this next authority, and may include further joint force activities in support of that authority. This includes coordination of joint force actions with other supporting or supported participants. Since redeployment operations for interdiction forces will most often begin during this phase, redeployment requirements should be identified as early as possible. The military end state(s) are achieved during this phase, signaling the end of the operation.

e. **Weapons of Mass Destruction-Interdiction Termination or Transfer Criteria.** When and under what circumstances to suspend or terminate military operations remain political decisions. Even so, it is essential that the commander ensure higher authorities understand the implications, both immediate and long term, of a suspension of operations at any point along the operational continuum. For DOD purposes, WMD interdiction of specific shipments terminates on handoff (transfer) from interdiction forces to the appropriate civilian or international authority for final disposition of material and persons. Handoff may occur to a third country government, US law enforcement, or to other civil authorities. Successful transition usually requires extensive interagency coordination through OSD and JS before, during, and after interdiction of a shipment.

SECTION D. CONSIDERATIONS

10. Intelligence Planning and Coordination

a. **Strategic Intelligence.** Strategic intelligence for WMD interdiction focuses on identifying and characterizing a state or non-state actor of proliferation concern's WMD network. This network encompasses the national leadership guiding the WMD program (see Section C "Weapons of Mass Destruction Interdiction Operational Planning"); the R&D complex designing and developing WMD; the infrastructure which produces precursors, components, and weaponized WMD; the operating forces which employ WMD; and the networks of front companies or agents that acquire and distribute WMD technology and materials from foreign sources. It is these acquisition networks and transportation and financial links among and between them that are the focus of WMD interdiction. Locations and descriptions of any known WMD worldwide are identified in the DIA Modernized Intelligence Database. Any planned interdiction must start with a request to update the data base with all-source intelligence to insure currency and accuracy of the data.

(1) Combatant commands can influence the intelligence planning process through the Concept Plan 8099 National Intelligence Support Plan (NISP). CJCSI 3110.02E, *Intelligence Planning Guidance, Objectives and Tasks*, outlines this process.

NISP identifies key intelligence requirements supporting CWMD operations to the overall intelligence community.

(2) The NISP is the mechanism by which CCDRs communicate those intelligence requirements needing defense wide and national intelligence support to the Director, Defense Intelligence Operations Center. WMD issues are in Band A, the highest level of the National Intelligence Priorities Framework. Requests for information are the mechanism used to request collection and/or provision of tactical intelligence to support specific WMD interdiction cases.

b. **Cueing.** WMD interdiction relies on indications and warning to cue forces for appropriate action. Often, initial cues are vague and incomplete and will require a focused effort to gather intelligence specific enough to enable the desired action. Cues can include evidence of ongoing transactions, loading of cargo, transit of shipping, or route and destination information. Rarely will they include information on the specific nature of cargo or security arrangements.

c. **Priority Intelligence Requirements for Weapons of Mass Destruction-Interdiction.** Commanders will need to establish priority intelligence requirements (PIRs) for WMD interdiction and communicate them, together with operational or tactical implications of intelligence gaps, not only to intelligence collectors but also to the policy community. PIRs may include, but are not limited to:

(1) Destination of WMD (or related) shipment;

(2) Timing, route, and mode of transport to include intermediate stops of WMD shipments/movements;

(3) Security arrangements of WMD shipments/movements;

(4) Nature of WMD type cargo and item(s) or person(s) of interest;

(5) Specific location of WMD type cargo aboard large vessels (e.g., which container);

(6) Specific individuals of interest related to WMD program or shipment; and

(7) WMD interdiction capabilities or shortfalls of potential international partners.

d. **Intelligence or Information Sharing.** Successful multinational action requires the sharing of selected information and intelligence with international partners. The United States will share information and intelligence either to build international partners' will to take action against WMD proliferation or to build their capability. Intelligence sharing is governed by specific regulations determining what intelligence will be shared, and with whom the United States will share it. Military staffs must consult closely with senior intelligence personnel, foreign disclosure office personnel, and SJA when considering sharing intelligence.

(1) Execution of WMD interdiction may require additional disclosure of intelligence data beyond routine dissemination. This requires determination, on a case-by-case basis, of the risk to comprising intelligence sources and methods versus the expected gain.

(2) This determination is a policy decision made in conjunction with the intelligence community. The required coordination may prove lengthy. Also, many partners may not have the automated information services capabilities necessary to receive, protect, and process classified information. This dramatically slows the intelligence or information sharing process.

e. **Exploitation of Seized Material.** Exploitation of seized personnel and material is a critical element of WMD interdiction. It enables development of additional strategic intelligence; identifies proliferation network nodes; may lead to future WMD interdiction opportunities; and supports potential diplomatic, economic, or legal action against proliferators. Planners should carefully consider the impact of various legal regimes on the ability to exploit material and personnel when determining disposition of the seized transport vehicle, personnel, and cargo. Legal issues including the right to question persons, the right to inspect documents and cargo, and potential requirements to maintain a chain of custody will impact exploitation. Exploitation is primarily an intelligence function and may require specific capabilities beyond those routinely available in theater. Planning must consider the need to reach back to, or bring forward, these capabilities, timing constraints, and the logistics required to do so.

11. Security Cooperation and Partner Activities

a. **Integration with Security Cooperation Activities.** The security cooperation guidance (SCG) included in the Global Employment of the Force describes SecDef priorities for creating new partnerships and enhancing existing partnerships with military allies and friendly nations. These relationships establish, enhance, and encourage partner nations and organizations to cooperate with the US military, thereby improving their ability to prosecute the WOT and to combat WMD. The SCG establishes priority partners with whom commanders should emphasize WMD interdiction capacity building activities. PSI partner nations are strong candidates for such capacity building. The ultimate goal is to develop partners who are willing and able to actively conduct WMD interdiction, are willing to work with US forces, or will enable US forces to take action through their territory.

b. **Building Capacity and Will for Weapons of Mass Destruction-Interdiction.**

(1) **The Proliferation Security Initiative.** The PSI provides a framework specifically for WMD interdiction. As of its fifth anniversary in May 2008, 94 countries have endorsed the PSI Statement of Interdiction Principles. This agreement between

like-minded nations serves as a means to leverage the support of key international partners to interdict WMD by employing the instruments of national power on a global scale. PSI provides a basis for CP-related activities of the USG and serves as a mechanism that allows the USG and foreign partners to share information and to discuss pertinent operational constraints to conducting WMD interdiction missions. Contacts built through this informal information sharing venue have often provided the necessary information during critical stages of actual WMD interdiction successes.

(2) The operational experts group (OEG) includes core countries that conduct international and regional meetings to bring together PSI countries for discussion aimed at enhancing their collective capabilities to prevent the proliferation of WMD materials, technologies, and related items. The PSI OEG builds capacity, confidence, and support for international information exchange through quarterly meetings to discuss exercise and operations priorities. It identifies possible legal constraints to conducting WMD interdiction missions, commercial implications concerning delays of shipments of goods, and options for disposition of any confiscated material. The PSI OEG also establishes PSI exercise schedules and goals. PSI exercises are important for developing international confidence by validating and codifying actual WMD interdiction capabilities, communication processes, and national-level legal authorities and limitations.

(3) **Non-PSI Partners.** For a variety of regional and domestic political reasons, several US allies and partners do not subscribe to the interdiction principles of the PSI but play important roles in facilitating WMD interdiction. Many of these nations lie along key trade routes and will, on a case-by-case basis, support WMD interdiction activities. These states likely have acceded to key treaties, agreements, and UN Security Council resolutions, which provide a basis for action. Early engagement of and information sharing with, non-PSI partners are necessary to build their will to conduct WMD interdiction in support of enforcement of their international commitments. In many cases, nations will require specific, detailed evidence that a shipment is WMD-related and will only act in accordance with strict interpretation of their domestic laws. Commanders should identify opportunities to include non-PSI nations in combined exercise events which have a WMD interdiction component to identify those nation's information needs, legal and political thresholds for action, and capabilities to actually track, intercept, search, and coordinate disposition of WMD-related cargo and personnel.

c. **Multinational Operations.** JP 3-16, *Multinational Operations*, discusses the implications of working in a multinational environment. Key among a number of issues is the ability to share information in a timely and secure fashion. In many instances, states supporting a WMD interdiction activity will not have the ability to communicate rapidly in a secure environment either with their own forces or with the United States. Multinational operations may involve US military forces with nonmilitary law enforcement, border control, or customs entities of a partner nation. Commanders should identify and forward to the JS requirements for liaison elements to ensure interoperability or required interagency augmentation to enhance liaison capabilities early in the planning process.

12. Interagency Coordination

Interagency relationships are ones of coordination and mutual support, not direction. A commander may request support, but the degree to which OGAs or departments can or will provide support is conditional upon federal statutes, policy decisions, departmental or agency resources, and memoranda of agreement/memoranda of understanding. Commanders must plan collaboratively to identify where and how they and OGAs or departments can provide mutually beneficial support and work through the OSD and JS to develop standing relationships with the requisite organizations. For almost all WMD interdiction related activities, CCDR coordination with the JS and OSD will ensure proper liaison with USG interagency resources. CJCSI 5715.01B, *Joint Staff Participation in Interagency Affairs,* provides guidance and JP 3-08, *Interorganizational Coordination During Joint Operations*, provides doctrine for interagency coordination. Annex V (Interagency Coordination) of a supported commander's operation plan enables a commander to identify interagency support requirements during planning. Annex V should specify for interagency partners not only the capabilities that military planners have determined the military may need, but also the shared understanding of the situation, and common objectives required to resolve the situation.

a. **Support to Campaign or Specific Operations.** Commanders should identify tasks requiring interagency support early in the planning process. These may include diplomatic, economic, law enforcement, and informational support required from interagency partners. For example, in support of security cooperation, a commander may require DOS and DOJ engagement with their political and legal counterparts in the partner state in parallel with military diplomacy and combined exercises. A commander would forward this request for support to OSD and JS so they can engage their interagency counterparts to build a unified USG plan of action.

b. **Role of Theater Joint Interagency Coordination Group or a Joint Interagency Task Force (JIATF).** A commander may also employ a JIACG or a JIATF. A JIACG enables theater-level coordination of interagency activities based on existing agreements. The JIACG performs a liaison function enabling civilian and military operational planners to establish regular, timely, and collaborative working relationships. Originally formed to coordinate counterterrorism activities, JIACGs can be expanded to cover the full spectrum of theater-level interagency coordination requirements (e.g., CWMD, MOTR, humanitarian assistance or disaster relief). Commanders must ensure JIACG personnel are linked to their parent agencies' subject matter experts for various interagency processes (e.g., NSPD-20, *Counterproliferation Interdiction,* and MOTR) and understand their agencies' authorities, capabilities, and capacity to assist in given situations.

c. A JIATF differs from a JIACG in that it exercises tactical control over attached elements when executing a mission. Created as part of the US strategy to defeat narcotics trafficking, JIATFs perform a dual detection or monitoring and partner capacity building role. JIATFs derive their authority from a formally coordinated interagency memorandum signed by the head of each participating department or agency. JIATFs currently do not have authority to conduct WMD interdiction.

13. Strategic Communication

SC is an essential element of WMD interdiction in that it provides a means of reinforcing or extending interdiction effects through dissuasion and deterrence. SC are focused United States Government efforts to understand and engage key audiences to create, strengthen, or preserve conditions favorable for the advancement of United States Government interests, policies, and objectives through the use of coordinated programs, plans, themes, messages, and products synchronized with the actions of all instruments of national power SC must be a responsive and agile whole-of-government effort with synchronization of crucial themes, messages, images, and actions. The predominant military activities that support SC are IO, PA, and DSPD. JP 5-0, *Joint Operation Planning*, provides current doctrine on SC.

a. **Coordination with Interagency.** OSD is responsible for coordinating DOD SC with interagency efforts. The NSC includes a PCC for Public Diplomacy and Strategic Communication (PDSC) where this coordination can occur. Ideally, DOD SC activities will complement other interagency SC. CCDRs consider SC during peacetime security cooperation planning, and incorporate themes, messages, images, actions, and other relevant factors in their theater campaign plans. For example, a commander may undertake WMD interdiction training with a partner nation. Simultaneously, the combatant command JIACG would coordinate diplomatic activity, with the training, to establish a diplomatic and legal basis for WMD interdiction against business entities used by a country for WMD acquisition and with economic measures publicly designating these business entities under Executive Order 13382, *Blocking Property of Weapons of Mass Destruction Proliferators and Their Supporters*. The PDSC PCC would coordinate a DOS and Department of Commerce effort to highlight these events to the larger business community engaged in manufacture of dual-use items to dissuade and deter cooperation with the target country's business entities.

b. **Selected Audiences and Tailored Themes.** There exist multiple potential audiences for SC. It is important to tailor themes and supporting messages to the appropriate audience and ensure the audience can receive the message through the chosen mode of transmission. Potential audiences for WMD interdiction SC include:

(1) Leaders of states of proliferation concern and their principle advisors.

(2) Technical experts required to produce and employ WMD such as scientists; commanders of units employing WMD; and managers of industrial enterprises producing WMD, precursors, and dual-use materials.

(3) Technicians involved in the details of WMD production and employment such as laboratory technicians, officer cadre, and factory personnel.

(4) Each audience has a unique set of interests (recognition or prestige within the international scientific community, for example) that SC planners should leverage in crafting specific messages.

c. **Phasing of Efforts.** Commanders should ensure that their military activities support SC themes and addresses audiences appropriate to the phase of their operation. During phase 0 (Shape), both potential proliferators and regional allies or partners can be key audiences. Themes targeted toward entities of proliferation concern focus on dissuasion both by demonstrating US resolve, capability, and readiness and by identifying mechanisms through which the entity can come into compliance with US and global NP goals, thus attaining the benefits of that compliance. For allies and partners, themes should enhance cohesion and build will by highlighting their NP obligations and demonstrating the benefits of adherence, communicating US resolve to deal with WMD proliferation, and assuring allies and partners that the United States will assist them in meeting their obligations and work to build justifications for action. As commanders enhance their posture to conduct WMD interdiction in later phases, SC should ensure tight synchronization of crucial themes, messages, images, and actions to strongly influence entities of proliferation concern and disrupt their ability to counter US actions. For allies, partners, and others, themes should work to justify US actions and counter adversary disinformation.

APPENDIX C
REFERENCES

The development of JP 3-40 is based on the following primary references:

1. **General**

   a. *The National Security Strategy.*

   b. *National Military Strategy to Combat Weapons of Mass Destruction.*

   c. *National Strategy to Combat Weapons of Mass Destruction.*

   d. NSPD-17/Homeland Security Presidential Directive (HSPD)-4: *National Strategy to Combat Weapons of Mass Destruction.*

   e. *The Proliferation Security Initiative: Statement of Interdiction Principles.*

   f. *National Strategy for Homeland Security.*

   g. HSPD-5: *Management of Domestic Incidents.*

   h. *National Response Framework.*

   i. HSPD-7: *Critical Infrastructure Identification, Prioritization, and Protection.*

   j. HSPD-8: *National Preparedness.*

   k. *National Incident Management System.*

   l. Presidential Decision Directive/NSC-62, *Protection Against Unconventional Threats to the Homeland and Americans Overseas* (U). Document is classified SECRET.

   m. Title 10, US Code, Section 12304.

   n. Title 50, US Code, Chapter 40, *Defense Against Weapons of Mass Destruction.*

   o. *Unified Command Plan (UCP).*

   p. *Joint Strategic Capabilities Plan (JSCP).*

   q. *Maritime Operational Threat Response for the National Strategy for Maritime Security.*

   r. *Aviation Operational Threat Response Plan.*

2. **Department of Defense**

   a. *National Defense Strategy.*

b. Counterproliferation Program Review Committee (CPRC), *Activities and Programs for Countering Proliferation and NBC Terrorism.*

c. DODD 2060.02, *Department of Defense Combating Weapons of Mass Destruction (WMD) Policy.*

d. DODD 3025.1, *Military Support to Civil Authorities (MSCA).*

e. DODD 3025.15, *Military Assistance to Civil Authorities.*

f. DODI 2000.21, *Foreign Consequence Management (FCM).*

g. DOD Instruction 6490.03, *Deployment Health.*

h. Office of the Deputy Secretary of Defense, *Nonproliferation and Counterproliferation Activities and Programs.*

i. *Quadrennial Defense Review Report.*

j. Office of the Secretary of Defense, *Defense Planning Guidance* (U). Document is classified SECRET.

k. DODD S-2060.ee, *DOD Support to the National Technical Nuclear Forensics (NTNF) Program.*

3. **Joint Publications**

a. JP 1, *Doctrine for the Armed Forces of the United States.*

b. JP 1-02, *DOD Dictionary of Military and Associated Terms.*

c. JP 2-01.3, *Joint Intelligence Preparation of the Operational Environment.*

d. JP 3-0, *Joint Operations.*

e. JP 3-01, *Countering Air and Missile Threats.*

f. JP 3-03, *Joint Interdiction.*

g. JP 3-07.2, *Antiterrorism (FOUO).*

h. JP 3-29, *Foreign Humanitarian Assistance.*

i. JP 3-08.VI, *Interorganizational Coordination During Joint Operations, Volume I.*

j. JP 3-10, *Joint Security Operations in Theater*.

k. JP 3-11, *Operations in Chemical, Biological, Radiological, and Nuclear (CBRN) Environments*.

l. JP 3-13, *Information Operations*.

m. JP 3-27, *Homeland Defense*.

n. JP 3-28, *Civil Support*.

o. JP 3-33, *Joint Task Force Headquarters*.

p. JP 3-41, *Chemical, Biological, Radiological, Nuclear, and High-Yield Explosives Consequence Management*.

q. JP 3-50, *Personnel Recovery*.

r. JP 4-0, *Joint Logistics*.

s. JP 4-02, *Health Service Support*.

t. JP 4-06, *Mortuary Affairs in Joint Operations*.

u. JP 5-0, *Joint Operation Planning*.

v. JP 6-0, *Joint Communications System*.

4. **Chairman of the Joint Chiefs of Staff Instructions and Manuals**

a. CJCSI 2030.01B, *Chemical Weapons Convention Compliance Policy Guidance*.

b. CJCSI 2110.01D, *International Transfer of US Defense-Related Technology and Munitions*.

c. CJCSI 3100.01B, *Joint Strategic Planning System*.

d. CJCSI 3110.16A, *Military Capabilities, Assets, and Units for Chemical, Biological, Radiological, Nuclear, and High Yield Explosive Consequence Management Operations* (FOUO).

e. CJCSI 3125.01A, Military Assistance to *Domestic Consequence Management (CM) Operations in Response to a Chemical, Biological, Radiological, Nuclear, or High-Yield Explosive (CBRNE) Situation*.

f. CJCSI 3137.01C, *The Functional Capabilities Board Process*.

g. CJCSI 3214.01C, *Military Support to Foreign Consequence Management Operations for Chemical, Biological, Radiological, and Nuclear Incidents.*

h. CJCSI 3401.02A, *Global Status of Resources and Training System (GSORTS).*

i. CJCSI 3500.01E, *Joint Training Policy and Guidance for the Armed Forces of the United States.*

j. Chairman of the Joint Chiefs of Staff Manual 3500.04E, *Universal Joint Task List (UJTL).*

k. CJCSI 3520.02A, *Proliferation Security Initiative (PSI) Activity Program.*

l. CJCSM 5225.01B, *Classification Guide for Combating WMD Information.*

5. Multi-Service

a. FM 3-11.3/MCRP 3-27.2A/NTTP 3-11.25/AFTTP(I) 3-2.25, *Multi-Service Tactics, Techniques, and Procedures for Chemical, Biological, Radiological, and Nuclear Contamination Avoidance.*

b. FM 3-11.5/Marine Corps Warfighting Publication (MCWP) 3-37.3/NTTP 3-11.26/AFTTP(I) 3-2.60, *Multi-Service Tactics, Techniques, and Procedures for Chemical, Biological Radiological, and Nuclear Decontamination.*

c. FM 3-6/MCRP 3-37B/Air Force Manual 105-7, Field Behavior of NBC Agents.

d. FM 3-11/ MCWP 3-37.1/NWP 3-11/AFTTP(I) 3-2.42, *Multi-Service Tactics, Techniques, and Procedures for Nuclear, Biological, and Chemical Defense Operations.*

e. FM 3-11.21/MCRP 3-37.2C/NTTP 3-11.24/AFTTP(I) 3-2.37, *Multi-Service Tactics, Techniques, and Procedures for Chemical, Biological, Radiological, and Nuclear Consequence Management Operations.*

f. FM 3-11.4 /MCWP 3-37.2/NTTP 3-11.27/AFTTP(I) 3-2.46, *Multi-Service Tactics, Techniques, and Procedures for Nuclear, Biological, and Chemical (NBC) Protection.*

g. FM 3-11.14/MCRP 3-37.1A/NTTP 3-11.28/AFTTP(I) 3-2.54, *Multi-Service, Tactics, Techniques, and Procedures for Chemical, Biological, Radiological, and Nuclear Decontamination Nuclear, Biological, and Chemical Vulnerability Analysis.*

h. FM 4-02.283/MCRP 4-11.1B/NTRP 4-02.21/AFMAN 44-161 (I), *Treatment of Nuclear and Radiological Casualties.*

i. FM 8-284/NAVMED P-5042/AFMAN (I) 44-156/MCRP 4-11.1C, *Treatment of Biological Warfare Casualties.*

j. FM 4-02.285/MCRP 4-11.1A/Navy Technical Reference Publication 4-02.22/AFTTP(I) 3-2.69, *Multi-Service Tactics, Techniques, and Procedures for Treatment of Chemical Agent Casualties and Conventional Military Chemical Injuries.*

k. FM 8-9/NAVMED P-5059/AFJMAN 44-151, *NATO Handbook on the Medical Aspects of NBC Defensive Operations AMedP-6(B).*

l. FM 100-23-1/FMFRP 7-16/NDC TACNOTE 3-07-6/ACCP 50-56/PACAFP 50-56/USAFEP 50-56, *Multiservice Procedures for Humanitarian Assistance Operations.*

m. FM 101-4/MCRP 6-23A/NWP 3-13.1.16/AFTTP (I) 3-2.22, *Multi-Service Procedures for Joint Task Force—Information Management.*

6. **Army**

a. Army Regulation 385-61, *The Army Chemical Agent Safety Program.*

b. FM 3-0, *Operations.*

c. FM 3-07, *Stability Operations and Support Operations.*

d. FM 3-7, *NBC Field Handbook.*

e. FM 3-13, *Information Operations: Doctrine, Tactics, Techniques, and Procedures.*

f. FM 3-101, *Chemical Staffs and Units.*

g. FM 4-02.7, *Health Services Support in a Nuclear, Biological, and Chemical Environment: Tactics, Techniques, and Procedures.*

h. FM 5-0, *Army Planning and Orders Production.*

7. **Marine Corps**

MCWP 3-37, *Marine Air-Ground Task Force (MAGTF) Nuclear, Biological, and Chemical Defensive Operations.*

8. **Navy**

a. Navy Doctrine Publication (NDP) 1, *Naval Warfare.*

b. NDP 2, *Naval Intelligence.*

c. NDP 5, *Naval Planning*.

9. **Air Force**

a. Air Force Doctrine Document (AFDD)-1, *Air Force Basic Doctrine*.

b. AFDD 2, *Operations and Organization*.

c. AFDD 2-1.8, *Counter-CBRN Operations*.

d. Air Force Instruction 10-2501, *Air Force Emergency Management (EM) Program Planning and Operations*.

e. Air Force Handbook 10-2502, *USAF Weapons of Mass Destruction (WMD) Threat Planning and Response Handbook*.

f. Air Force Manual (AFMAN) 10-2602, *Nuclear, Biological, Chemical, and Conventional (NBCC) Defense Operations and Standards*.

g. AFMAN 32-4004, *Emergency Response Operations*.

h. AFMAN 32-4005, *Personnel Protection and Attack Actions*.

i. Air Force Policy Directive (AFPD) 10-25, *Emergency Management*.

j. AFPD 10-26, *Counter-Chemical, Biological, Radiological and Nuclear Operations*.

k. AFPD 32-40, *Disaster Preparedness*.

l. Air Mobility Command C-CBRN CONOPS.

10. **Other Sources**

a. Chandler, Robert W., *Deliberate Planning for Attack Operations Against Weapons of Mass Destruction*.

b. National Defense University (NDU), Center for Counterproliferation Research, *Deterrence and Defense in a Nuclear, Biological, and Chemical Environment*.

c. NDU, Center for Counter-Proliferation Research, *The Effects of Chemical and Biological Warfare on Operations: What We Know and Don't Know*.

d. NDU, Center for Counter-Proliferation Research, *The NBC Threat in 2025: Concepts and Strategies for Adversarial Use*.

e. Schneider, Barry R., *Future War and Counterproliferation: US Military Responses to NBC Proliferation Threats* (Washington, DC: Praeger).

f. Weaver, Greg and Glass J. David, *Inviting Disaster: How Weapons of Mass Destruction Undermine US Strategy for Projecting Military Power* (Washington, DC: AMCODA Press).

g. Wirtz, James, Scott Sagan and Peter Lavoy, *Planning the Unthinkable: How New Powers Will Use Nuclear, Biological, and Chemical Weapons* (Ithaca, NY: Cornell University Press).

h. *Handbook for Joint Weapons of Mass Destruction (WMD) Elimination Operations.*

i. DTRA-AR-40H-4, *WMD Facility, Equipment and Munitions Identification Handbook.*

j. DOD Chemical and Biological Defense Program (CBDP) Overview.

k. Joint Program Executive Office for Chemical and Biological Defense Overview.

Intentionally Blank

APPENDIX D
ADMINISTRATIVE INSTRUCTIONS

1. **User Comments**

Users in the field are highly encouraged to submit comments on this publication to: Commander, United States Joint Forces Command, Joint Warfighting Center, –Doctrine and Education Group, 116 Lake View Parkway, Suffolk, VA 23435-2697. These comments should address content (accuracy, usefulness, consistency, and organization), writing, and appearance.

2. **Authorship**

The lead agent for this publication is the US Strategic Command. The Joint Staff doctrine sponsor for this publication is the Director for Strategic Plans and Policy (J-5).

3. **Supersession**

This publication supersedes JP 3-40, *Joint Doctrine for Combating Weapons of Mass Destruction*, 8 July 2004.

4. **Change Recommendations**

a. Recommendations for urgent changes to this publication should be submitted:

```
TO:     HQ USSTRATCOM OFFUTT AFB NE//CC//
INFO:   JOINT STAFF WASHINGTON DC//J7-JEDD//
        CDRUSJFCOM SUFFOLK VA//DJT10//
```

Routine changes should be submitted electronically to Commander, Joint Warfighting Center, Doctrine and Education Group and info the Lead Agent and the Director for Operational Plans and Joint Force Development (J-7/JEDD) via the CJCS JEL at http://www.dtic.mil/doctrine.

b. When a Joint Staff directorate submits a proposal to the Chairman of the Joint Chiefs of Staff that would change source document information reflected in this publication, that directorate will include a proposed change to this publication as an enclosure to its proposal. The Military Services and other organizations are requested to notify the Joint Staff J-7 when changes to source documents reflected in this publication are initiated.

c. Record of Changes:

CHANGE NUMBER	COPY NUMBER	DATE OF CHANGE	DATE ENTERED	POSTED BY	REMARKS

5. Distribution of Publications

Local reproduction is authorized and access to unclassified publications is unrestricted. However, access to and reproduction authorization for classified joint publications must be in accordance with DOD Regulation 5200.1-R, *Information Security Program.*

6. Distribution of Electronic Publications

a. Joint Staff J-7 will not print copies of JPs for distribution. Electronic versions are available on JDEIS at https://jdeis.js.mil (NIPRNET) and https://jdeis.js.smil.mil (SIPRNET), and on the JEL at http://www.dtic.mil/doctrine (NIPRNET).

b. Only approved joint publications and joint test publications are releasable outside the combatant commands, Services, and Joint Staff. Release of any classified joint publication to foreign governments or foreign nationals must be requested through the local embassy (Defense Attaché Office) to DIA Foreign Liaison Office, PO-FL, Room 1E811, 7400 Pentagon, Washington, DC 20301-7400.

c. CD-ROM. Upon request of a JDDC member, the Joint Staff J-7 will produce and deliver one CD-ROM with current joint publications.

GLOSSARY
PART I – ABBREVIATIONS AND ACRONYMS

AFTTP(I)	Air Force tactics, techniques, and procedures (instruction)
AOR	area of responsibility
APOD	aerial port of debarkation
BIS	Bureau of Industry and Security
C2	command and control
CBP	Customs and Border Protection
CBRN	chemical, biological, radiological, and nuclear
CBRNE	chemical, biological, radiological, nuclear, and high-yield explosives
CCD	camouflage, concealment, and deception
CCDR	combatant commander
CDRUSJFCOM	Commander, United States Joint Forces Command
CDRUSPACOM	Commander, United States Pacific Command
CDRUSSTRATCOM	Commander, United States Strategic Command
CDRUSTRANSCOM	Commander, United States Transportation Command
CJCS	Chairman of the Joint Chiefs of Staff
CJCSI	Chairman of the Joint Chiefs of Staff instruction
CJCSM	Chairman of the Joint Chiefs of Staff manual
CJTF	commander, joint task force
CM	consequence management
CMOC	civil-military operations center
COA	course of action
COG	center of gravity
COM	chief of mission
CONOPS	concept of operations
COOP	continuity of operations
CP	counterproliferation
CS	civil support
CSA	combat support agency
CTR	cooperative threat reduction
CWC	Chemical Weapons Convention
CWMD	combating weapons of mass destruction
DHS	Department of Homeland Security
DIA	Defense Intelligence Agency
DNDO	Domestic Nuclear Detection Office
DOD	Department of Defense
DODD	Department of Defense directive
DODI	Department of Defense instruction
DOE	Department of Energy
DOJ	Department of Justice
DOS	Department of State
DSCA	defense support of civil authorities

DTRA	Defense Threat Reduction Agency
EP	emergency preparedness
FBI	Federal Bureau of Investigation
FCM	foreign consequence management
FDO	flexible deterrent option
FHP	force health protection
FID	foreign internal defense
FinCEN	Financial Crimes Enforcement Network
FM	field manual (Army)
FSU	former Soviet Union
GCC	geographic combatant commander
HD	homeland defense
HN	host nation
HQ	headquarters
HSC	Homeland Security Council
HSS	health service support
HYE	high-yield explosives
ICE	Immigration and Customs Enforcement
IED	improvised explosive device
IGO	intergovernmental organization
INDRAC	Interagency Combating Weapons of Mass Destruction Database of Responsibilities, Authorities, and Capabilities
IO	information operations
ISR	intelligence, surveillance, and reconnaissance
JECE	Joint Elimination Coordination Element
JFC	joint force commander
JIACG	joint interagency coordination group
JIATF	joint interagency task force
JIPOE	joint intelligence preparation of the operational environment
JOPES	Joint Operation Planning and Execution System
JOPP	joint operation planning process
JP	joint publication
JS	the Joint Staff
JTF	joint task force
JTF-E	joint task force elimination
LFA	lead federal agency
LOO	line of operations

METOC	meteorological and oceanographic
MMA	military mission area
MOTR	maritime operational threat response
MSO	military strategic objective
MTCR	missile technology control regime
NGO	nongovernmental organization
NIMS	National Incident Management System
NISP	national intelligence support plan
NMS-CWMD	National Military Strategy to Combat Weapons of Mass Destruction
NNSA	National Nuclear Security Administration
NP	nonproliferation
NPT	Treaty on the Nonproliferation of Nuclear Weapons
NRF	National Response Framework
NSC	National Security Council
NS-CWMD	National Strategy to Combat Weapons of Mass Destruction
NSPD	national security Presidential directive
NSS	National Security Strategy
OEG	operational experts group
OFAC	Office of Foreign Assets Control
OGA	other government agency
OPSEC	operations security
OSD	Office of the Secretary of Defense
PA	public affairs
PB	peace building
PCC	policy coordination committee
PDSC	public diplomacy and strategic communication
PEO	peace enforcement operations
PIR	priority intelligence requirement
PKO	peacekeeping operations
PO	peace operations
PSI	Proliferation Security Initiative
R&D	research and development
ROE	rules of engagement
RUF	rules for the use of force
SC	strategic communication
SCC-WMD	United States Strategic Command Center for Combating Weapons of Mass Destruction
SCG	Security Cooperation Guidance
SecDef	Secretary of Defense

SJA	staff judge advocate
SOF	special operations forces
SPOD	seaport of debarkation
TIM	toxic industrial material
UAS	unmanned aircraft system
UN	United Nations
UNCLOS	United Nations Convention on the Law of the Sea
US	United States
USA	United States Army
USAF	United States Air Force
USC	United States Code
USCG	United States Coast Guard
USG	United States Government
USJFCOM	United States Joint Forces Command
USMC	United States Marine Corps
USN	United States Navy
USNORTHCOM	United States Northern Command
USPACOM	Unites States Pacific Command
USSOCOM	United States Special Operations Command
USSTRATCOM	United States Strategic Command
USTRANSCOM	United States Transportation Command
VEO	violent extremist organization
WOT	war on terrorism
WMD	weapons of mass destruction
WMD CM	weapons of mass destruction consequence management

Unless otherwise annotated, this publication is the proponent for all terms and definitions found in the glossary. Upon approval, JP 1-02 will reflect this publication as the source document for these terms and definitions.

balance. None. (Approved for removal from JP1-02.)

chemical, biological, radiological, and nuclear hazard. Chemical, biological, radiological, and nuclear hazard elements that could cause an adverse affect through their accidental or deliberate release, dissemination, or impacts. Also called CBRN hazard. (JP 1-02. SOURCE: JP 3-11)

chemical, biological, radiological, and nuclear passive defense. Passive measures taken to minimize or negate the vulnerability to, and effects of, chemical, biological, radiological, or nuclear attacks. This mission area focuses on maintaining the joint force's ability to continue military operations in a chemical, biological, radiological, or nuclear environment. Also called **CBRN passive defense.** (JP 1-02. SOURCE: JP 3-40) (Approved for inclusion in JP 1-02.)

counterproliferation. Those actions taken to defeat the threat and/or use of weapons of mass destruction against the United States, our forces, allies, and partners. Also called **CP.** (JP 1-02. SOURCE: JP 3-40) (This term and its definition modify the existing term and its definition and are approved for inclusion in JP 1-02.)

deterrence. The prevention from action by fear of the consequences. Deterrence is a state of mind brought about by the existence of a credible threat of unacceptable counteraction. (JP 1-02. SOURCE: JP 3-40)

exploitation. 1. Taking full advantage of success in military operations, following up initial gains, and making permanent the temporary effects already achieved. 2. Taking full advantage of any information that has come to hand for tactical, operational, or strategic purposes. 3. An offensive operation that usually follows a successful attack and is designed to disorganize the enemy in depth. (JP 1-02. SOURCE: JP 2-01.3)

hostile environment. Operational environment in which hostile forces have control as well as the intent and capability to effectively oppose or react to the operations a unit intends to conduct. (JP 1-02 SOURCE: JP 3-0).

nonproliferation. Actions to prevent the proliferation of weapons of mass destruction by dissuading or impeding access to, or distribution of, sensitive technologies, material, and expertise. Also called **NP.** (JP 1-02. SOURCE: JP 3-40) (This term and its definition modify the existing term and its definition and are approved for inclusion in JP 1-02.)

nuclear reactor. A facility in which fissile material is used in a self-supporting chain reaction (nuclear fission) to produce heat and/or radiation for both practical application and research and development. (JP 1-02. SOURCE: JP 3-40)

permissive environment. Operational environment in which host country military and law enforcement agencies have control as well as the intent and capability to assist operations that a unit intends to conduct. (JP 1-02 SOURCE: JP 3-0)

proliferation. The transfer of weapons of mass destruction, related materials, technology, and expertise from suppliers to hostile state or non-state actors. (JP 1-02. SOURCE: JP 3-40) (This term and its definition modify the existing term 'proliferation (nuclear weapons)' and its definition and are approved for inclusion in JP 1-02.)

readiness. The ability of United States military forces to fight and meet the demands of the national military strategy. Readiness is the synthesis of two distinct but interrelated levels. a. unit readiness—The ability to provide capabilities required by the combatant commanders to execute their assigned missions. This is derived from the ability of each unit to deliver the outputs for which it was designed. b. joint readiness—The combatant commander's ability to integrate and synchronize ready combat and support forces to execute his or her assigned missions. (JP 1-02)

tacit arms control agreement. None. (Approved for removal from JP 1-02.)

threat reduction cooperation. Activities undertaken with the consent and cooperation of host nation authorities in a permissive environment to enhance physical security, and to reduce, dismantle, redirect, and/or improve protection of a state's existing weapons of mass destruction program, stockpiles, and capabilities. Also called **TRC.** (JP 1-02. SOURCE: JP 3-40) (Approved for inclusion in JP 1-02.)

uncertain environment. Operational environment in which host government forces, whether opposed to or receptive to operations that a unit intends to conduct, do not have totally effective control or the territory and population in the intended operational area. (JP 1-02. SOURCE: JP 3-0)

unilateral arms control measure. None. (Approved for removal from JP 1-02.)

weapons of mass destruction. Chemical, biological, radiological, or nuclear weapons capable of a high order of destruction or causing mass casualties and exclude the means of transporting or propelling the weapon where such means is a separable and divisible part from the weapon. Also called **WMD.** (JP 1-02. SOURCE: JP 3-40) (This term and its definition modify the existing term and its definition and are approved for inclusion in JP 1-02.)

weapons of mass destruction active defense. Active measures to defeat an attack with chemical, biological, radiological, or nuclear weapons by employing actions to divert, neutralize, or destroy those weapons or their means of delivery while en route to their target. Also called **WMD active defense.** (JP 1-02. SOURCE: JP 3-40) (Approved for inclusion in JP 1-02.)

weapons of mass destruction consequence management. Actions authorized by the Secretary of Defense to mitigate the effects of a weapon of mass destruction attack or event and, if necessary, provide temporary essential operations and services at home and abroad. Also called **WMD CM.** (JP 1-02. SOURCE: JP 3-40) (Approved for inclusion in JP 1-02.)

weapons of mass destruction elimination. Actions undertaken in a hostile or uncertain environment to systematically locate, characterize, secure, and disable, or destroy weapons of mass destruction programs and related capabilities. Also called **WMD elimination.** (JP 1-02. SOURCE: JP 3-40) (Approved for inclusion in JP 1-02.)

weapons of mass destruction interdiction. Operations to track, intercept, search, divert, seize, or otherwise stop the transit of weapons of mass destruction, its delivery systems, or related materials, technologies, and expertise. **Also called WMD interdiction.** (JP 1-02. SOURCE: JP 3-40) (Approved for inclusion in JP 1-02.)

weapons of mass destruction offensive operations. Actions to disrupt, neutralize, or destroy a weapon of mass destruction threat before it can be used, or to deter subsequent use of such weapons. Also called **WMD offensive operations.** (JP 1-02. SOURCE: JP 3-40) (Approved for inclusion in JP 1-02.)

weapons of mass destruction security cooperation and partner activities. Activities to improve or promote defense relationships and capacity of allied and partner nations to execute or support the other military mission areas to combat weapons of mass destruction through military-to military contact, burden sharing arrangements, combined military activities, and support to international activities. Also called **WMD security cooperation.** (JP 1-02. SOURCE: JP 3-40) (Approved for inclusion in JP 1-02.)

Intentionally Blank

JOINT DOCTRINE PUBLICATIONS HIERARCHY

```
                          ┌─────────────┐
                          │    JP 1     │
                          │             │
                          │   JOINT     │
                          │  DOCTRINE   │
                          └─────────────┘
```

JP 1-0	JP 2-0	JP 3-0	JP 4-0	JP 5-0	JP 6-0
PERSONNEL	INTELLIGENCE	OPERATIONS	LOGISTICS	PLANS	COMMUNICATION SYSTEMS

All joint publications are organized into a comprehensive hierarchy as shown in the chart above. **Joint Publication (JP) 3-40** is in the **Operations** series of joint doctrine publications. The diagram below illustrates an overview of the development process:

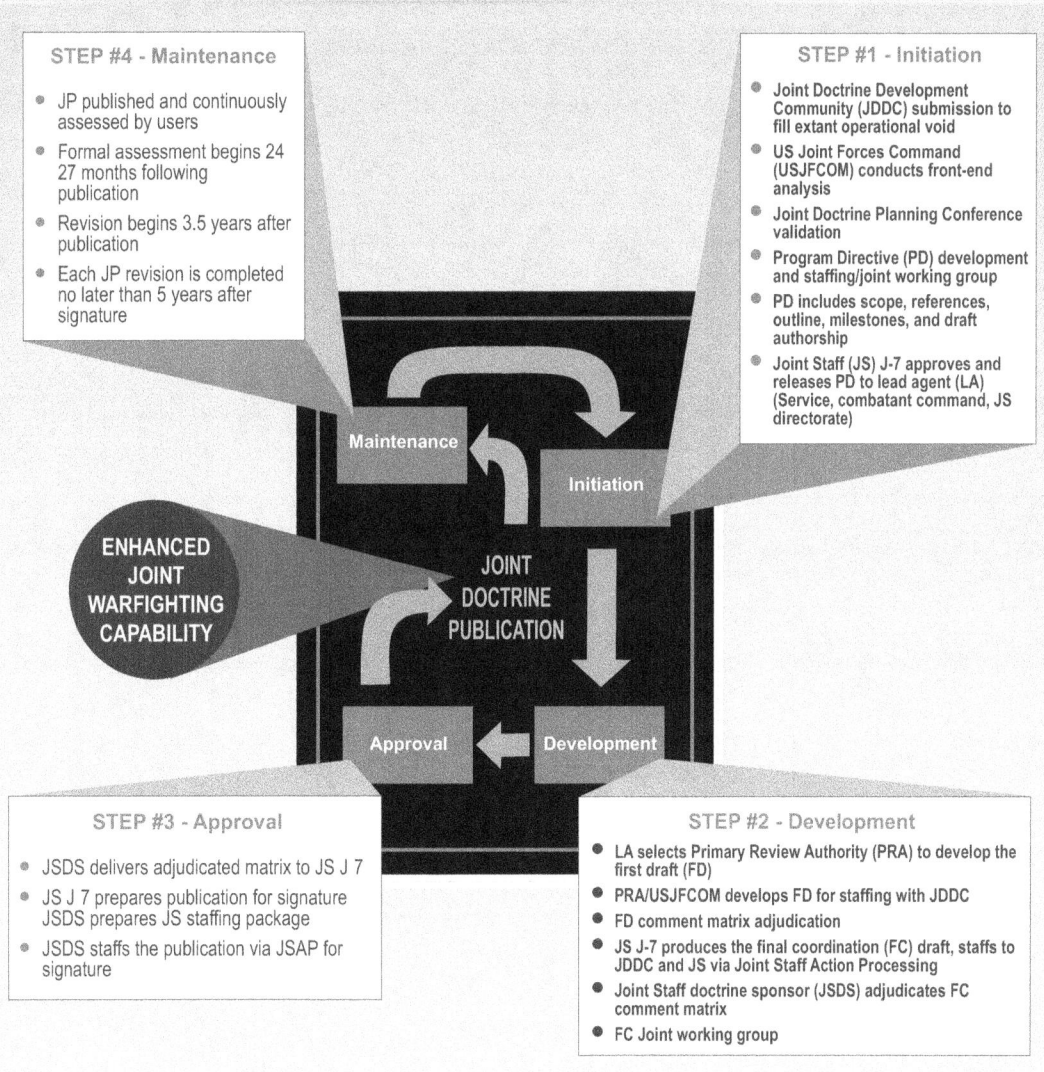

STEP #4 - Maintenance

- JP published and continuously assessed by users
- Formal assessment begins 24 27 months following publication
- Revision begins 3.5 years after publication
- Each JP revision is completed no later than 5 years after signature

STEP #1 - Initiation

- Joint Doctrine Development Community (JDDC) submission to fill extant operational void
- US Joint Forces Command (USJFCOM) conducts front-end analysis
- Joint Doctrine Planning Conference validation
- Program Directive (PD) development and staffing/joint working group
- PD includes scope, references, outline, milestones, and draft authorship
- Joint Staff (JS) J-7 approves and releases PD to lead agent (LA) (Service, combatant command, JS directorate)

STEP #3 - Approval

- JSDS delivers adjudicated matrix to JS J 7
- JS J 7 prepares publication for signature JSDS prepares JS staffing package
- JSDS staffs the publication via JSAP for signature

STEP #2 - Development

- LA selects Primary Review Authority (PRA) to develop the first draft (FD)
- PRA/USJFCOM develops FD for staffing with JDDC
- FD comment matrix adjudication
- JS J-7 produces the final coordination (FC) draft, staffs to JDDC and JS via Joint Staff Action Processing
- Joint Staff doctrine sponsor (JSDS) adjudicates FC comment matrix
- FC Joint working group